REASON AND EXISTENCE

# REASON
# AND EXISTENCE

SCHELLING'S PHILOSOPHY OF HISTORY

BY

PAUL COLLINS HAYNER

LEIDEN
E. J. BRILL
1967

# TABLE OF CONTENTS

# PREFACE

No less a historian of ideas than A. O. Lovejoy has pointed out that Schelling's later philosophy (from 1812 on), to the extent that it expresses an "evolutionary theology,"[1] is the first philosophy in the Western tradition to make a complete break with the static, "devolutionist" metaphysics stemming from Plato and Plotinos. The aim of this study is to show in some detail how this observation is borne out in an examination of the development of Schelling's philosophy as a whole, and to show in particular how this construction of an evolutionary, or "historical," ontology affects Schelling's interpretation of human history. When Schelling's efforts in this direction are seen against the background of the conception of history which prevailed generally during the Enlightenment, as well as the conceptions of history which were suggested by the Romantic and other critics of the Enlightenment, it will be seen that Schelling's views represent a culmination, in many respects, of a tendency to substitute a dynamic for a static metaphysics as a means to the interpretation of the social, political and religious history of mankind. In this way, it is hoped, a higher appreciation of Schelling's philosophy may be evoked than has generally been accorded it by historians of philosophy. For Schelling's philosophy represents an important link in the process by which evolutionary conceptions became established in the natural and social sciences in the nineteenth century.

Schelling's views on the significance of human history underwent considerable development during the course of his philosophic labors. In fact, in this respect, his doctrines more or less recapitulate the general pattern followed by European thought in its shift from the point of view of the Enlightenment to that of Romanticism. From the position taken in 1797–98, when he declared, in effect, that a philosophy of history is an impossibility, to that of 1812 and after, when he attempted to describe in detail the history of the universe as a whole, there is a considerable reorientation in philosophical perspective. Coupled with this there is to be noted, also, the gradual shift from philosophical to theological categories in Schelling's expli-

---

[1] Arthur O. Lovejoy, *The Great Chain of Being* (Cambridge: Harvard University Press, 1936), p. 323.

cation of the content of history. And while this trend in Schelling's thinking does not necessarily match any broader pattern of European thought, it is at least an interesting example of the way in which an evolutionary ontology may be employed in the service of illuminating the religious history of the human race. It is also, for this reason, an instructive illustration of the Romantic approach in Germany to the philosophy of religion, and invites comparison, on the one hand, with Schelling's better-known contemporary, Schleiermacher.

The first section of this study consists of an examination of more or less typical expressions of the conceptions of history which were put forth in Europe in the eighteenth century. Here an attempt is made, first, to characterize "the" Enlightenment conception of history, emphasizing the metaphysical preconceptions which guided some of its outstanding formulators such as Tindal, Voltaire and Montesquieu. In general, it seems, the Enlightenment commentators on history were guided by the assumption that history is the scene of immutable law, of "eternal truths" regarding human nature and human activities—of a progressive achievement of rationality, to be sure—but not of a developing process wherein genuine novelty appears at a certain point in time. It was this world-view, stemming from the influence of Newtonian science with its emphasis upon universal law and fixed patterns, that was gradually undermined from around the middle of the eighteenth century. Here, in the latter part of this section, illustrations are set forth of the way in which European and, especially, German thinkers tended more and more to embrace a developmental conception of social, political and religious history. By the end of the eighteenth century, with the appearance of the Romantic movement in Germany, the stage is set for the formulation of an evolutionary metaphysics which will serve to give full expression to the emphasis, which had been growing for some time, upon the processing character of human history. And while Schelling's philosophy, even in its final form, preserves a rationalistic tinge, it nevertheless does bring to a climax in many respects the attempt to conceive of human history in genuinely "historical" terms.

In the next two sections, an examination is made of Schelling's philosophy during his "first period," i.e. to the appearance of his most important work, *Of Human Freedom*, in 1809. It is pointed out how Schelling's work during this period was centered around the

development of a philosophy of nature, somewhat as a corrective to
the one-sided views of Fichte. Nevertheless, Schelling shared at this
time the dynamic views of Fichte and other German idealists; and
while he considers history only more or less parenthetically, he
does so with the assumption that it shares in the development which
the Absolute undergoes in its achievement of full expression. The
"philosophy of identity" which eventually appears as a culmination
of his philosophical labors during this period is, to be sure, a system
which is rationally perfect, a-temporal in character, in spite of the
dialectical movement of its constitutive elements. But at the same
time, the view of history which is developed within the context of the
system of identity is such that, in the first place, it does have, at
least from a finite point of view, the character of a developing
process; and in the second place, Schelling argues, it is most adequately illuminated by concepts drawn directly from Christian
theology. By combining these two emphases, Schelling achieves in
his second period a philosophy which reaches full expression only in
reference to the religious history of mankind.

The remainder of the study is devoted to an examination of
Schelling's "positive" philosophy. Here the historical orientation
achieves its complete expression. Through his doctrine of freedom,
Schelling erects a critique of his own earlier "negative" philosophy,
and in so doing he also attacks Hegel's rationalism as representing
the fundamentally non-historical type of philosophy which had
previously dominated the European scene. The "metaphysical
empiricism" which is finally developed by Schelling is offered by him
as a method for dealing adequately with the fundamentally "historical" character of reality. Coupled with this method is the doctrine
that human history is one aspect of the larger whole of the process
which the universe itself undergoes. Moreover, while man and his
history are now placed in the center of the universe, the universe itself
is to be understood as a history which can be fully understood only
from the point of view of the Christian drama of salvation. And by
appealing to the "facts" of the mythological and religious traditions
of mankind, Schelling claims to offer verification for the speculative
scheme which his philosophy as a whole entails. Thus, while in large
measure supplanting the static metaphysics by which the Enlightenment had interpreted the social, political, and especially the religious,
history of mankind, Schelling also, it would seem, saw many of the
defects of German rationalistic idealism; and while his attempts to

overcome some of these defects may be regarded as of dubious merit, he was at least able to point the direction in which much of later European thought was to go.

CHAPTER ONE

# THE ENLIGHTENMENT CONCEPTION OF HISTORY
# AND ITS EIGHTEENTH CENTURY CRITICS

### I. THE ENLIGHTENMENT CONCEPTION OF HISTORY

In the late eighteenth and early nineteenth centuries in Germany, there took place gradually that change in the intellectual climate which is usually referred to as the transition from the *Aufklärung* to Romanticism. Many critics and students have pointed out the distinctive features of this transition, especially with reference to its impact upon literature, religion and philosophy. Its effect upon the conception and evaluation of human history has also been noted, but somewhat more cursorily. And yet it would appear, from a study of the literature produced during the hundred-odd years between 1700 or thereabouts and 1820 or 1830, that one of the fundamental changes which transpired during this era was the change in attitude toward history and historical studies. Moreover it would seem that this shift was certainly accompanied by, and was probably influenced by, a quite distinctive revision of metaphysical outlook. More specifically, we may note the gradual replacement of a static by a dynamic conception of the universe; and it is with this tendency to assign to process a much higher place in the scheme of things that we find a growing awareness of the significance of history.

It is the aim of this study to show how the philosophy of Schelling implements, and in many ways brings to fruition, the trend toward the affirmation of a dynamic metaphysics and with it a heightened regard for human history in the late eighteenth and early nineteenth centuries. But before turning to Schelling's philosophy itself, we must scrutinize briefly the attitudes toward history, and the metaphysical views in which such attitudes were grounded, during the Englightenment and during the time when the Romantic movement, so-called, was raising questons about these views.

It is well to observe at the outset that in many ways, of course, it is a grave mistake to identify the *Aufklärung* in Germany with the Enlightenment in England and in France. For while it is true that foreign influence provided much of the intitial impetus, the *Auf-*

*klärung* was "not... a simple reflection of French and English doctrines," It was, rather, "a complete system of ideas, sentiments and of government encountered in Prussia at the end of the reign of Frederck II..."[1] If we would be historically exact, we must refer to the *Aufklärung* only as a specifically German phenomenon, native to Prussia, and dating from the accession of Frederick II in 1740, under whose leadership a distinctive type of liberalism flourished under the "triple aspect of rationalist philosophy, tolerant religion and enlightened despotism."[2]

Nevertheless, while keeping in mind the unique social and political features which distinguished the German *Aufklärung* from the Enlightenment in general, we must also take account of the influence exercised by English and French thought in this period in Germany. Many of those who became the leaders in the *Aufklärung* were influenced at an early age by such well-known foreign writers as Locke and Shaftesbury, Rousseau and Voltaire. As one historian has noted, if one studies the biography of a well-educated German of the *Aufklärung*, "one always finds in his youth a period when he discovered English and French authors."[3] Locke and Rousseau especially seem to have influenced the thinking of the younger generation of German Enlighteners. And as has recently been pointed out, it was John Locke who, probably more than any other single thinker, was instrumental in shaping the religious views of the *Aufklärung*.[4] Indeed, "foreign influence seems... to have been universal, like reason itself."[5] Certainly the basic philosophic principles embraced by German thinkers in the eighteenth century were not peculiar to Germany.

In seeking, then, to come to grips with what may most properly be designated as "the" Enlightenment conception of history, we must take into account those ideas which seem to have been held by a large number of the prominent thinkers of that age. As we have already noted, Germany was, to a large extent, influenced by the views of English and French thinkers; and—as we shall see—this circumstance served to make the philosophy of the German Enlightenment,

---

[1] Henri Brunschwig, *La crise de l'état prussien a la fin du XVIIIᵉ siècle et la genèse de la mentalité romantique* (Paris, 1947), p. vii.
[2] *Ibid.*, p. 23.
[3] *Ibid.*, p. 5.
[4] Andrew Brown, "John Locke and the Religious 'Aufklärung'." *The Review of Religion*, XIII, 2 (January, 1949).
[5] Brunschwig, *op. cit.*, p. 7.

in its early stages, at least, quite similar to its counterpart elsewhere, especially England. Even as in England, where competing sects had long disturbed the peace, the religious wars and theological disputes of the seventeenth century had made Germany ready for religiously "liberal" views. In the face of the growing antipathy toward religious fanaticism, German Pietism had already opposed itself to the dogmatism of the official churches. But it was the rationalism which was beginning to be imported around 1700 which seemed to offer to many of the leaders of the intellectual life of Germany the greatest promise of resolving the conflict among the creeds.

It is at this point that one of the chief factors determining the Enlightenment attitude toward history emerges. Other factors, as we shall note, were at work too. But at first, it seems, it was the ready acceptance given to the views of those who proposed a method of harmonizing the differences between religious creeds which resulted in the shaping of a widely held and influential Enlightenment attitude toward one kind of historical development. To those who were surfeited with dogma and who regarded the competing claims to correct doctrine as not only fallacious but politically dangerous, the ideas of a thinker like John Locke seemed particularly acceptable. He had suggested that it ought to be possible by means of rational analysis to recover the "essential" truth of Christianity from the mass of dogma which had grown up since its establishment. When, as the result of such a rational analysis, positive, historical Christianity had been made to yield its eternal, "reasonable" principles, Locke argued, a basic core of Christian truth would be available for acceptance by all reasonable men. But—while Locke himself does not explicitly draw this implication—the very nature of his enterprise suggests a judgment upon the history of religion: that it is essentially a record of the corruption by irrational dogma of the rational core of Christian truth. Whatever else history may contain, the history of religious doctrines is a table of falsehood and superstition.

Locke's own religious investigations are confined, more or less, to proving that Christianity, rightly understood, is a system of morality rather than dogma, and—at least in *The Reasonableness of Christianity as Deliver'd in the Scriptures* (1695)—that the Christian revelation was necessary because "human reason, unassisted, failed men in its great and proper business of morality."[1] In other works, such as

---

[1] *The Worke of John Locke*, 9 vols. (9th ed., London, 1791), VI, 140. Quoted by Brown, *op. cit.*, p. 129.

his *Paraphrases of St. Paul* (1705–1707) and his *Essay Concerning Human Understanding* (1690), while tending to give greater authority to reason in establishing religious truth, Locke continues to maintain that Christianity is primarily a matter of morality and that moral truth, rationally apprehended, is the most valuable possession of man.

But others did not hesitate to draw out the implication contained in this approach to Christian doctrine. John Toland, for example, in his *Christianity not Mysterious* (1696) argued that Christ "preached the purest Morals," together with those conceptions of divine things which the rational worshipper required to know.[1] Thus "having stripp'd the Truth of all external Types and Ceremonies which made it difficult before, he rendered it easy and obvious to the meanest Capacities."[2] But while Christ's disciples managed for a time to adhere to this pure and simple Truth, it wasn't long before abuses began to creep in. Converted Jews wished to retain their ancient rites, so that "what at the Beginning was but only tolerated in weaker Brethren became afterwards a part of *Christianity* itself, under the Pretence of *Apostolick* Prescription or Tradition."[3] As time went on and large numbers of Gentiles were converted to Christianity, the simplicity of the original Gospel was only further corrupted. It became a thing of mysteries, ceremonies and creeds—in short, of superstition. The historical development of Christianity, far from adding anything of value, had but increased the degree of its corruption.

The significant feature of Toland's argument is that he makes a sharp distinction between the essential truth of Christianity—the pure morality taught by Christ—and the rites and dogmas which in time were added to, were confused with, and thus caused the corruption of, original Christianity. Hence the historical development of Christianity is regarded as a process of adulteration of Christian truth. Moreover, in distinguishing original truth and its historical corruption in this fashion, Toland is obviously committing himself to a rather specific doctrine regarding the nature of moral and religious truth. In this Toland was but repeating an assumption common to the age in which he lived, but it is important for our purposes to

---

[1] Reprinted in Creed and Boys Smith, *Religious Thought in the Eighteenth Century* (Cambridge, 1934), pp. 16f.

[2] *Ibid.*, p. 21.

[3] *Ibid.*

point it out. The assumption in question is that the truth or truths of morality and religion can be subject to no development—that such truth is, by nature, "eternal." By the same token—although this would seem to be a quite separate assumption—it is believed that man's *apprehension* of moral and religious truth is not only not made easier by the passage of time, but that, on the contrary, those who lived at an earlier age were in a better position to apprehend such truth than those who lived later. Such "primitivism," as it has been called,[1] was a pervasive feature of the Enlightenment and served in large measure to determine the prevailing attitude toward history and historical development.

Both assumptions became an integral part of the doctrines of English Deism and, through the influence of numerous translations of Deistic writings, of the German *Aufklärung*. Matthew Tindal's *Christianity as Old as the Creation, or the Gospel a Republication of the Religion of Nature* (1730) is a typical expression of the attitude of this age toward the variety of historical forms of Christianity. Tindal is quite explicit in his affirmation of the "eternal" nature of moral and religious truth and of its apprehension by mankind "from the beginning." The gist of his argument is that the nature of God is "eternally the same" and that "his laws at all times must be the same" since "God, at no time, cou'd have any Motive to give laws to Mankind, but for their Good"—He being equally good at all times and acting upon the same motives.[2] Hence the moral law contained in Christianity is but "a republication of the religion of nature" which has been corrupted by historical accretions. If one would avoid the conclusion "that God created the greatest Part of Mankind to be damn'd,"[3] he must affirm the eternal benevolence of God and with it the absolute perfection of the religion with which mankind was originally endowed. Any addition or diminution to this religion during the course of history must have been a change for the worse.

Such doctrines were enthusiastically welcomed in Germany in the first part of the eighteenth century; and while they did undergo some modification during the course of the *Aufklärung*, we find them being purveyed practically intact from around 1741 when Johann

---

[1] Notably by A. O. Lovejoy. See. e.g., "The Parallel of Deism and Classicism" in *Essays in the History of Ideas*.

[2] Creed and Boys Smith, *op. cit.*, p. 34.

[3] *Ibid.*

Lorenz Schmidt issued a German translation of Tindal's work.[1] A writing of Lessing's from his early period, the *Gedanken über die Herrnhuter* (1750), will serve to illustrate how closely the views of many *Aufklärer* followed those of Tindal and other English Deists:

> Turn back to the earliest ages. How simple, easy, and living was the religion of Adam! But how long did such religion continue? Each of his descendants added something to it, according to his own liking. The essential was submerged in a deluge (*Sündflut*) of arbitrary doctrines. All were disloyal to the truth, though a few men, the posterity of Abraham, less so than others.

It was Christ's work, according to Lessing,

> to restore religion to its original purity, and to confine it within those limits in which it brings forth effects the more holy and universal, the more narrow the limits. God is a spirit, ye shall worship him in spirit and in truth; upon what beyond this did he insist, and what truth is more capable than this of binding together all the varieties of religion?[2]

Lessing's views, as we shall note, underwent considerable modification at a later date. But at first he shared the two assumptions of the English Deists noted above, viz. that religious truth undergoes no development, and that mankind's apprehension of it was more adequate before the corruption introduced by historical change had set in.

It is not necessary to cite in detail the views of the numerous eighteenth century writers who subscribed to this thesis. Many, of course, did not; and the literature of the eighteenth century was considerably enlarged by the contributions of those who rushed to the defense of the orthodox position. The Deists, however, were the aggressors; and even when their orthodox opponents did not share their conclusions, they frequently argued from the same assumption. On the whole, as far as the history of mankind's religious expressions was concerned, the Enlightenment tended to adopt a negative approach. Assuming, as they did, that religious truth is embodied in a few moral principles which are, by nature, "eternal," and that "original" mankind was in full possession of these principles, the Enlighteners were prone to deny that the varieties of religious expression, past and present, had any intrinsic worth. As long as "the religion of nature" was regarded as the ideal, with its connotation of

---

[1] Andrew Brown, *op. cit.*, p. 141.
[2] Quoted by Lovejoy, *op. cit.*, p. 88.

uniformity, simplicity and universality of belief and practice, it was generally held "that the entire moral and religious history of civilized mankind, most of all in the West, had been worse than barren—had not only yielded no enrichment of ethical insight or religious understanding or experience, but had been a long tale of multiplying error and increasing departure from the uniformity and simplicity of 'nature'."[1]

It would, of course, be grossly misleading to suggest that the Enlightenment was concerned only with the religious history of mankind. Indeed, as we shall attempt to indicate, its preoccupation with other phases of human history is, in some ways, more characteristic of this era as a whole. But it seems well to focus attention upon this aspect of Enlightenment philosophy at the outset for two reasons. In the first place, as we shall note, it was a prime concern of many Romantic writers in Germany to combat the Enlightenment's negative judgment upon religious history, and Schelling was in the vanguard of those who made this their own concern. A clear statement of the prevailing Enlightenment attitude toward the religious history of mankind would therefore appear to be essential to the nature of this study. But, in the second place, it seems essential to an understanding of the Enlightenment conception of history as a whole to see it as the result of an attempt to achieve a perspective on social and political institutions on the basis of the Christian religious tradition. This attempt must be seen as, in many instances, a reaction against what was understood as the Christian, or at least Biblical, conception of human history. But whether it was a revolt from such a history or, as in some cases, an effort to reinterpret it and thus infuse it with new significance, eighteenth century philosophy invariably reflected the influence of the Christian Biblical tradition.

When the Enlightenment's views on human history are considered from this perspective, they exhibit, again, certain features which tend to supplement those which we have already noted in connection with its interpretation of the religious history of mankind. As in the case of this latter aspect of history, its social and political dimensions were, on the whole, subjected by the Enlightenment thinkers to rigorous critical analysis—not, as with many of the Romantics, because they loved the past for its own sake, or regarded it in any way as an ideal, but because "they wanted to prepare a better future."[2]

---

[1] Lovejoy, *op. cit.*, p. 89.
[2] Ernst Cassirer, *The Myth of the State*. New Haven, 1946. p. 181.

Since "the future of mankind, the rise of a new political and social order, was their great theme and real concern,"[1] Enlightenment philosophers studied history with a view to correcting its mistakes and directing its course into better channels.

As we have already noted, the Enlightenment was sharply critical of the diversities of belief and practice which are associated with the history of religions. Moreover, its criticism was based upon the conviction that the universal and eternal truths of morality are only confusedly, if at all, reflected in the inherited religious tradition, and that, at any rate, reason, as the Enlightenment understood the term, is the ultimate judge if not the sole authority in such matters. John Locke, for example, while recognizing that the truths of revelation, which are "above reason", are legitimate truths, nevertheless stipulated that they be not contrary to reason and that any religious truths, so-called, be in accord with reason.[2] The Deists and many others went even farther than Locke, abolishing reliance upon revelation, and either confining moral truth to "natural religion" alone or even dispensing with religion entirely. But this approach to history was not confined to the religious tradition. Essentially the same presuppositions were effective in the Enlightenment treatment of the history of social and political institutions.

We cannot here treat in detail all the Enlightenment writings dealing with the social and political history of mankind. But a few examples will serve to illustrate the approach that most of these writers made to this field. Since, as Cassirer has pointed out,[3] the main concern of Enlightenment thinkers was not the idealization of the past but the direction of society toward a better future, human history was invariably consulted with the assumption that it contained, if rightly analyzed, valuable lessons regarding the rise and fall of human societies; and since it was generally assumed that human nature remains the same throughout all ages, it was also believed that a knowledge of the causes of human success and failure in the past could serve as a means of securing a better social order in the future. The notion that "history is philosophy teaching by example," as Bolinbroke put it in his *Letters on the Study and Use of History*

---

[1] *Ibid.*

[2] John Locke, *An Essay Concerning Human Understanding* (1690). Bk. IV, Ch. 17, sec. 23.

[3] Ernst Cassirer, *op. cit.*, p. 181ff.

(1735),[1] became a favorite one of the Enlightenment commentators on this subject.

Such statements, of course, have led many to conclude that the Enlightenment was singularly devoid of sympathetic understanding of the past. It became a favorite theme of Romantic writers, for example, that the Enlightenment was an entirely unhistorical age. But such a charge can hardly be substantiated when one considers the work of men like Hume, Gibbon, Voltaire and Montesquieu.[2] On the contrary, much of the labor of these writers was devoted to the establishment of a new scientific method for understanding history. It was not that such men were lacking in historical understanding or interest but that their historical studies were undertaken with rather definite preconceptions. In general they were motivated by the belief that through rational analysis of historical records it is possible, first, to weed out the myths, fables and superstitions and, second, to discover the true causes of the rise and fall of human societies. When analyzed in this fashion, history could be made to yield those principles which would serve as a guide for the direction of social and political affairs.

The method of historical investigation undertaken by Enlightenment writers was essentially the same, whether it was the religious tradition or the cultural heritage in a broad sense which was subjected to rational scrutiny. For the most part, history was expected to teach useful lessons to be applied to individual and social conduct. Thus Voltaire in his *Dictionnaire Philosophique* in the article "Histoire," in answer to the question, "What would be useful history?" replies, "That which would inform us of our duties and our rights, without appearing to teach them to us."[3] So also, in his introduction to *The Philosophy of History*, dedicated to Catherine II of Russia, Voltaire undertakes to supply her Highness with "useful truths" about ancient history to take the place of the "useless errors" she had hitherto had to accept.[4] Much of Bolingbroke's work, previously cited, is also devoted to pointing out the fundamental truths governing the relations between the conduct of government and the prosperity of states.[5]

---

[1] Quoted by A. O. Lovejoy, "Herder and the Englightenment Conception of History," *op. cit.*, p. 177.

[2] As pointed out by Cassirer, *op. cit.*, p. 180.

[3] *Oeuvres completes*. Paris, 1818, p. 331.

[4] *Essays and Criticisms*, by M. de Voltaire. New York, 1915.

[5] Lovejoy, *op. cit.*, pp. 176–178.

By and large, such investigations of past history were guided by quite definite metaphysical preconceptions of the kind already noted in connection with the study of man's religious history. The main interest of the majority of the Enlighteners was not to uncover the variety and diversity of mankind's institutions and beliefs, but to discover, if possible, universal laws and fixed patterns of conduct. Voltaire, for example, assumes in his *Philosophy of History* that all men at all times must have reacted in the same way to similar phenomena. As he puts its, "Nature being everywhere the same, men must necessarily have adopted the same truths, and fallen into the same errors, in regard to those things which are the immediate objects of sense and the most striking to the imagination."[1] Likewise, and for the same reason, he assumes that "the notion of something just" is "universally received by all men," and is "independent of all law, of all compact, of all religion."[2] In spite of the differences he has observed in climate, manners, languages, laws and other circumstances, he claims to have observed that all men "have the same fund of morality."[3] Such an approach to history is well illustrated in the work of another eighteenth century writer, Mascon, in his *Geschichte der Teutschen*:

> The stage-setting in different periods of history is, indeed, altered, the actors change their garb and their appearances; but their inward motions arise from the same desires and passions of men, and produce their effects in the vicissitudes of kingdoms and peoples.[4]

Of all the political thinkers of the Enlightenment, Montesquieu stands practically alone as a student of history who did not leap to hasty generalizations but spent many years collecting facts and amassing information about the past. His *Spirit of the Laws* was unique in his age in its wealth of information about the customs and laws of various times and places. Still, while more painstaking than most of his contemporaries, Montesquieu shared their objectives. He too sought the universal laws embodied in the growth and decline of social and political institutions. Rome in particular attracted him— not because of any antiquarian interest on his part—but because it

---

[1] *Essays and Criticisms, op. cit.,* p. 22.
[2] "The Ignorant Philosopher" in *Essays and Criticisms, op. cit.,* p. 40.
[3] *Ibid.,* p. 38.
[4] Quoted by Lovejoy, *op. cit.,* p. 173.

"seemed to offer a complete specimen of the rise and fall of a society."[1]
Like the majority of the Enlighteners, Montesquieu believed that
the relevance of his historical studies consisted in large measure in
the homogeneity of the subject-matter with which he dealt. As he
expressed it in his *Considérations sur les causes de la grandeur des
romains et de leur décadence*, "while men have had in all times the
same passions, the occasions which have produced great changes are
different, but the causes are always the same."[2]

Tempting though it is, it would be hazardous to suggest a single
formula purporting to characterize all expressions of *the* Enlightenment conception of history. Probably the most we can say is that on
the whole, and in most cases, the leading spokesmen for the Enlightenment, when they considered history at all, did so from the
point of view of certain preconceptions which were generally shared
in Europe during the first half of the eighteenth century. It was suggested at the outset that a fundamental difference between the outlook of the early and of the late eighteenth century was the difference
in the general metaphysical orientation—in the shift from a relatively static to a relatively dynamic conception of the universe. It was
also suggested that this change in viewpoint had a direct bearing
upon the attitude toward, and conception of, history and historical
studies. We have yet to show in some detail how this transformation
was effected. But we are now, perhaps, in a better position to estimate the prevailing metaphysical outlook of Enlightenment writers
on history.

If our survey so far is at all representative of the Enlightenment
attitude toward history, it would seem quite evident that most of the
writers who dealt with this theme were strongly under the influence
of a world-view which emphasized the unchanging nature of ultimate
reality. One need only to call to mind the more general philosophic
situation of the early eighteenth century in order to realize how
pervasive was the influence in that age of conceptions stemming from
Newtonian science, and how strong, accordingly, was the hold which
a static world-view had on men's thinking. The development of the
social sciences, of which the "science" of history formed a part, was
undertaken by Enlightenment thinkers in large measure by "combining... the two strains of the humanistic emphasis upon the dignity

---

[1] J. H. Randall, Jr., *The Making of the Modern Mind*. Boston, New York...
1940, p. 320.
[2] *Considerations... von Montesquieu*, ed. by Erzgraeber. Berlin, 1885, p. 5.

and worth of man's life upon this earth, and of the scientific emphasis upon the universal law and a harmonious causal order in every part of nature."[1] It is not surprising, therefore, to find historians and philosophers of history looking for "eternal truths", universal laws and fixed patterns in the development of social and political institutions. The Deists and other critics of the religious tradition who sought by rational analysis to uncover "eternal truths" of morality were not essentially different in their approach from the philosophers and historians who studied cultural history with the expectation of discovering universal principles governing the rise and fall of human institutions. It would seem fair to suggest, therefore, that to the extent that the overwhelming majority of Enlighteners conceived themselves to be living in a universe governed by universal and immutable law—a universe wherein no change of *ultimate* significance occurs—they tended to view human history as a realm within which, as a part of the unchanging universe, one may find light for guidance in the future but no principle or law which is not forever true.

## II. Eighteenth Century Criticism of the Enlightenment Conception of History

Toward the latter part of the eighteenth century there began to appear in Europe what may, broadly speaking, be called "developmental" conceptions of history. We mean by this term only so much as may be suggested by the notion that in the course of history mankind has gradually achieved, and is achieving, higher and higher levels of religious insight, knowledge of the arts and sciences, and social and political competence, and that, furthermore, this achievement is the result of a developing historical process. This is not to imply that there was not what may be designated as a latent "progressivism" in the thought of the Enlightenment, especially in the assumption that in that age mankind had at last achieved in the natural sciences, and was about to achieve in the social sciences, complete rationality. But while the Enlighteners were prone to regard their own age as a definite improvement over earlier ones, they did not, on the whole, think of their era as occupying a definite position in a connected sequence of eras within which there was to be

---

[1] Randall, *op. cit.*, p. 309.

traced a *developing* pattern of culture. The idea of historical process was largely alien to the thought of the Enlightenment.

To this generalisation one noteworth exception should be made— although it is extremely doubtful whether the philosopher in question should be classed as an exponent of Enlightenment views. Giambattista Vico should be regarded, rather, as the first outstanding critic of the Enlightenment conception of history; and while his *Scienza Nuova*, which first appeared in 1725, was practically ignored by his contemporaries, it was in many respects prophetic of those philosophies of history which were to grace the European scene within the next hundred years. For Vico protested vehemently against the Cartesian attempt to confine all reliable knowledge to the sphere of nature, maintaining, on the contrary, that certainty is not guaranteed by "clear and distinct ideas", but only by the circumstance that the subject of investigation has been created by the investigator. Hence both nature and the supernatural are hidden from man's knowledge and only the social world, he claimed, can be known with certainty:

> If this is admitted, everyone who reflects will be astonished that the philosophers have seriously undertaken to know the *world of nature* which God has made, and the science of which he has kept to himself, and that they have neglected to meditate on this *social world*, which men can know since it is their own work.[1]

It is on the basis of this criticism that Vico proceeds to an exposition of a "metaphysic of the human spirit".[2] What is significant about this "metaphysic", however, is that it is not a description of merely static entities. To be sure, its principles have an "eternal" status, but the "new science... traces the eternal circle of an ideal *history*, around which turn, *in time*, the histories of all the nations, with their birth, progress, decadence and end..."[3] Vico thus seeks to construct *"a history of human ideas"*[4] which, though decidedly Platonic in metaphysical orientation, is nevertheless concerned to conceive of the universe of human affairs as guided by a non-recurring historical process. As a pious Christian, Vico ascribes the creation of the eternal principles and the order of their manifestation in human

---

[1] G. B. Vico, *Principes de la philosophie de l'Histoire*, trans. of *La Scienza Nuova* of 1774 by Jules Michelet, (Brussels, 1835), I, 162.

[2] *Ibid.*, p. 174.

[3] *Ibid.*, p. 175. (Italics in the original).

[4] *Ibid.*, p. 174.

affairs to Providence, with the result that, as he notes, the new science becomes "under one of its principal aspects, a civil theology of Divine Providence..."[1] In deference to the religious tradition, Vico divides human history into "sacred" and "secular", reserving to the former the account of the Hebrews who, unlike the rest of mankind, were preserved by Divine Grace from returning to the state of bestiality after the Fall. In secular history, however, there is to be traced the gradual development of the Gentiles from a state of barbarity to civilization, under the guidance of Providence, until at last all mankind shall dwell together in the perfect state of Justice.

Unfortunately, Vico's *Scienza Nuova* was little known and less appreciated in his own day. But in the last half of the eighteenth century ideas very much like Vico's gained greater prominence. At first, to be sure, the metaphysics of human progress—if it may be called that—was not explicitly formulated. But the static universalism and uniformitarianism of the Enlightenment became the frequent target of those who professed to find evidence of historical development in human institutions. In particular, the notion that this development is the result of a gradual unfolding, or realization, of human potentialities became more and more widely accepted as a substitute for the Enlightenment idea that history is a scene of more or less recurrent exemplifications of fixed laws and patterns. And while the favorite conceptions of the Enlightenment lingered on for a long time, the attitude toward history gradually underwent major revision.

An example of the change in approach to human history is manifested, in some respects, in Rousseau's *Discourse on Inequality* of 1754. To term Rousseau's view of history in this writing as "progressivistic" might be misleading, if it were suggested that Rousseau here avows the superiority of his own age to preceding ones. On the contrary, Rousseau, as is well known, makes much of the distinction between the "natural" and the "civilized", and regards the former as of much greater worth. Still this writing contains one of the earliest expressions of the belief that society has developed, is still developing, and can be in some ways guided in its future development; and for this reason it is to be contrasted with prevalent Enlightenment doctrines.

The *Discourse* is primarily concerned with social criticism. The

[1] *Ibid.*, p. 170.

device employed for this purpose by Rousseau is the idea of the "state of nature" which he conceived somewhat hypothetically, but which he believed to be a necessary presupposition of gaining a perspective on society;

> for it is not a light enterprise to disentangle that which is original and that which is artificial in the actual nature of man, and to know well a state which no longer exists, which perhaps never did exist, probably never will exist, but of which it is nevertheless necessary to have some correct ideas in order to judge rightly our present state.[1]

In other words, for Rousseau man in the "state of nature" is "original man",[2] not so much in the historical sense, but in the sense of what man may be conceived to be, stripped of that with which social life has endowed him. As Rousseau himself remarks, "it is not necessary to take the investigations into which one can enter on this subject for historical verities, but only for hypothetical and conditional reasonings, in order to clarify more properly the nature of things than to show the true origin of them".[3]

Stripped of "all the artificial faculties which he has been able to acquire only by long progress",[4]—the notion of progress here is significant—man appears for Rousseau as in all respects a superior animal, differing from the beasts in "the quality of free agent",[5] i.e. in his freedom to choose, and in "the faculty of perfecting himself",[6] i.e. his capacity of developing himself, both as an individual and as a species, in the course of time so that he is able to think, feel and do things of which formerly he was incapable. Thus Rousseau not only affirms the goodness of natural man,[7] but also his power, or capacity of self-development. The wickedness which man displays is a result of the corruptive power of social living, and not—as Hobbes believed—an original part of his nature.[8] In fact, when left to themselves, man's natural instincts of pity and sympathy for his fellows lead him to be sollicitous for their welfare. It is only when man

---

[1] Preface to *Discours sur l'origine et les fondements de l'inégalité parmi les hommes*, V. D. Musset-Pathay, ed., Paris, 1823, p. 216.
[2] *Ibid.*, p. 219.
[3] *Ibid.*, p. 225–26.
[4] *Ibid.*, Part I, p. 228.
[5] *Ibid.*, p. 238.
[6] *Ibid.*
[7] *Ibid.*, note 9, p. 328.
[8] *Ibid.*, p. 257 and note 15, p. 351.

emerges from his natural state, when he ceases to be guided by instinct and is guided by reason, that self-love makes of him a hater and a despoiler of his fellow men.

Historical development begins, for Rousseau, with the institution of property: "The first man who, having enclosed a piece of land, bethought himself to say *This is mine*, and found people simple enough to believe him, was the true founder of civil society".[1] Immediately the simplicity and goodness of the state of nature began to disappear, their place being taken by the artificiality and wickedness of social intercourse. The rule of instinct gave way to the rule of reason "which engenders self-love".[2] Whereas "formerly", by the natural sentiment of pity, and the unreflective avoidance of that which would harm his neighbor, men had lived with a minimum of injury to each other, now they became rational, calculating, proud. Natural differences of climate, terrain and seasons become reflected in men's manner of living. Through the power of reason, man becomes self-conscious, and with the development of self-consciousness he plots his own advantage and the detriment of his neighbor's. New needs, or at least desires for new commodities, spring up, and the social fabric becomes more complex as the means to their satisfaction are developed. The family appears, and gradually all the other social ties come into being. But here, where the beginnings of human society are to be found—the point at which "most savage people have arrived which we know"[3]—"this period of the development of human faculties, keeping to an equitable mean between the indolence of the primitive state and the petulance of our self-love, must have been the most happy and enduring epoch".[4] This—and *not* the "state of nature", as most critics of Rousseau have assumed[5]—was regarded by him as the "least subject to revolutions, the best for man..."[6] The departure from this state—"the true youth of the world"—and the subsequent development of civilization was the worst historical evil suffered by the human race. From this point on, history is a sad tale of the accumulation and abuse of riches, the

---

[1] *Ibid.*, p. 271.
[2] *Ibid.*, p. 260.
[3] *Ibid.*, p. 281.
[4] *Ibid.*, p. 282.
[5] As pointed out by A. O. Lovejoy, "The Supposed Primitivism of Rousseau's *Discourse on Inequality*", *Essays in the History of Ideas*, Baltimore, 1948.
[6] *loc. cit.*, p. 282.

development of the arts and sciences, the institution of social systems which benefit the rich and powerful and which grind the poor—in short, of all the evils of social inequality which are henceforth heaped upon hapless mankind.

What is significant about Rousseau's *Discourse* is not his employment of the idea of "the state of nature" which, by his time, in one form or another, had become a commonplace, and which, anyway, was conceived by him as a principle of social criticism rather than as a historical fact, but rather his doctrine that human society has *developed*; that this development coincides with the development of human reason; that stages within this development—e.g. the stage of savagery versus the state of civilization—are to be distinguished; and that the achievement of rationality is not, as the Enlightenment had assumed, a good, but rather a source of all human evil. And, in even more general terms, we may agree with Lovejoy that this work of Rousseau's "is chiefly notable in the history of ideas as an early contribution to the formulation and diffusion of an evolutionary conception of human history".[1]

From this time forward, especially in Germany, "evolutionary" conceptions of human history are given more and more frequent expression. In fact, it seems that a large part of the criticism of Enlightenment philosophy is delivered from this point of view. The idea of historical process is employed by various writers in widely differing connections, but invariably with the understanding that mankind's present condition is the result of a connected development, teleologically fashioned, and designed so that the passage of time is an integral part of the realization of value. Truth is not delivered and apprehended once and for all, but is slowly and laboriously acquired. Civilization did not spring miraculously into being, but grew and developed by the slow transmission of ideas and customs. It is no longer possible to study examples of human societies, such as Rome, with the expectation of finding therein the complete story of the decline and fall of all human societies; for Rome and its civilization represent one stage in historical process. Its civilization is unique; and while it contributes to the realization of the cultural whole, which, eventually, is humanity, it cannot be considered as an end in itself. Mankind has evolved through its institutions; and in this over-all evolution, we are to look for the thread which binds all cultures

---

[1] Lovejoy, *op. cit.*, p. 25.

together, and which will find its ultimate expression in the full flowering of the arts and sciences, and all that has made humanity's development significant. Whether it was religion, art, science, morality or social and political institutions in general that the writers of the late eighteenth century discussed, they did so increasingly with the assumption that diversity, change, development and purpose characterize all these fields. And as we shall see, Schelling's philosophy in the late eighteenth and early nineteenth century is in many respects a culmination of this post-Enlightenment emphasis upon history and historical development.

At this point, however, we must sketch briefly the pattern which this trend followed in Germany. And here, with the appearance of Johann Gottfried Herder's *Auch eine Philosophie der Geschichte zur Bildung der Menschheit* in 1774, the distinctive features of the new "progressivism" have begun to make their appearance. Herder vigorously denounces the historical viewpoint of the *Aufklärung*, charging it with an inability to appreciate the uniqueness of individual nations of the past. For the attempt of the *Aufklärung* to compare all nations with a common standard, Herder would substitute sympathetic insight into the uniqueness of each culture. They cannot, he maintains, be compared to one another or to the European nations of the eighteenth century, for every culture has its own value and worth. For instance, the question as to which nation in human history has been the happiest is meaningless: "each nation has its midpoint of happiness in itself, just as every sphere has its own center of gravity".[1] Consistently applied, this view would seem to lead to a kind of historical atomism. But Herder claims to avoid this conclusion by assuming an over-all progress and development "in a higher sense than has yet been imagined".[2] Like a stream which contains individual drops of water, each of which is to be regarded as a totality in itself, while the stream as a whole nevertheless has a pattern and direction, human history moves according to the "plan of an unfathomable Providence", directed toward "the general cultivation of mankind".[3]

The optimistic progressivism which Herder embraces here, and in his *Ideen zur Philosophie der Geschichte der Menschheit* of 1784–91, is

---

[1] J. G. Herder, "Auch eine Philosophie der Geschichte zur Bildung der Menschheit" (1774), *Werke*, ed. Suphan, V, 509.

[2] *Ibid.*, p. 512.

[3] *Ibid.*, pp. 585–86.

in practically every respect a complete break with the views on history of the *Aufklärung*. To be sure, Herder wavers somewhat and is inclined, at times, to raise questions about the value of contemporary civilization. But on the whole he is guided by the vision of history as an organically developing unit. As such, he maintains, it is to be conceived as a teleologically determined process, the goal of which is the realization of all of mankind's capacities for rational expression. In his earlier work, the *Auch eine Philosophie...*, he sees mankind beginning from a pair of humans, and, under the guidance of Providence, progressing from the state of childhood innocence through the various stages of boyhood, adolescence, and maturity to a complete development of its rational faculties. All of the earlier nations represented levels of ever-increasing maturity. Even as Providence "beguiled and educated [the nations] through religion",[1] and schooled them in the arts of civilization, so the Orientals, Egyptians and Greeks in succession contributed something to the over-all development of mankind. The same theme, with a somewhat more naturalistic emphasis, is taken up and expanded in the *Ideen...* wherein mankind is represented as proceeding by gradual development to the goal of *Humanität*. In large measure a product of organic Nature, man also brings to full expression the *telos* of Nature in his display of rationality. Since man alone is "organized for rational abilities",[2] i.e. for art, speech, freedom and expansion throughout the earth—in short, for "humanity", the highest expression of which is religion—the progress of nations is to be measured by their approximation to this ideal. And while it is a goal which is yet to be realized in the future, already the race has advanced toward that end in the achievement of the arts of civilization, and especially in the art of equitable social organization. "All doubt and complaint among men about the confusion and imperceptible progress of good in history is owing to the fact that the sad wanderer looks at too small an expanse of his way".[3]

Meanwhile, Lessing was also working out a kind of evolutionism for the religious history of mankind in his *Erziehung des Menschengeschlechts*. This work, which was to have a considerable impact on Romantic philosophy in Germany, and especially upon the Romantic conception of religious history, was a major factor in undermining the Deistic interpretation of religion. For while many of Lessing's

---

[1] *Ibid.*, p. 489.                      [2] *Ibid.*, XIII, 115.
[3] *Ibid.*, p. 235.

views were shaped by the assumptions of the *Aufklärung*, especially, as we have noted,[1] in his earlier period, his later philosophic expressions, at least as regards religion, were modified considerably in the direction of developmental, or dynamistic, notions. Accordingly at this time, in 1780, Lessing no longer regards the history of positive religions as merely a story of the corruption of originally pure revealed truth. Rather does he look upon history, in one of its more important aspects, as a process in which mankind has become *progressively* more enlightened, or educated, by revelation. In other words, Lessing comes to stand in the company of those who regard history as a significant process of the development of mankind toward progressively higher achievement.

While Lessing's espousal of a developmental conception of history in his *Die Erziehung des Menschengeschlechts* is not without notable dependence, at the same time, upon a generally static world-view stemming from the *Aufklärung*, he is able nevertheless to combine these two somewhat antithetic tendencies rather ingeniously. For while he regards the truths of revelation themselves as "eternal" truths, unaffected by any process, he yet conceives mankind's *apprehension* of these truths as a progressive development marked by temporal sequence. As with so many of the *Aufklärung* he assumes a pristine—although not necessarily historical—state of rational perfection. The first man "was equipped with a concept of a single God."[2] But as soon as man's reason, left to itself, began to elaborate this concept, "it dissected the Infinite into several finite things, and gave to each of these parts a designating mark."[3] Thus arose polytheism and idolatry, and mankind might have remained forever in darkness and error had not God chosen to recommunicate his truth by revelation. Since "that which is education for the individual man is revelation for the whole human race,"[4] however, and since God out of His goodness chose to educate mankind through the revelation of His truths, human history is to be seen as the realm within which man has been enlightened and brought back to knowledge of God. In the childhood of the human race, God chose the Jews to educate the human race in the knowledge of His oneness.[5] This concept,

---

[1] *Supra.*, p. 6.
[2] Works, ed. Olshausen (Berlin, Leipzig, n.d.), VI, 65.
[3] *Ibid.*, p. 64.
[4] *Ibid.*
[5] *Ibid.*, p. 67.

though far below "the true transcendental concept... which Reason so much later learned to infer with certainty from the concept of the Infinite,"[1] was nevertheless a step in the right direction, and the human race had made a significant advance. But in that the Old Testament, "the elementary book of... the Israelites,"[2] contained nothing about the immortality of the soul and future reward and punishment, a new stage in the education of the human race had to be reached. With Christ, "the first trustworthy, practical teacher of the immortality of the soul,"[3] mankind reaches its adolescence, and the more advanced text of the New Testament becomes the source of man's enlightenment. But full maturity will be reached only when man is able, by reason alone, to demonstrate not only the unity of God and the immortality of the soul as he is able at present, but also such higher truths as the doctrine of the Trinity and original sin. For after all,

> ...the cultivation of revealed truths into truths of reason is absolutely necessary if the human race is to be benefitted by them. As they were revealed, doubtless they were not truths of reason; but they were revealed *in order to become such*. They were like the sum which the mathematics teacher tells his students in advance in order that they can thereby somewhat direct their computation. If the students were satisfied with the sum given in advance, they would never learn how to add, and the intention with which the good teacher gave them a guide for their work would be badly fulfilled.[4]

As we shall see, Lessing is important as foreshadowing the work not only of later German thinkers in general in laying stress upon the significance of historical process, but also of Schelling in particular in making the content of history to consist in the rational realization of revealed religious truth.

It was, however, Immanuel Kant who was to lay the philosophic foundations for the emphasis upon history and historical process which characterizes later German thought. To attribute this role to Kant's philosophy, at first glance, may seem somewhat absurd, especially in view of Kant's stress upon the universality and uni-formity of nature's laws as this is developed in his theoretical philosophy. But, as in so many other respects, so also in respect to the subsequent attitude of German writers toward history, Kant's

---

[1] *Ibid.*, p. 66.
[2] *Ibid.*, p. 67.
[3] *Ibid.*, p. 75.
[4] *Ibid.*, p. 79.

philosophy was to prove to be a watershed between the *Aufklärung* and Romanticism. To be sure, from the point of view of the theoretical philosophy, nature's laws undergo no development. The categories of the understanding are not subject to change or process of any kind: a position which gives the fullest affirmation possible to the *Aufklärung's* belief in the necessity, universality and—above all—the "eternity" of the truths of nature's operations. But from the point of view of the practical philosophy, the situation, as Kant views it, is considerably different. For here, even though the moral law and its demands remain constant, the human race as a whole may nevertheless be conceived as progressing, through conflict, toward an ever more complete rationality in its social and political relations. Thus, while refusing to construct a "metaphysics" of history, Kant nevertheless does construe history as a whole in developmental terms, and in so doing continues the trend we have been tracing.

Thus, while sharply crticial of Herder's attempt in the latter's *Ideen* to erect an overall metaphysics which will explain both nature and history,[1] Kant himself proceeds in his *Idee zu einer allgemeinen Geschichte in weltbürgerlichen Absicht* of 1784 to "a philosophical attempt to construct the general world history according to a plan of Nature which is aimed at the complete unification of the human race."[2] But Kant makes certain critical distinctions at the outset regarding the kind of history he proposes to construct. While avoiding the speculation which is connected with understanding "noumenal" man as an autonomous moral creature, i.e. as endowned with free will, one may nevertheless adhere to a strictly empirical point of view, says Kant, and subject to investigation the free will's *appearances*, "human deeds, just as much as all other natural events [which] are determined according to general laws of nature."[3] So conceived, human history "allows the hope that when the play of the freedom of the human will is regarded *in toto*, a law-abiding process can therein be discovered."[4]

History becomes "a law-abiding process" for Kant when it is seen to be teleologically determined. In spite of the indeterminacy of indi-

---

[1] "Recensionen von J. G. Herders Ideen zur Philosophie der Geschichte der Menschheit" (1785); *Werke*, ed. Koninglich Precissischen Akademie der Wissenschaften, (Berlin, 1912), vol. VIII.

[2] *Ibid.*, p. 29.

[3] *Ibid.*, p. 17.

[4] *Ibid.*

vidual events, the actions of mankind taken collectively fall into a patterned process which has as its goal the establishment of an international constitution as the basis for the political association of all men. But this is the final stage of human development, and the complete realization of this goal of Nature lies still in the future. Meanwhile man has already made significant progress in that direction. Through the endowment of reason, which "is a faculty for extending... the use of all his powers beyond natural instinct,"[1] man has been able to gain increasing control over his physical environment so that later generations have been able to enjoy ever larger benefits from the arts and sciences. In his social relationships, however, man has experienced only discord. From a narrow point of view this may seem like an evil; but since "it is this opposition which awakens all the powers of man,"[2] social antagonisms are really blessings in disguise. Were it not for the selfish arrogance which men possess, they would have been content with a sheep-like existence, and civilization, culture, morality and social justice would never have developed. "Man wants concord; but Nature knows better what is good for the race; it wants discord."[3] Thus even as the natural unsociability of men has presented them with the problem of constructing local and national constitutions in order to mediate their antagonisms, so in the future an international constitution must be constructed to resolve the conflicts among nations. But history as a whole is to be seen, from Kant's point of view, as a gradual achievement of social harmony, a rationalization of social intercourse, and with it a progressive realization of man's capacities for rational self-expression.

This outline remained for Kant the more or less definite statement of the meaning of empirical history; and as such it served to set the pattern for much that is found in the writings of Fichte, Schelling and Hegel. Kant himself, however, was cautious in speculating about human history—as, indeed, he was about any and all metaphysics. And while he believed that an empirical science of human actions could be established along the lines laid down in his *Idee zu einer allgemeinen Geschichte*, he could not conscientiously accord more than a merely speculative status to any attempt to relate "a history of the first development of freedom from its original situation in the nature

---

[1] *Ibid.*, p. 19.
[2] *Ibid.*, p. 21.
[3] *Ibid.*

of man."[1] With this reservation, however, he did set forth such a "history" in his *Muthmasslicher Anfang der Menschengeschichte* of 1786, primarily as a supplement to his earlier work.

The *Muthmasslicher Anfang* gives a somewhat more extended treatment of the course of human history than does the *Idee zu einer allgemeinen Geschichte*, but its basic point of view is the same. "Originally"—and again, as with Rousseau, not necessarily historically—man is endowed with instinct; and "as long as man obeyed this [instinct], he prospered."[2] But as his reason developed his desires multiplied; and with the growth of desires arose the need for their rational control. Hence man develops a conscience. He also becomes able to anticipate the future; and while this enables him to control the future, it also exposes him to the pangs of anxiety and the fear of death. Finally man becomes conscious of himself as "actually the goal of Nature"[3] and hence as having all things placed at his disposal. It is with somewhat greater difficulty that he grasps the converse of this fact, viz. that *all* men are ends in themselves, are "to be valued by all others and to be used by none merely as means to other ends."[4]

The tendency which had been growing for some time to conceive of history in dynamic terms, as a developing process, and not as a realm where the same laws of human behavior are repeatedly exemplified, is, therefore, given renewed emphasis by Kant's writings on this subject. In this respect, at least, Kant shares the point of view, in general, of those who opposed the conception of history favored by the *Aufklärung*. Like Rousseau, whose writings he greatly admired,[5] Kant employs the notion of the "state of nature" as a contrast to man's historical development. It was the transition from the guidance by instinct to control by reason which Kant regards as the change "from the guardianship of Nature to the condition of Freedom,"[6] i.e. to the condition of historical existence. But there are two aspects of this transition which must be kept in mind: "The history of *nature* begins with good, for it is the work of

---

[1] "Muthmasslicher Anfang der Menschengeschichte" in *Werke, op. cit.* VIII, 109ff.

[2] *Ibid.*, p. 111.

[3] *Ibid.*, p. 114.

[4] *Ibid.*

[5] See, for example, Ernst Cassirer, *Rousseau-Kant-Goethe : Two Essays,* Princeton, 1945.

[6] *Op. cit.*, p. 115.

*God*; the history of freedom begins with *evil*, for it is a human work."[3] From the point of view of the individual, the acquisition of freedom entails consciousness of the demands of the moral law and the failure to achieve the required conformity. But from the point of view of the race, this step was a gain. For the change from the state of innocence to that of rational freedom is marked by the appearance of divisions among men according to their various modes of livelihood; and as men advance from nomadic to agricultural and other types of economy, not only do all the various aspects of culture develop, but warfare between groups becomes the instrument for the development of law. It is in the extension of legal arrangements to ever more inclusive social units, until an international state is finally realized, that the progressive development of human history chiefly consists.

The philosophy of Kant was to stand as the main source of inspiration for the writers of the next generation in Germany. Such was the wealth of undeveloped suggestion to be found in him, not only, or even primarily, in his brief writings touching on our main theme, but just as much in what was taken to be his philosophical position as a whole, that those who followed him, however diverse their views might be, believed that they could claim verification for their ideas in Kant himself. Not only Fichte and Schelling, but a whole host of lesser writers, sought to perpetuate and extend the Kantian philosophy.

Cognizance also should be taken, however, of the development in Germany in the last two decades of the eighteenth century of what is commonly referred to as the Romantic movement. For while, as a fashion of thought which first made its appearance among the younger literary lights, it was at the outset too broad and inchoate to be called a philosophy, it nevertheless did influence the philosophical expressions of this period and in time achieved a distinctive kind of formulation, by no means inadequately exemplified in the philosophy of Schelling himself. While it seems rather futile to attempt a formula or definition which will adequately identify all the diverse tendencies of German Romanticism, it nevertheless possesses certain common features which serve to distinquish it from the viewpoint of the age which preceded it, and especially the viewpoint of the *Aufklärung*.

As we have already noted, many of the favorite conceptions of the *Aufklärung* had suffered attack from around the middle of the eigh-

---

[1] *Ibid.*

teenth century. It was, therefore, largely as a culmination of a trend that had been growing for some time that Romanticism finally established itself as a movement of thought in the late eighteenth and early nineteenth centuries. Brunschwig contends that Romanticism "is defined essentially by its faith in miracle,"[1] in contrast to the Enlightenment's faith in reason, and that all its other traits of character, in literature, politics and religion, derive from this basic point of view. And indeed many of the expressions of Romantic writers would seem to justify this estimate. But a somewhat less misleading observation is made by the same author in noting "that the manner of thinking of the Romantics appears to be dominated by their conception of time."[2] It is this trait of the Romantic movement which, from our point of view, it is important to stress. For in their preoccupation with the problem of time, in their vivid sense of the developing, processing, unstable character of reality, the Romantics bring to fruition, in many respects, the trend toward a dynamic conception of the universe which had already found expression in recent German thought.

To quote Brunschwig again:

> The problem of time does not interest the multitude during the epoch of the Enlightenment. Reason has no age, and the men of the *Aufklärung* are not conscious of the passage of the hours. Their universe is immovable and perfect. Their progress is a putting in place, in a rigid frame, where the positions to be occupied have been marked in advance.[3]

But the Romantics, on the contrary, are keenly aware of the passage of time. For them, not only each moment, but each age, is charged with possibilities; and in the continuous passage from one instant to another there is to be found developing, changing, growing and expanding a manifold of ever new forms and unique expressions. Thus no one immutable standard is adequate to a representation of the richness of reality. One must seek, rather, to give expression to the diversity, past, present, and future, of the world, and abandon the attempt to confine the universe to a static system of eternal forms. Hence, for Lovejoy, "the shift from the uniformitarian to the diversitarian preconception [is] the most significant and distinctive

---

[1] *Op. cit.*, p. 220.
[2] *Ibid.*, p. 275.
[3] *Ibid.*, pp. 275–76.

single feature of the Romantic revolution."[1] And since the diversity of forms could never be fully realized in any one age, the Romantics turned to the past to recapture vanished modes of thought and behavior, and to seek to come in contact with the developing stream of reality.

The Romantic movement serves, thus, to give renewed impetus to the study of history and the fostering of evolutionistic ideas. A cursory examination of the leading ideas of a few of Schelling's immediate predecessors and contemporaries will help to illustrate how this is so. As early as 1789, for example, Schiller set forth a progressivistic conception of history in his inaugural address at Jena: *Was heisst und zu welchem Ende studiert man Universalgeschichte?* Here, with obvious dependence upon the doctrines of Kant, Schiller praises the advance which the eighteenth century has made over previous ages in the development of culture and the establishment of stable political relations; and in a vein reminiscent of Lessing and Herder, he compares the maturity of his own society with the primitives whose child-like immaturity serve the modern man as a reminder of "what he himself was formerly, and whence he has departed."[2]

By 1795, however, Schiller had become much more interested in aesthetic theory and had sought, through a Kantian approach, to express some of the insights thus obtained in an analysis of the development of civilization. This attempt is made in *Üeber naive und sentimentalische Dichtung*. Here Schiller develops as his fundamental conception the antithesis between the natural and the artificial, the naive and the sentimental, the real and the ideal, as the basis for comparing and contrasting the spirit of the ancient and the modern world. This antithesis between the natural and the artificial was, of course, an extremely well-worn notion by this time. But Schiller's employment of it is an instructive example of the contrast between the approach of Romanticism and the Enlightenment to social criticism, and serves, furthermore, to indicate the nature of that restless dissatisfaction with contemporary society which was so characteristic of early Romantic writers. Such restlessness is part and parcel of the Romantic taste for change, diversity, and dynamic, rather than static, conceptions of the ultimate nature of things.

---

[1] A. O. Lovejoy, *The Great Chain of Being*, (Cambridge, 1936), p. 297.
[2] *Werke*, (Stuttgart and Tübingen, 1847), X, p. 363.

The age of reason, the Enlightenment, had, on the whole, tended to compliment itself on the advance it had made over previous ages. It did not, therefore, idealize the past but sought, rather, to avoid the errors of the past in shaping the course which society was to take in the future. But with Schiller the past becomes an object of admiration; and it does so, in large measure, because he locates the "natural" in a specific historical epoch, viz. Greek, or "ancient", civilization. In contrast to Rousseau and Kant, for example, both of whom regarded the "state of nature" as a useful standard for achieving a perspective on society, but by no means as a necessarily historical condition of mankind, Schiller uses it as a means of comparing one historical era with another. Thus, while preserving the euphemistic connotations of the word "natural", and applying them to Greek civilization, he also manages to impart a nostalgic significance to a by-gone age. By the same token, modern civilization suffers by comparison and becomes, hence, an object, if not of contempt, at least of dissatisfaction.

In general, for Schiller, nature is absolutely opposed to the artificial, "all the advantage remaining on the side of nature."[1] When correctly understood, "nature is for us nothing but existence in all its freedom; it is the constitution of things taken in themselves; it is existence according to its proper and immutable laws."[2] Art, on the other hand, is the product of human activity. That which has been constructed, deliberately and rationally, by man, whether it be a particular object, or civilization and culture, is artificial. Nature is simple, or "naive," while art is complex and sophisticated. And of the two, it is nature, or natural objects, which has the power to awaken in us "not a satisfaction of the aesthetical taste, but a satisfaction of the moral sense."[3] For this reason, natural objects represent the norm to which we, as moral beings, aspire, as well as the original essence of our own being. "These natural objects which captivate us *are* what we once *were*, what we *must be* again some day."[4] Applied to historical development, this means, according to Schiller, that the naive simplicity of the childhood of the human race has been corrupted by the artificiality of civilization:

---

[1] Friedrich Schiller, "Simple and Sentimental Poetry" in *Essays Aesthetical and Philosophical*; English translation in Bohn Library, London, 1875, p. 263.
[2] *Ibid.*
[3] *Ibid.*
[4] *Ibid.*

> As long as man dwells in a state of pure nature,... all his being acts at once like a simple sensuous unity, like a harmonious whole. The senses and reason, the receptive faculty and the spontaneously active faculty, have not been as yet separated in their respective functions; *a fortiori* they are not yet in contradiction with each other... But when man enters the state of civilization, and art has fashioned him, this *sensuous* harmony which was in him disappears, and henceforth he can only manifest himself as a *moral unity*, that is, as aspiring to unity. The harmony that existed as a *fact* in the former state, the harmony of feeling and thought, only exists now in an *ideal* state.[1]

The historical locus of "the state of pure nature," for Schiller, is Greek civilization: "the Greeks had not lost sight of nature in humanity... in accord with themselves, happy in feeling themselves men, they would of necessity keep to humanity as to what was greatest to them..."[2] In contrast, modern civilized man, instead of being spontaneously conformed to nature, is in opposition to it, and the original unity of himself with himself, as well as with other men, has been destroyed. But Schiller did not advocate a return to the state of nature; and in this he displays his sense of the inevitability of historical development. He saw that it is man's destiny to pass from the state of nature to that of culture and to pursue through history the ideal which "nature" presents to him:

> ...we know... that humanity cannot reach its final end except by *progress*, and that the man of nature cannot make progress save through culture, and consequently by passing himself through the way of civilization.[3]

Thus, in still another way, Schiller contributes to the sense of movement and change which fills the consciousness of the young Romantics. Along with Friedrich Schlegel, Fichte and the early Schelling, who stressed this even more than did Schiller, the man of history cannot remain at rest in any given age. He cannot find fulfillment of all his potentialities in any point of time. Rather does time itself bear him along in a continual striving for a goal which always recedes. As Schiller expresses it, natural objects, in their immutable perfection, offer us an ideal which we, as ever-changing creatures, must ever pursue but never reach:

> ...we perceive eternally *in them* that which we have not, but which we are continually forced to strive after; that which we can

---

[1] *Ibid.*, p. 285.
[2] *Ibid.*, p. 279.
[3] *Ibid.*, p. 287.

never reach, but which we can hope to approach by continual progress.[1]

Not to labor the point, but in order to indicate how closely bound up with the thinking of other leaders of the Romantic movement these conceptions were, we may cite the views of Friedrich Schlegel in one of his earlier writings on the subject of history: his *Vom Wert des Studiums der Griechen und Römer* of 1794. Here, in even more clearly defined terms than those proposed by Schiller, Schlegel seeks to explain, by means of a theory based upon the Kantian philosophy, the nature of the difference between ancient and modern conceptions of history. In general, he observes, there are two ways of conceiving the movement of history: either as a finite, circular movement, which always returns to the point of departure, or as an infinitely progressing movement which never reaches a terminus. The former conception satisfies the requirements of the theoretical reason in that it allows us to view history as a "completed synthesis." But only the latter conception satisfies the demands of the practical reaon, for here the requirement is for an infinitely closer approximation to an unattainable perfection. Thus, on Kantian grounds,

> it is manifest *a priori* that there must exist two types of culture, according as the *representative* faculty or the *conative* faculty is primary and preponderant: a natural and artificial culture; that the former must come first in time, and is a necessary antecedent of the latter; and that the system of cicular movement (*System des Kreislaufes*) is possible only in the natural type of culture, the system of infinite progress (*System der unendlichen Fortschreitung*) only in the artificial type.[2]

The similarity of these views to those, just cited, of Schiller is manifest. According to Schlegel's principle of discrimination, the civilization of the Greeks and Romans was based upon the conception of history as a system of circular movement; and since, accordingly, it was based upon the achievement of a finite goal, it suffered inevitable decline when the goal was reached. Modern civilization, however, is based upon the conception of history as a "system of infinite progress"; and since its goal is ever receding,"...our history must remain ever uncompleted, ...our striving unsatisfied..."[3]

---

[1] *Ibid.*, p. 264–265.
[2] Quoted by A. O. Lovejoy, "Schiller and the Genesis of German Romanticism," in *Essays in the History of Ideas*, p. 212.
[3] *Ibid.*, p. 213.

All that was needed, in effect, was to incorporate this infinite
striving for an unattainable ideal into a metaphysical principle, as it
was by Fichte, Schelling and Hegel, in order to produce the type of
ontology which became characteristic of German idealism. With the
publication of Schelling's *System des transcendentalen Idealismus* in
1800, and Fichte's *Wissenschaftslehre* in 1801, wherein the whole of
existence is to be seen as an expression of the endless striving of the
Absolute, the spirit of the Enlightenment had been almost completely eclipsed by the contrasting spirit of Romanticism. As Lovejoy
succinctly puts it:

> The notion of infinity thus took precedence in philosophy over
> that of the finite and determinate, the category of Becoming over
> that of Being, the ideal of activity over that of achieved comple-
> tion, the mood of endless longing over that of quietude and
> collectedness of mind.[1]

It is, finally, with the appearance of Schleiermacher's *Reden* in
1799 and his *Monologen* in 1800 that the full circle of the development which we have been tracing is completed. As will become evident, Schelling's religious-historical conceptions are, in many ways,
but an extension and amplification of the views of the Romanticists
which we have noted up to this point. Schleiermacher's *Reden* in
particular, which were "greeted by the votaries of Romanticism as a
gospel,"[2] served to fix in broad outline, at least, the views on religion
of the Romantic movement. Not only are these writings of Schleiermacher an outspoken attack upon the religious theories of Deism and
the Enlightenment in general, but also—and most significantly, from
the point of view of this study—an affirmation of the essentially
historical character of religion.

The *Reden* of Schleiermacher, as is well known, deny that the
distinctive feature of religious piety is either intellectual belief or
moral action. Rather, while it includes both of these elements in its
manifestation, "it affirms its own territory and its own character in
that it falls entirely outside science as well as practice."[3] Religion has
to do primarily with a third element in man's nature, besides his
intellect and will, viz. his feeling. As Schleiermacher put it:

> Your feeling, insofar as it expresses the common being and life of
> the All, insofar as you have mediated its particular moments as a

---

[1] *Ibid.*, p. 211.
[2] Quoted by A. O. Lovejoy, *The Great Chain of Being* (*op. cit.*), p. 307.
[3] Schleiermacher, *Reden über die Religion*. Rede II.

working of God within yourself... this is your piety... Your feelings... are the exclusive elements of religion.[1]

Thus "true science is completed intuition; true praxis is self-engendered education and art; true religion is sense and taste for the Infinite."[2]

An essential feature of Schleiermacher's theory of religion, however, is the metaphysical setting within which he places man and his various faculties. For him, the universe is not a static system of fixed forms.

> The universe is in an uninterrupted activity, and reveals itself to us at every moment. Every form which it produces, every being to which it gives an independent existence according to the fullness of its life, every event which it pours forth constantly out of its rich, ever fruitful womb is its activity upon us...[3]

The Infinite, or All, the apprehension of which through feeling produces religious piety, is itself fundamentally dynamic in character. Back of each particular thing which is the product of this infinite activity lies the all-encompassing One as its source. Religion, therefore, has as its peculiar function the apprehension, through feeling, of the higher unity of the Infinite:

> ...to take each particular not in itself but as a part of the Whole, everything limited not in its difference towards others but as a representation of the Infinite in our life, and to let ourselves be moved thereby—that is religion.[4]

When applied to the variety of particular historical religions, these conceptions relating to religion in general make of its individual manifestations "a work of the Spirit which reveals itself in all human history."[5] It is of the nature of the Infinite Spirit, according to Schleiermacher, to express itself outwardly in an unlimited variety of forms. All religions, hence, represent various ways of apprehending the one World Spirit; and since these apprehensions are not limited to any one time or place, the widest extent possible of spatial, and especially temporal, variety is necessary for the expression of the fullness of religion. Thus "...history in the most exact sense is the richest source of religion."[6] The variety and plurality of religions, which seemed to the Enlightenment one of its worst features, is that which Schleiermacher regards as its crowning glory. For all of them

---

[1] *Ibid.*    [2] *Ibid.*    [3] *Ibid.*    [4] *Ibid.*    [5] Rede V.    [6] Rede II.

are equally "good" and "true" if approached from the point of view of their being progressive manifestations of the one Infinite Spirit. For since "only in the totality of all... possible forms can the whole of religion actually be given," and since religion "will be represented only in an infinite series, in various points of space as well as of time, of gradually developing forms,"[1] the religious history of mankind is to be seen as a progressive unfolding of the Absolute Spirit's activity.

When, now Schelling's conceptions relating to history and historical development are placed against the background, not only of Schleiermacher's theory but also of the more general viewpoint of the Romantic movement, it will be readily seen how he brings to a culmination the emphasis upon a dynamic metaphysics—and with it a heightened regard for historical process—which had grown up in conjunction with the later eighteenth century's criticism of the static world-view of the Enlightenment. And as we trace the development of Schelling's doctrines relating to the social, political and especially the religious history of mankind, we shall be in a better position to estimate the contributions which he made to these fields.

---

[1] Rede V.

# CHAPTER TWO

# THE ROLE OF HISTORY IN SCHELLING'S PHILO-SOPHY TO 1809

## I. Schelling as Disciple of Fichte

The earliest philosophical expressions of Friedrich Wilhelm Joseph von Schelling (1775–1854) rest upon an attempt to extend the implications of the Kantian criticism in the direction and spirit of the Fichtean "science of knowledge." However much Schelling was to diverge from Fichte's position later on, it is certainly true that "at the outset... Schelling was regarded by Fichte and others as his best commentator."[1] It is against this background, hence, that Schelling's first contributions are to be judged and evaluated.

Schelling no less than Fichte believed himself to be among the few followers of Kant who really understood and appreciated the master's critical investigations. In all his early works, but especially in his *Philosophical Letters on Dogmatism and Criticism* (1795),[2] Schelling set himself the task of explaining to his contemporaries the significance of Kant's *Critique of Pure Reason* in particular, and of the Kantian philosophy in general, in the face of what he felt was a general misunderstanding. Briefly stated, this misunderstanding, in Schelling's view, rested upon the failure to see that the *Critique of Pure Reason* was an investigation of the cognitive faculty in general, and that it did not establish any particular metaphysical system whatsoever. There was, Schelling believed, an "almost universal belief" that Kant had laid the foundations of "one system alone, whereas it must be the very peculiarity of a critique of reason that it favor *no* system exclusively, but instead... prepare the canon for *all*."[3] To be sure, Kant's investigations had demonstrated with finality the weakness of human reason, but in so doing they had established certain conclusions about "the idea of system *in general*, not [about]

---

[1] F. de W. Bolman, *Schelling : The Ages of the World* (New York: Columbia University Press, 1942), p. 12.

[2] Schelling's *Sämmtliche Werke*, edited by K. F. A. Schelling (J. G. Cotta, Stuttgart and Augsburg: 1856–61), I, p. 283–341.

[3] *Ibid.*, p. 301.

the idea of a particular system."[1] The time had come to set forth Kant's work in its true light and to destroy the misconceptions which threatened to undermine the fruits of all his labors.

According to Schelling, Kant proved once and for all that human reason cannot construct a philosophical system which can claim to be a complete transcript of reality as an object of *knowledge*. Knowledge extends only to objects of possible experience, and what lies beyond experience cannot be known. Hence one result of the Kantian criticism is the demonstration of the limited character of all (scientific) cognition. But Kant had also, and at the same time, shown that as soon as the knowing subject attempts to judge objectively, it "egresses from itself and is compelled to engage in a synthesis," whence it follows that "no absolutely objective knowledge is possible, i.e. that the object is knowable at all only under the *conditioning of the subject*."[2] Thus Kant had also irrefutably established idealism. Where there is knowledge it must take place under conditions which the knowing subject, the ego, imposes.

These results of the Kantian criticism are then employed by Schelling to elucidate the course of philosophic speculation. Following a distinction laid down by Fichte,[3] Schelling notes two opposed systems of thought: dogmatism and criticism, which are more commonly known as realism and idealism. Dogmatism has as its principle a "non-ego [or object] which is posited as prior to everything which is ego [or subject]. The principle of criticism [on the other hand] is an ego posited prior to, and exclusive of, all non-ego."[4] If ultimate reality is affirmed of the object, or non-ego, the resulting system is realistic; but if the ego, or subject, is regarded as ultimately real and as the condition for everything called "objective," a system of idealism is the result. In terms of this distinction, the problem is to determine which system is true.

It is at this point, according to Schelling, that Kant's critique, if properly understood, is able once and for all to indicate the direction in which a solution may be found. In his criticism of the idea of system as such, he has effectively closed one door through which many have sought to enter. Neither idealism nor realism can be proved demonstratively. For *as systems* which seek by means of

[1] *Ibid.*, p. 305.
[2] *Ibid.*, p. 296.
[3] Among other places, in his two *Introductions to the Wissenschaftslehre*.
[4] "On the Ego as a Principle of Philosophy," (1895), S. W. I, 170.

theoretical reason to ground the series of conditioned objects (synthesis) in an absolute (thesis)—"the goal of all synthesis is thesis"[1]—they are doomed to failure in that they leave the realm of possible experience wherein alone cognition is effective. But if at this point "philosophy makes a transition to the realm of demands, i.e. to the realm of *practical* philosophy,"[2] a clear cut decision can be made.

Kant himself had noted, as Schelling recalls, that reason possesses an irresistible inclination to bring unity into its cognitions by grounding them in an Absolute. This inclination of human reason "to transgress its boundaries, so that transcendental ideas are as natural to it ["*Vernunft*"] as the categories are to the understanding ["*Verstand*"]",[3] results only in vain and empty concepts with no grasp of reality. Nevertheless the impulse which finds expression in the transcendental ideas cannot be denied, even though the ideas themselves fail to achieve objectivity. In place of the transcendental ideas which make a spurious claim to extend our knowledge beyond the sphere of empirical experience, Kant substituted the *postulates* of God, freedom and immortality in order to allow reason to expand to the universality which it "unavoidably requires from a moral point of view."[4] Thus, Schelling maintains, following Kant, where reason fails to obtain knowledge for the theoretical question of the Absolute, "that theoretical question necessarily becomes a *practical postulate*, and the problem of all philosophy leads us necessarily to a demand which can be fulfilled only outside of all experience."[5] Both dogmatism and criticism *as systems* must reap embarrassment in attempting to arrive at knowledge of the Absolute. But when the basis for choosing between them is an *ethical* one, the whole complexion of the inquiry is changed and an unambiguous decision about their relative worth can be made.

Both dogmatism and criticism take their rise from the question, "Why is there a world of experience?" The empirical world, to which synthetic propositions apply, is obviously not self-explanatory. As a conditioned series, it presents us with the question of the Un-

---

[1] "Philosophical Letters...," S. W. I, 297.

[2] *Ibid.*, p. 299.

[3] "Kritik der reinen Vernunft" in *Kant's Gesammelte Schriften*, (Berlin: 1911), III, p. 426.

[4] *Prolegomena to any Future Metaphysics*, tr. by P. Carus, (Chicago; 1933), p. 136.

[5] "Philosophical Letters...", S. W. I, p. 311.

conditioned, the Absolute, the Thesis which lies beyond the subject-
object antithesis. Dogmatism, whose outstanding representative was
Spinoza, assumed an Absolute *Object* as original, and with this there
followed necessarily "the demand that the finite strive to become
identical with the Infinite, and to merge in the infinity of the Absolute Object."[1] But Spinoza is merely typical of a host of philosophers
who have counseled "the return into the Deity, into the fountain-
head of all existence, the unification with the Absolute, the annihilation of selfhood."[2] Such "enthusiasm" has consistently maintained
that the subject should "be absolutely passive toward absolute
causality"[3] and thereby has produced that type of mysticism which
ends in denying all freedom, all causality, for the ego. In effect, it
degrades the human subject by making it a mere mode of the Absolute Object—a mode which is to be swallowed up in the all-embracing
one.[4]

Criticism does not begin with a different problem, but its approach
and solution are directly opposite to dogmatism's. Dogmatism mis-
takenly believes that there is an objective Absolute opposed to our
subjectivity and in which our subjectivity must lose itself. This error
arises in the first instance because of the theoretical demand that
there be a thesis as the basis for the series of conditioned objects
presented in experience. But further than that, the human ego has
an ability to intuit itself: "we all have a secret and wondrous capacity
of withdrawing from temporal change into our innermost self which
we divest of every exterior accretion: there, in the form of immuta-
bility, we intuit the eternal in us." This "intellectual intuition" provides the link between the theoretical Absolute and the ego's own
subjectivity. It is not a postulate, but "an *immediate* experience in
the strictest sense, i.e.... an experience produced by ourselves and
independent of any objective causality,"[5] In the intellectual intuition, we are no longer an object for ourselves, "the intuiting object
is identical with the intuited,"[6] time and space vanish; and in that
consciousness is possible only by means of the opposition of subject
and object, all consciousness must vanish in this "absolute identity."[7]
In fact, as Schelling expresses it, "we awake from the intellectual
intuition as from the state of death."[8]

It is this intellectual intuition which, Schelling suggests, is the

---

[1] *Ibid.*, p. 315.   [2] *Ibid.*, p. 317.   [3] *Ibid.*, p. 316.   [4] *Ibid.*, p. 318.
[5] *Ibid.*   [6] *Ibid.*, p. 319.   [7] *Ibid.*, p. 327.   [8] *Ibid.*, p. 325.

goal of all mystical systems and of those religions which advocate absorption in Deity, or, like Buddhism, entrance into Nirvana. But in philosophical dogmatism it is viewed as the means to union with the Absolute Object. Spinoza, the typical dogmatist, objectified this intellectual intuition, believing thereby that he had, or could, become identical with the Absolute (God) and thus his selfhood might be completely swallowed up in object. But Spinoza, no less than all other dogmatists, in "believing this... deceived himself. It was not he who had vanished in the intuition of the Absolute Object. On the contrary, everything objective had vanished for him in the intuition of himself,"[1] This is the error to which all dogmatism has succumbed: in taking "the intuition of oneself for an intuition of an object outside of oneself, the intuition of the inner intellectual world for an intuition of a supersensual world outside oneself."[2] Idealism, on the other hand, recognizes and affirms the subjective character of this intuition, and thereby proclaims the ultimate reality of Ego.

Again we must note, however, that in Schelling's view the *goal* of both dogmatism and criticism is the same. Whether I vanish in the object, or everything objective vanish for me, the end result is absolute identity. At this final stage, the subject-object antithesis is abrogated in the Absolute, and it matters not, in effect, whether the subject or the object has become all-in-all. In the case of criticism, wherein freedom (as that which is unconditioned) is attributed to the subject, *complete* freedom would mean annihilation of all objectivity. With dogmatism, where necessity is attributed to the object, *complete* necessity would mean annihilation of all subjectivity (i.e. the overcoming of all causality outside of that possessed by the object). But the freedom-necessity antithesis has meaning only as long as there exists an opposition of subject and object. Both subject and object, freedom and necessity, vanish at the point of absolute identity, so that "absolute freedom and absolute necessity are identical."[3] If criticism, therefore, represents the goal of its system as that of complete freedom, its fate is the same as dogmatism's. In fact, "criticism itself necessarily turns into dogmatism as soon as it sets up the ultimate goal as realized (in an object), or as realizable (at any particular time)".[4]

Idealism displays its superiority to realism in two respects. In the first place, idealism bases its claim to truth upon the fact, originally

---

[1] *Ibid.*, p. 319.    [2] *Ibid.*, p. 321.    [3] *Ibid.*, p. 331.    [4] *Ibid.*

pointed out by Kant, of the autonomy of the practical reason. Man as a moral being, as that being which owes allegiance to no higher law than that of his own selfhood, is (at least potentially) free. At least in principle, and according, to his own essence, man is not determined by anything outside of himself. He is (or should be) autonomous, hence absolute. Thus idealism accords, as realism does not, with the nature of man as a free being whose *will* is destined to become supreme as an expression of egohood. In the second place, idealism provides a system, or at least a point of view, whereby the expression of man's autonomy becomes possible. As an autonomous being, man must express himself through activity, Dogmatism claims to present a system whose realization through practical activity is assured, but actually, in that its ultimate demand is for complete *passivity* on the part of the subject, it destroys what it claims to offer. Only criticism is faithful to the demand of man's inner essence for free activity, for "in criticism my vocation is to strive for immutable selfhood, unconditional freedom, unlimited activity."[1] And this is the demand of the moral law. Criticism stands for self-realization, while dogmatism leads to self-destruction.

During the years 1795–97, Schelling's work consisted largely of an amplification of the views set forth in his *Philosophical Letters on Dogmatism and Criticism*. Still strongly under the influence of Fichte, he sought to show in various ways how the presuppositions of the "science of knowledge" must issue in a metaphysics which will solve the manifold problems which had plagued philosophers from the earliest times. It is evident that Schelling, like Fichte, in elevating the Ego to the position of absolute first principle, was convinced that the means were now at hand for the inauguration of that great period in human history when "all the gleams of human knowledge and the experience of many centuries will finally unite in one focal point of truth,"[2] when the sciences would be brought to completion, and when all mankind would be united through its possession of the one science which underlies all, but which had, until the labors of Kant and Fichte, remained concealed from human view.

This attitude, which amounts at times to an exuberant faith in the all-embracing efficacy of the *Wissenschaftslehre* to solve the riddles of the universe, is decisive for Schelling in his early period, no less

---

[1] *Ibid.*, p. 335.
[2] "On the Ego as a Principle of Philosophy," *op. cit.*, S. W. I, p. 158.

than it was for Hegel and Fichte. One cannot understand German idealism without a grasp of this spirit which inspired its chief representatives. What has, perhaps rightly, been denounced as metaphysical arrogance on the part of Fichte, the early Schelling, and Hegel stems directly from this belief that a new era of human history had dawned as a result of the critical investigations of Kant. For Kant had furnished the principles and the method whereby all the sciences and philosophies could be understood and coordinated, while his philosophy itself represented the peak achievement of human knowledge. In the "critical philosophy" of Kant and Fichte, human knowledge had finally arrived at self-consciousness. The task which was set for Schelling in his early period, accordingly, was to show in detail how this philosophy is able to solve all the traditional problems which had beset mankind on the assumption that *at last* the key to these problems had been discovered. It is only somewhat later that he seeks to show concretely how the human race has progressed in its discovery (or recovery) of the Truth.

The extension of the point of view set forth in the *Philosophical Letters* was accomplished by Schelling in two major works of the same period: *On the Ego as a Principle of Philosophy* (1795) and *Discussions toward Elucidation of the Idealism of the Wissenschaftslehre* (1796–97). Imbued with the conviction that mankind is on the point of achieving unity through the unification of its knowledge,[1] he sets out to describe the manner in which ultimate reality must be conceived if it is to be understood from the standpoint of critical idealism. Having already established "criticism" on moral grounds, his efforts are now bent toward an elaboration of that system which presupposes, as a first principle, "the final ground of all reality,"[2] the Absolute Ego. This Ego, as that which is Unconditioned, cannot be conceived as an object, for an object always presupposes a subject of which it is the object. And by the same token, the Absolute cannot be a subject, if this be conceived as that which is conditioned by an object. Rather, "the completed system of science proceeds from the Absolute, from the Ego exclusive of all antithesis."[3] The Absolute Ego is that which conditions everything else, but which itself is unconditioned. It is not appearance, nor is it "thing-in-itself" "because as such it is nothing, but absolute ego, and pure ego is that which excludes all non-ego."[4]

---

[1] *Ibid.*, pp. 158–9.    [3] *Ibid.*, p. 163.    [4] *Ibid.*, p. 176.
[2] *Ibid.*, p. 177.

In attempting, thus, to set forth what he called "a counterpart to Spinoza's Ethics,"[1] Schelling was aiming at nothing less than a complete metaphysics. It differed from Spinoza's only in that the latter presupposed an Absolute Object, while Schelling offered an Absolute Subject as first principle. Furthermore reality is not to be conceived as an aggregate of disparate substances, for "the Ego contains all being, all reality,"[2] "The Ego is the only substance..." hence "everything that is, is merely accident of the Ego."[3] In short, "the Ego is... not only first principle of being (*Esse*), but also of the essence (*Essentia*) of everything that is."[4] Schelling's monism thus is aptly characterized as panpsychism.

The problem, now, is to explain the manifold structures and elements of reality in terms of the Absolute Ego—a task which, though difficult in execution, held promise, as Schelling believed, of bringing to an end the controversies which had beset the world of philosophy from the beginning. Assuming that Ego is original and all else derivative, it becomes possible to deduce further characteristics which reality possesses. Ego, or Mind (*"Geist"*), is "pure activity."[5] It is by no means a static structure. And since the pure activity of Mind cannot be other than purposeful—or, we might say, since the ego by its nature displays a rationally directed, rather than a chaotic activity, and furthermore is determined in its activity by no external factor—Mind is self-determined activity. But if this is true, then Mind's activity takes the form of willing: "That self-determination of mind is called willing."[6] *That* reality should manifest itself in this form cannot be accounted for by appeal to any more ultimate principle. Reality as encountered absolutely is free (self-determined) activity which we denote as willing.

We may better understand Schelling's endeavors at this point if we see that he is now attempting to give expression to the metaphysical postulates which are involved in the system of "criticism" he had set forth in the *Philosophical Letters*. In this latter work, as we noted, the defense of idealism is undertaken from the standpoint

[1] *Ibid.*, p. 159.
[2] *Ibid.*, p. 186.
[3] *Ibid.*, pp. 192–3.
[4] *Ibid.*, p. 195.
[5] "Discussions toward Elucidation of the Idealism of the Wissenschaftslehre, S. W. I, p. 390.
[6] *Ibid.*, p. 395.

of the morally self-determined subject who seeks to establish a system which will provide scope for his activity. Now the situation is reversed in that the system itself, which answers to these specifications, is elaborated in such a way that the willing subject appears as a deduced element in the total scheme of things. Granting, now, that Ego is the ultimate principle of reality, the question still remains of how this *Geist* produces a world—the question *par excellence* of philosophy. The empirical world, the world of "appearance", must be deduced from the Absolute Ego.

The detailed elaboration of this deduction need not concern us here. We may note, briefly, that Mind, as that which is original and productive at the same time, must by its very nature express itself in such a way that consciousness, which is lacking to it at the outset, come to full expression. That consciousness—or, more exactly, *self-consciousness*—is the goal of Mind's activity is to be understood through the inner constitution of ego as autonomous. This autonomy, which is identical with freedom conceived as self-determination, cannot achieve expression, however, unless there be "another" in contrast to which its complete independence can be portrayed. Thus Ego, or Subject, must oppose to itself a Non-ego, or Object; the Infinite must set itself off against a Finite; the Unconscious must achieve consciousness.

> Hence we shall think of the soul as an activity which is continually endeavoring to produce the finite out of the infinite. It is as though an infinite were concentrated in it which it is compelled to represent outside of itself. This can be explained only as the steady endeavor of Mind to become *finite* for itself, i.e. conscious of itself.[1]

In this way, following almost exactly the course laid out by Fichte, Schelling attempts to explain human consciousness. It is, for both philosophers, an attempt to assign an ultimate reason, not only for human cognition in the specialized sense of scientific knowing, but for the whole series of representations from the barest awareness of sensed objects to the pinnacle of mental activity displayed in the *Critique of Pure Reason*. But if such philosophizing is properly termed epistemological investigation, it is also, and none the less, ontological speculation. For if the world is that which is object of the ego's consciousness, and object itself is nothing but a self-projection of the ego, then an analysis of the activity of the ego is also an

---

[1] *Ibid.*, p. 382.

analysis of the world. Naive realism assigns an independent objectivity to the non-ego. But criticism, the "transcendental philosophy",[1] recognizes the so-called objective world as a mere projection of the Ego, and, in fact, seeks to make explicit the point of view from which this judgment is rendered.

Such a judgement can be rendered only from an absolute point of view, i.e. a point of view which transcends the subject-object antithesis. This "absolute situation"[2] of Mind is that which is achieved by the "intellectual intuition".[3] In this intellectual intuition, "the mind becomes immediately aware of itself".[4] It was this faculty which was exhibited by Kant in his transcendental investigations in which, as a result of this power, he was able to render a scientific account of the mind's operations. What Kant failed to do was to show explicitly that, since Mind is the pure activity of absolute willing, the intellectual intuition achieves union with the primal source of reality itself. Whereas Kant maintained that the things-in-themselves are "those things which provide the ground of our representations"[5] and thus stand as symbols of the supersensible, Fichte dispenses with this symbolic representation "since he does not, like Kant, deal with the theoretical philosophy in separation from the practical".[6] Instead, Fichte makes the principle which Kant placed at the summit of the *practical* philosophy (the autonomy of the will) the principle of the *entire* philosophy, "and thus becomes the author of a philosophy which can rightly be called the *higher philosophy*, since in spirit it is *neither theoretical nor practical alone*, but, as it were, *both*".[7] Thus Fichte and (at this stage) his disciple, Schelling, seek to deduce the finite appearance of the Will from the position established by what they believe was Kant's transcendental idealism.

The question to be posed at this point—which is more immediately relevant to the special concern of this investigation—is: what is the status of the *empirical* world, the world of "appearance", in this metaphysical scheme? Above all, where does history fit into the picture? The answers to these questions are contained in the nature

---

[1] *Ibid.*, p. 401.
[2] *Ibid.*, p. 399.
[3] *Supra*, pp. 50–1.
[4] "Discussions..." *op. cit.*, p. 401.
[5] *Ibid.*, p. 409.
[6] *Ibid.*
[7] *Ibid.*, Underscoring in the original.

of the Ego's activity. In the endeavor of Mind to become finite for, and thereby conscious of, itself—in order to realize itself as un- conditionally free—it seeks a foil for its activity. If the activity of the Absolute Will is understood as the expression of the moral law, then the foil for its activity must be understood as an activity which is, at least potentially, lawless and hence immoral. Strictly speaking, the supersensible Will, "in so far as it is legislative, i.e. absolute, can be neither free nor unfree, since it expresses merely itself in the law".[1] It *becomes* free by separating from itself phenomenally (but not essentially) a part of itself which is endowed with spontaneity. The freedom with which Will is endowed when it becomes finite, or phenomenal, is "freedom to choose".[2] This freedom, which Schelling designates as spontaneity (*"Willkür"*), is distinguished from the free- dom of the Absolute which is completely self-determined.

Freedom of choice, therefore, is the condition of self-consciousness. It is the freedom to act unmorally, to act contrary to the moral law. Indeed, the moral law would have no meaning if there were not some way of acting contrary to its dictates. But even in recognizing this possibility, the human subject must acknowledge the authority of the Absolute Will. It is through this possibility that we achieve "consciousness of the supersensible",[3] and thereby we also recognize our finitude. The *empirical* ego, therefore, is to be understood as "the transcendental place where the intellectual in us passes over into the empirical".[4] It is in the empirical, or finite, ego that the subject- object antithesis is experienced and provisionally—at least in the intellectual intuition—overcome.

This is the context within which human history must be seen. For "the whole history of our race... belongs only to finitude".[5] There- fore, whatever qualifications are imposed upon finitude, the empiri- cal realm, will apply also to history. History is the scene wherein the Absolute expresses itself in the human subject as the subject's free- dom to choose, to separate himself from objectivity, to make this objectivity subordinate to his freedom, and thereby to achieve self- consciousness. Thus history plays an essential role in the Absolute's scheme of expressing its (moral) activity. History as a whole has a definite significance: "it [history] begins with the Fall, i.e. with the first spontaneous act, and ends with the reign of reason, i.e. when all

---

[1] *Ibid.*, p. 440.    [2] *Ibid.*, p. 435.    [3] *Ibid.*, p. 439.    [4] *Ibid.*, p. 440.
[5] *Ibid.*, p. 439.

spontaneity disappears from the earth".[1] What is referred to as the Fall in the Christian tradition becomes, therefore, in Schelling's view, the beginning of the Absolute's self-limitation, the place where freedom as spontaneous choice creates the possibility of the anti-thesis between "good" and "evil" through an activity which, poten-tially at least, runs counter to the direction of that established by the Absolute Will. History as the scene of spontaneity is to be understood as the point where the Will becomes phenomenal. This is the meta-physical framework within which history is to be placed.

From the point of view of the historical subject, history represents the scene of moral struggle. It may mean other things, but its es-sential significance is grasped when from the multitude of decisions with which the individual is confronted there is extracted the basic drive toward identification of the empirical willing with the Absolute Will. The phenomenal world presents itself as the limit against which our subjectivity strives. But the very striving of our subjec-tivity bespeaks a goal which is supra-empirical. The human spirit cannot find rest in the empirical realm. We finally reach a point where, "no longer finding objects, we make ourself into an object."[2] But the self, or ego, is not an object *as such*. It can become objective to the extent that it realizes itself as subject of a given objectivity, and thus achieve self-consciousness. But it can never become a completely limited object.

From the point of view of *theoretical* reason, therefore, the goal of Mind's activity is its consciousness *of* that activity. Thus history, from the theoretical side, is "none other than the history of the various situations through which it [Mind] gradually arrives at the intuition of itself, at *pure* self-consciousness."[3] This has been the goal of all philosophizing from the beginning; and as we have seen,[4] Schel-ling believed that, primarily through the investigations of Kant, the groundwork had been laid whereby mankind at last was able to ar-rive at the completed system of the sciences and to achieve, thereby, a final statement of the riddles of the universe.

From the *practical* side, however, whereby history is viewed as the realm of spontaneous *activity*, and accordingly as the scene wherein empirical willing seeks identification with the Absolute Will, there

---

[1] *Ibid.*
[2] *Ibid.*, p. 431.
[3] *Ibid.*, p. 382.
[4] *Supra.*, pp. 52–3.

can be no practical state corresponding to the theoretical state of the intellectual intuition. For to achieve identity of willing and Will would mean the end of spontaneity and with it the end of history. As long as history endures, the presupposition of its existence, viz. the cleavage of spontaneity and Absolute Freedom, must also obtain. The activity of the willing subject is the *sine qua non* of history. Its object, or goal, must therefore be infinite; it "can be realized only in endless progress, i.e. empirically."[1] There is no point within history where the goal of history can be considered as realized. As long as history lasts, it is the scene of endless moral struggle, of progress but not fulfillment.

Ultimately, of course, the view of history which emerges in this treatment of it is of a realm which is not endowed with true significance. Nothing novel or decisive is produced by historical events, except the production of self-consciousness on the part of the spontaneously willing subject. Eventually the moral activity of the subject must be seen as a mere episode in the drama of the Absolute's self-development. Finitude as such exists merely to be overcome; and since history is identified with the sphere of finitude, or appearance, it too has only relative worth. To be sure, history is not merely illusory, any more than is finitude in general.[2] Nevertheless, it is the Absolute which achieves ultimate significance rather than the subject whose spontaneous activity must finally disappear in the synthesis of Absolute Reason. At this point in his development, Schelling had failed to arrive at a philosophy of history.

## II. THE PHILOSOPHY OF NATURE

Schelling's interests, from around 1797, were largely confined to the construction of a philosophy of nature along the lines laid down previously in his exposition of transcendental idealism. In his *Ideas for a Philosophy of Nature* (1797), as well as in the supplementary work, *The World Soul* (1798), Schelling proceeds, as he believes, with an application of the principles of the *Science of Knowledge* to nature, little heeding, at the time, the possibility that here he was laying the basis for a break with the Fichtean philosophy. For to the extent

---

[1] "Discussions...", *op. cit.*, p. 431.
[2] *Ibid.*, p. 439.

that nature is conceived, as it is by Fichte, as the objective and hence as non-ego, and therefore as an opposition to be overcome by moral struggle, it is accorded no more than a provisional status in the ultimate nature of things. But for Schelling, during this period of his thought, "nature is not the epitome of lack of content, non-ego, to which the Ego stands in complete contrast, but rather in its inmost depths it is nothing other than mind and will, creative identity."[1] Certainly by the time that Schelling had produced the contents of his *First Sketch of a System of the Philosophy of Nature* (1799) and his *System of Transcendental Idealism* (1800), he had passed beyond the point where he and Fichte could agree on fundamentals.

Schelling's philosophy of nature, as it appears at this time, is based upon a complete identification of mind and nature. The Cartesian dualism of thought and extension, mind and matter, is a dichotomy which must be seen within the ultimate context of that one Unity, the Absolute. In effect, Schelling was attempting to reinstate the vision of Spinoza, whose virtue it had been to see that "ideal and real (idea and object) are internally united."[2] But Spinoza's had been a system of absolute realism, whereas Schelling was proposing the view that "the whole... is *absolute idealism*."[3] The Absolute, as such, is "an eternal act of knowing,"[4] a total activity, as opposed to the ultimately static nature of Spinozism. Whereas Spinoza had conceived the ultimate as absolute non-ego, within which all subjectivity is destined to be absorbed, Schelling maintains the equation, the All equals Ego, within which all objectivity is, in the final analysis, illusory. Hence while Schelling still is able to maintain the distinction between his philosophy of nature and that of Spinoza's, he has now moved closer to him in spirit and intent. At least, whereas in 1795 he had spoken out vigorously against "the abomination of Spinozism,"[5] he was now ready to recognize the basic affinity between his quest for a systematic exposition of the Absolute and Spinoza's.

What, then, are the presuppositions which the philosopher brings to his understanding of "the idea of nature as a whole"?[6] He must have some key by which the mystery of nature's hidden springs may be penetrated, some vision which will illuminate the depths of the

---

[1] Paul Tillich, *Mystik und Schuldbewusstsein in Schellings Philosophischer Entwicklung*, (Gütersloh: 1912), p. 49.

[2] "Ideen zu einer Philosophie der Natur," S. W. I, 2: 35.

[3] *Ibid.*, p. 68.    [4] *Ibid.*, p. 62.    [5] I, 1, 309.    [6] I, 2, 348.

productive force of which only the manifestations are ordinarily glimpsed. He must explain the series of representations which ordinarily is accepted as the pattern of events upon which our experience of a "world" is based. This is the task which philosophy has faced from the beginning: "whoever first noticed that he could separate himself from external things and thus his representations from the objects, and vice versa... was the first philosopher."[1] The standpoint of earlier philosophers, on the whole, however, has been that of the assumption that the succession of events and their representations are co-ordinates of a system external to the mind which knows that system. Such was the position of Spinoza, and Hume's skepticism was a more or less fitting culmination of the type of philosophy which rests upon that assumption. Only one alternative remains: "to derive the necessity of [the mind's] representations from the nature of our mind, and to that extent of the finite mind in general."[2] Once we assume that "the system of nature is at the same time the system of our mind,"[3] that mind and nature are, in fact, identical, the problem of their inter-relation is solved.

Spinoza's philosophy is thus corrected, as it were, in order that the true transcendental perspective may be achieved. Spinoza erred in not "entering into the depths of his self-consciousness and from there viewing the genesis in us of two worlds, the ideal and the real."[4] Having "lost himself in the idea of an infinite outside of us,"[5] he was unable to grasp the true nature, of the Absolute. "From now on" Schelling proclaims, "all dogmatism is completely reversed."[6] Philosophy must proceed from the concept of the Absolute-as-Ideal, from the activity of absolute knowing, and thus itself become the instrument by which the One Absolute achieves expression. Thereby the character of philosophy itself is transformed: it "becomes *genetic*, i.e. it lets the entire necessary series of our representations, as it were, arise and end before our eyes."[7] And as such, philosophy is to be understood as itself the means whereby the Absolute reaches its highest mode of expression.

The dynamism of the Absolute, as it expresses itself, "has two sides, a real and an ideal."[8] The real side is that which has commonly been called "nature," and represents the dead product of the Absolute's activity, *natura naturata*.[9] In other words, "nature" is the

---

[1] I, 2, 15.    [2] I, 2, 35.    [3] I, 2, 39.    [4] I, 2, 36.    [5] *Ibid.*
[6] I, 2, 39.    [7] *Ibid.*    [8] I, 2, 66.    [9] I, 2, 67.

object as opposed to the subject, or "visible Mind."[1] It *appears* as extended being, as something outside of the Absolute. As *natura rerum*, the real world wherein eternal ideas come to birth as finite things, it is to be understood philosophically as the objectivation, or objective appearance, of the Absolute, and by no means as an independent realm of existences. Likewise the ideal side of the Absolute is that which has commonly been called "mind," as something which, as such, is opposed to "nature". But this ideal world, as such, as something independent of the objective realm, as this is conceived in "relative idealism,"[2] is not a separate realm either. Both nature and the ideal world are but "potencies" of the One Absolute.[3] Philosophy maintains "the absolute identity of mind *in us* and nature *outside of us*."[4]

The "potentiation" of the Absolute, however, provides Schelling with a means to the explanation of nature's products as stages in a general teleological schematization. The fact that nature is organized, or teleologically related in all of its parts, is itself accounted for by the purposefulness which is characteristic of Mind's activity. It is because one no longer "allows purposefulness to enter it from outside"[5] that nature is bound to express itself as organic. When, furthermore, the teleology of nature is analyzed into its constituents, man is seen to occupy a commanding position within the whole. The real world of *natura naturata*, the world of (relative) non-ego, reveals itself as a "system of world bodies" which, as such, is "none other than the visible realm of ideas."[6] But the real world, as the objective aspect of the Absolute, is destined to be transcended from the point of view furnished by the standpoint of idealism itself. In that man is the focal point wherein the Absolute's objectivation is manifested—*and understood*—man becomes both the end of natural process and the center of the Absolute's activity. For it is in man that the Absolute Identity of real and ideal is expressed. As identical with nature, the philosopher himself is the vehicle by which Nature's activity reaches the highest stage of development.[7] The philosopher of nature creates nature,[8] for here he knows that he and Nature are one. In fact, to know this identity is to become, as a philosopher, the instrument by which the Absolute achieves perfect freedom.

Such nature mysticism, as Tillich has pointed out,[9] has the effect

---

[1] I, 2, 56.    [2] I, 2, 68.    [3] I, 2, 66.    [4] I, 2, 56.    [5] I, 3, 45.
[6] I, 2, 189.    [7] I, 3, 47.    [8] I, 3, 13.    [9] *Op. cit.*, pp. 50ff.

of destroying all duality of God and the world. In man himself, the creative force of Nature breaks through to its highest expression and produces the feeling of mystic oneness with the All. The world is no longer the scene of moral struggle, in which the ego "uses" the non-ego as its foil for ethical activity. Rather does the philosopher who has been initiated into the mystery of the Absolute Identity submerge his individual activity in the creative activity of God, Nature, or the Absolute. As we shall see, the essential elements of aesthetic idealism were already present in this formulation of the philosophy of nature.

As yet, Schelling has failed to develop a genuine philosophy of history. Indeed, to the extent that during this period "Nature is viewed as unconditioned",[1] history as such is entirely ignored. Schelling has not yet interested himself in an understanding of the problems with which a philosophy of history deals. Nature represented the locus of philosophical interest, as witnessed by the extended discussion devoted to an analysis of various physical theories and the application of his philosophical views to the problems raised by natural science.

But one must not overlook, on the other hand, what may, broadly speaking, be called an historical interpretation of the subject-matter with which philosophy deals. Even at this early stage there is discernible in Schelling the impulse which was to be decisive for the entire gamut of his later metaphysics: the impulse to conceive reality as a whole as essentially historical. The word "historical," at this point, is hardly accurate as a description of Schelling's conception of the universe. But to the extent that the term connotes movement, change, development—in a word, process—it can be said that Schelling's view of reality is of a totality which displays these characteristics.

We noted earlier that Schelling's initial speculations were based on an analysis of the activity of the Ego. And as his thought developed, Schelling elaborated this theme. What must be stressed, though, is that Schelling conceives of Being as *active* rather than static, as dynamic rather than passive, and as displaying throughout its length and breadth movement, change, and creative power. While he has not yet freed himself from the view that Being is ulti-

---

[1] I, 3, 12.

mately an "eternal" system, he nevertheless lays strong emphasis upon the principle of dynamism by which the All comes to expression. Again and again, he uses the active form of the verb *"Wissen"* to denote the nature of the Absolute; and in his poem, *Epikurisch Glaubensbekenntniss Heinz Widerporstens*, which comes from this period, he rhapsodizes about the life, the ferment, which ceaselessly wells up as the "soul" of Nature and which finds its culmination in man: "in him, blind nature gets a voice; in him the spirit comes to himself. And all the universe is one glorious life, in whose contemplation the mystic soul rejoices."[1] This view of reality as dynamic was to be the basic principle which Schelling was to offer, throughout his career, for an understanding of the world.

But having noted the "historical", or genetic, orientation of Schelling's philosophy of nature, we are forced almost immediately to qualify this estimate of it. For the Absolute, *qua* Absolute is a finished, perfect unity. Once Nature's highest product, the subjective ego, is realized, there remains no further goal. The Absolute is "eternal activity"[2] and therefore it functions as a closed system. Though Nature may differentiate itself into real and ideal, and though the transition from real to ideal to their Identity is, from a finite perspective, a process, nevertheless the Absolute Identity is, as it were, the Alpha and Omega. Real and ideal, objective and subjective, are but provisional distinctions and constitute merely partial, and complementary, aspects engendered by a deceitful abstraction. It was reflection which was responsible for this dualism, and reflection must be overcome in order that the ultimate unity may again come into its own.

The result of this orientation in the philosophy of nature, therefore, is an essentially a-historical construction, in spite of the appearance of movement in the relation of the parts to the whole. Were it not that for Schelling the Absolute equals Ego, instead of object, his system in all essential respects would be a re-statement of Spinozism. It is, perhaps, in Schelling's view of the nature of time that the basically unhistorical character of the philosophy of nature is most strikingly displayed. Time characterizes the order of finitude, which by definition, is that which is limited and partial. From an essentially

---

[1] Josiah Royce, *The Spirit of Modern Philosophy* (New York: 1892), p. 187. See for translation of Schelling's *Heinz Widerporstens...*
[2] I, 2. 66.

Platonic point of view, Schelling regards the real (as contrasted to the ideal) world as "that area in which the eternal things, or ideas, come to existence."[1] As a result of "the eternal subject-becoming-object of the Absolute,"[2] the infinity within the Absolute becomes finite. The ideas, which are perfect forms of things, constitute the fulfillment of the condition for the Subject's becoming knowable. But the finite, as the order of appearance, is also the order of the corporeal, and that which is corporeal is, as such, always an imperfect replica of its idea or essence. Temporal things, therefore, are but partial expressions of the fullness which is contained in their idea; "temporality is... everything whose reality is surpassed by the essence, or in whose essence more is contained than can be expressed in reality."[3] If, therefore, history were placed in the same class with other temporal things, little worth could be accorded to it by Schelling during this period of his thought. It too, no doubt, would be swallowed up in the Absolute.

### III. The System of Transcendental Idealism

By 1800, when Schelling wrote his *System des transcendentalen Idealismus*, he had worked out in much greater detail the application of the basic philosophical position adopted in the philosophy of nature to the various problems occasioned by speculation. His interests now are centered not upon the relation of nature and the knowing subject so much as upon the more general question of the nature of all the forms of objectivity as this is manifested in natural science, morality, history, religion and art. Starting with the assumption that the Ego is the All, that "the first and only ground of all reality... is the *subjective*,"[4] the transcendental philosophy has as its task "*to proceed from the subjective, as from the first and absolute, and to let the objective arise out of it.*"[5] But to philosophize from this point of view is to undertake a truly *transcendental* investigation, "since to the transcendental philosopher only the subject has original reality."[6] Hence, like Kant, Schelling makes philosophy "*a knowing of knowing,*"[7] or a making of knowing itself the object of philosophical investigation. Transcendental philosophy *per se* is neither theoretical

---

[1] I, 2, 66.    [2] *Ibid.*    [3] I, 2, 364.    [4] I, 3, 343.    [5] I, 3, 342.
[6] I, 3, 345.    [7] *Ibid.*

nor practical, since it seeks to explain both points of view. Through the intellectual intuition, which "is the organ of all transcendental thinking,"[1] the transcendental philosopher sets forth "a transcendental history of consciousness,"[2] in which is brought to light all of the determinations by which the Ego constructs a world for its knowledge, its moral activity, and finally its aesthetic contemplation. Thus philosophy becomes, for Schelling, "a history of self-consciousness which has various epochs, and through which that one absolute synthesis is successively compounded."[3]

The elaboration of this history of self-consciousness is, in effect, an analysis of the "one absolute Act" with which is posited "not only the Ego itself with all of its determinations, but also... everything else which, in general, is posited for the Ego."[4] When the Ego with its determinations is further analyzed according to the types of relationship assumed to obtain between subject and object (which includes their identity), the result is a three-fold division of philosophy into theoretical, practical and aesthetic. Thus by a transcendental solution of the problems encountered in each of these three areas, the philosopher arrives at an exposition of the entire content of the Ego's activities in its various modes.

The theoretical philosophy has as its task "to investigate the possibility of experience."[5] In terms of the subject-object split, priority is assigned to the objective and philosophy's task, therefore, is to explain "how representations can correspond absolutely with objects (supposedly) existing completely independent of them."[6] This is the problem faced by the philosophy of nature—which thus appears as the theoretical branch of transcendental philosophy—and its goal is the "complete intellectualization of all the laws of nature into laws of perception and thought."[7] From within the larger perspective of the transcendental philosophy itself, the theoretical philosophy charts the first three stages, or epochs, in the history of self-consciousness: from the original sensation to the productive intuition, from this to reflection and thence to the absolute act of the will, at which point the transition to practical philosophy is made. All three epochs witness to the activity of Ego as unconscious, i.e. as producing an objective world of nature out of itself but without conciousness of itself as productive.[8] Thus the objective world appears as completely determined, as the limit against which the Ego

---

[1] I, 3, 369.     [2] I, 3, 398.     [3] I, 3, 399.     [4] I, 3, 388.     [5] I, 3, 347.
[6] *Ibid.*       [7] I, 3, 340.     [8] I, 3, 450.

is measured. Up to this point, none of the synthetic activities in which the Ego is engaged has made the Ego conscious of its *own* activity. While nature thus may be completely transparent to reason, the point of view is still that of the complete objectivity of nature and the passivity of the Ego in its representations. The Ego has not yet become conscious of the decisive character of its own activity.

The theoretical philosophy deals with the Ego's perception and reflection on an objective which is the order of nature. But to the extent that its attention is centered upon the object rather than the subject, it has not achieved the freedom which is demanded from a practical point of view. The Ego "can become conscious of itself as intelligence only by elevating itself above all that is object."[1] In other words, it must make itself an object. In doing so, however, the Ego realizes for the first time its power over the object. It becomes *self*-conscious rather than *object*-conscious. Hence "*the beginning of consciousness is explainable only from a self-determination, or from an activity of intelligence upon itself.*"[2] But since "self-determination of intelligence is called willing ["*Wollen*"],[3] it is at this stage that the Ego becomes aware of its character as Will. Thus the autonomy, or freedom, of the Ego emerges as a still "higher" stage in the history of self-consciousness and the problem of the practical philosophy, how can "representations which arise in us *without necessity, through freedom,*... pass over into the real world and achieve objective reality,"[4] is solved. In the practical philosophy, priority is assigned to the subject, and the willing subject affirms the power of the ideal to affect the real.

At this stage, however, there is needed a further elucidation of the relation between the ideal and real in order that the activity of willing, or the operation of the subject upon the object, be made understandable. It is also within the framework of the practical philosophy that Schelling expounds, deductively, the nature of the moral law, of government, history and religion. All of these are connected with one another and with the larger problem of freedom which appears at this point. When the problems of both the theoretical and the practical philosophy are understood from the transcendental perspective, the contradiction which emerges by the juxtaposition of their respective solutions can be removed. This contradiction, briefly stated, is that according to the theoretical philosophy,

---

[1] I, 3, 524.    [2] I, 3, 532.    [3] I, 3, 533.    [4] I, 3, 347.

the objects determine the representations, while in practical philosophy, the representations are believed to determine the objects. This
contradiction can be solved only by a philosophy which itself is
"neither theoretical nor practical but *both* at the same time,"[1] namely the transcendental philosophy.

From this latter point of view, the contradiction between theoretical and practical philosophy is solved by seeing that "the same
activity which is productive in the free activity *with consciousness* is
productive in the productivity of the world *without consciousness*."[2]
In other words, there is a pre-established harmony between real and
ideal. In terms of the relation between subject and object, it must be
affirmed that "the object which is acted upon and the activity [of the
subject] are identical."[3] In this way the means is provided for an
understanding of the content of practical philosophy in a unique
way. Assuming that in practical philosophy the Ego becomes
conscious of itself as Will, it thereby also becomes conscious of the
categorical imperative, or the moral law. What Kant had assumed as
a datum of the consciousness of all rational beings is here deduced
from the character of the Ego itself, as one stage in the history of
self-consciousness. For in that the ideal activity "directed solely toward pure self-determination must become object to the Ego as
*demand*,"[4] which demand is itself none other than that of becoming
fully conscious of self, the categorical imperative is thus deduced as a
necessary condition of self-consciousness in general. But this deduction entails the further deduction of the concept of happiness as
an element of the Ego's activity. If the moral law is an expression of
the demand to the Ego to become conscious of itself, and thus to become conscious of itself as Will, happiness is to be understood as "the
identity of that which is independent of willing with willing itself."[5]
But this identity is already presupposed in the transcendental
interpretation of the relation of subject and object: "if happiness is
only the identity of the external world with the pure will, then both
are one and the same object, only regarded from different sides."[6]

Thus the stage is set for the interpretation of government and
history. At the point in the history of self-consciousness at which the
idea of happiness appears, there is not yet realized the identity of
willing with that which is willed. Happiness is a desideratum, but the
condition for its achievement is still "future." In other words,

---

[1] I, 3, 348.    [2] *Ibid.*....    [3] I, 3, 580.    [4] I, 3, 573.    [5] I, 3, 581.
[6] I, 3, 582.

happiness has not yet become objective. In order to achieve this condition, the autonomy of the individual, which as such expresses itself as spontaneity, or arbitrary action, must be superseded by such an external arrangement as will require that "all rational beings limit their activity through the possibility of the free activity of all the rest."[8] Such an arrangement can take place only through the concept of right, or justice, which acts as the determinant of the free activity of rational beings. In spite of themselves, men are compelled toward the realization of a righteous order through the system of legality which universal constitutional government demands, and which, as "a federation of all states,"[9] stands as the realization of the moral law in its objective form.

It is at this point that Schelling's philosophy of history, during this period, appears as a deduction from the necessary course pursued by the "history" of self-consciousness. In substance, Schelling here presents Kant's *Idea of a Universal History from a Cosmopolitan Point of View*, although it is refurbished in terms of the fundamental assumptions of the transcendental philosophy as a whole. (Here we will indicate only the general character of the philosophy of history and will return later to a more detailed exposition of it.) History emerges in this context as ruled by "a blind necessity" which governs the play of freedom displayed by individuals and particular nations in their movement toward the realization of the universal legal constitution.[3] But the philosophy of history itself, which sets forth the various aspects of this development, assumes a commanding position within the practical philosophy. From the transcendental perspective, the philosophy of history "is to the practical philosophy what nature is to the theoretical".[3] For assuming the causality of the subjective, in opposition to the objective, the movement of history is to be understood as the gradual approximation to the identity of subjective and objective, the point where all opposition between willing and that which is willed is overcome—even as in the theoretical philosophy the goal is the identity of knower and known.

It must be emphasized, however, that for Schelling during the period of his transcendental philosophy, the highest synthesis is to be achieved neither in the theoretical nor the practical philosophy, but in the philosophy of art. Both nature and history, as real and ideal respectively, have as their goal an absolute identity. But such an

---

[1] *Ibid.*   [2] I, 3, 586.   [3] I, 3, 587.   [4] I, 3, 590.

identity, while it operates as a determinant in both nature and history, is itself beyond both. The identity of subjective and objective is achieved at two points: in the production of works of art and in the transcendental philosophy itself. Both disciplines "intuit" an identity of conscious and unconscious, the philosophic in the sphere of the subject and the aesthetic in the sphere of the object. But in that both operate via the same medium and in terms of the absolute identity, both achieve the highest expression which is possible. Here the Ego returns to itself, having completed its tour of the subjective and objective worlds, and thus loses itself in the mystic identity. Thus the historical appears, finally, as an incomplete phase of the Ego's activity.

## IV. The System of Absolute Identity

By the year 1801, Schelling, had, he believed, arrived at a full recognition of the difference between his brand of idealism and Fichte's. The contrast which had emerged as the two philosophers had worked out in detail the basic points of view of their respective systems had convinced Schelling that his should properly be termed *objective* idealism to distinguish it from Fichte's *subjective* idealism. For Fichte had approached idealism from the point of view of reflection, with the result that for him, the ego was everything. Schelling, on the other hand, maintained that "everything = ego and nothing exists but what = ego"[1]—a seemingly fine distinction, but one which was decisive in fixing the orientation of one's philosophical endeavors. Basically the distinction was manifested, according to Schelling, in the type of investigation one undertook. A subjec- \/ tive idealist, such as Fichte, begins with the ego and from a transcendental analysis of its structure and operations proceeds to an exposition of the contents of consciousness. Such idealism is epistemologically oriented, and must first settle the question of knowledge before proceeding to a statement of the nature of being. Schelling's objective idealism, on the other hand—as he contended at this time[2]—was

---

[1] *Darstellung meines Systems der Philosophie*, I, 4, 109.

[2] Schelling's estimate of his own philosophy must frequently be qualified. In this instance, he was answering the attacks of critics, and in doing so he ignored the fact that his earlier philosophy could, in most respects, be scarcely distinguished from Fichte's.

ontologically oriented, and hence was concerned only incidentally with epistemological questions.

Allowing for a slight exaggeration of emphasis in Schelling's view of his own work, it is nevertheless important to note that during this period, from 1801 to 1804, Schelling felt that he had forged and was presenting an independent system of philosophy. The uniqueness of his point of view did not become clear to him until the *Exposition of My System of Philosophy* (1801); but looking back upon both his philosophy of nature and his transcendental philosophy, he saw them as "opposed poles" of that one type of philosophizing which now emerged as "the system of absolute identity".[1] In other words, the philosophy of identity had been the presupposition of both the philosophy of nature and the transcendental philosophy. What was needed at this point, Schelling felt, was an explicit presentation of that system of philosophy which was uniquely his own, if for no other reason than that those critics who had accused him of instability of viewpoint might be informed of his true position.

The absolute reason, "or reason insofar as it is conceived as total indifference of the subjective and the objective",[2] is that in which all things are contained and outside of which there is nothing. It is the one absolute reason which is expressed in all the differentiations of being—not as divided into parts but as expressing itself complete-ly in each of its productions. Its nature is expressed in the law of identity; i.e. it is absolutely its own being and is posited in complete independence of any and all predicates. As pure being, it is inde-pendent of all spatial and temporal determinations. On the other hand, "everything which is, is the absolute identity itself."[3] In es-sence, the absolute identity is pure being itself: it is the Parmenidean One.

But while the *essence* of absolute reason is one and indivisible, it may be conceived according to various *forms*, or potencies. The chief distinction pertaining to the absolute identity according to form is that of subject and object. The one absolute identity which "accord-ing to the form of its being is posited as subject and as object"[4] can-not be differentiated qualitatively, or essentially, and hence must be represented as differentiable only in quantitative terms. Thus the original identity, by virtue of the quantitative ascendancy of one or the other potency, is expressed reciprocally either as nature or as

---

[1] I, 4, 110 and 113.    [2] I, 4, 114.    [3] I, 4, 119.    [4] I, 4, 123.

mind. The difference between them is established by the fact that the "power" which is characteristic of the absolute identity in the case of nature "has to combat the preponderance of the ideal".[1] Ideal and real, or thought and extension, are, accordingly, but different forms of the same absolute. The same essence expresses itself in both realms, even though the quantitative ascendancy of the respective potencies provides the basis for a realistic or an idealistic construction.

Realism and idealism thus find their places within the system of identity as merely relatively true expressions of the one absolute reason. They are relatively true expressions because they are but partial representations of the absolute identity. The very antithesis of real and ideal "appears as antithesis only to him who is outside the indifference".[2] Fundamentally, they are alternative ways of regarding, or interpreting, finite objects. They do not grasp the infinite essence of all finitude. As Schelling puts it, "The quantitative difference of the subjective and objective is the ground of all finitude, and, vice versa, the quantitative indifference of both is infinity".[3] The qualitative difference, so-called, between mind and body, knowledge and nature, is but a quantitative differentiation of the one essence.

From his basically Spinozistic standpoint, it is not difficult for Schelling to "explain" the type of philosophy which he had propounded earlier. The main difference which has emerged at this point is the desertion of the earlier Fichtean orientation in favor of what he called objective idealism, with emphasis upon ontology rather than epistemology. In fact, it would seem that it was the gradual emergence of a new epistemological approach which was instrumental in inducing Schelling to break with Fichte. The latter's moralism and his anti-mystical treatment of nature, coupled with his failure (in Schelling's view) to gain intellectual rapport with reality, all contributed to making the incipient break, noted in Schelling's philosophy of nature, into a permanent rift. For Schelling's interests, during the time of his espousal of the identity philosophy, were largely centered around the employment of the "intellectual intuition" as the instrument of philosophical construction; and the type of knowing which is thereby supplied is closely linked to aesthetic perceptivity.[4] As Tillich has pointed out,[5] the strong mystical strain which is present

---

[1] I, 4, 128.    [2] *Ibid.*    [3] I, 4, 131.    [4] See *supra*, p. 64.
[5] *Op. cit.*, pp. 74f *et passim.*

in Schelling's work during the major portion of his first period was ultimately decisive in impelling him toward the construction of a closed system in which rational intuition of the absolute is the highest form of expression. From a religious standpoint, certainly, moral activity is but a phase preliminary to mystical identity with God.

The details of the construction of the system of identity need not concern us here. Suffice it to note that the absolute identity becomes finite through the process of its own creativity by which the eternal ideas come into existence as potencies. The manifold of potencies constitutes the world of particular forms, the eternal prototypes of existing things. But even as finitude is a form of infinity, so time is but an image of eternity: "all potencies are absolutely simultaneous".[1] Hence, even while philosophy proceeds genetically to construct the objectification of the absolute, the philosopher works on the assumption that it is an eternal structure which he is describing. The universe with all its potencies is eternal and complete.

Turning, now, to a consideration of the role of history in the system of identity, we have to note that Schelling has both strengthened and weakened its importance. He has strengthened its importance by constructing a more comprehensive schematization for it by construing various historical epochs according to definite potencies. In this way he is able to fit history into the general framework of his philosophy, first by viewing history as the manifestation of the absolute under the potency of the ideal, and secondly by arranging the process of history according to subordinate potencies within the larger framework of the ideal. Moreover, in his *Philosophy and Religion* (1804), in his attempt to account more adequately for the finite, he also was able to give a more penetrating analysis of the beginning and end of history and to recognize the significance of history as not *merely* an imperfect image of ultimately static truth.

But Schelling has also weakened the importance of history in his system of identity. For as a mere form, or potency, of the absolute, history has no intrinsic reality. Moreover, since the potencies which mark the epochs of history are, as such, "without any relationship to time and absolutely eternal",[2] history displays no progress. It has a logical structure, but the structure is finished before the process of history begins. It is not history as such which is significant, but the absolute identity to which history points and which is but imperfect-

---

[1] I, 4, 135.    [2] *Ibid.*

ly revealed in that medium. The philosopher and/or the religious mystic looks beyond history to the absolute; and since "the highest goal for all rational beings is identity with God",[1] the philosopher seeks such mystical union through the intellectual intuition.

---

[1] I, 6, 562.

CHAPTER THREE

## SCHELLING'S PHILOSOPHY OF HISTORY TO 1809

The development of a philosophy of history during this period cannot be said to have been the exclusive aim of Schelling's endeavors. He was much more interested in arriving at a systematic view of nature, and only incidentally did he treat of history as a subject demanding philosophical treatment. Even then, history was generally assigned a subordinate place within the total scheme of things. For until 1809, when his "doctrine of freedom" emerged in clear-cut form, he was largely concerned with presenting reality's "idea", i.e. the rational structure which is embodied in all of the Absolute's productions. As yet, from the point of view of his later philosophy, he was concerned only with the rational form of being. The "positive" content, denoted by "will," representing the non-rational, or "extra-logical," character of being, had not emerged as a metaphysical principle. Accordingly, while he attributes to reality a movement, or development, such movement is largely phenomenal. From the point of view of the Absolute as such there can be no genuine movement. Change, or process, is robbed of ultimate significance when it is viewed merely as a phase of the Absolute's appearance, and as a transitory interlude whose program is prescribed in advance. Thus Schelling's first period is a-historically oriented. There is no fascination with history for its own sake, for it is subordinated to the over-all rational structure in which it appears.

Nevertheless Schelling does develop a philosophy of history during this period; and taken by itself, it furnishes some by no means insignificant observations on the problems—together with their possible solutions—which the philosophical understanding of history entails. An astute observer will, of course, recognize Schelling's dependence upon the investigations undertaken in this field by many of his predecessors and contemporaries, even though he does not often acknowledge such dependence.[1] It will be evident, too, however, that Schelling was beginning to recognize the possibilities inherent in a philosophical understanding of history, especially from the stand-

---

[1] See *supra*, pp. 27f.

point of concepts borrowed from the religious tradition of the West. It will, therefore, appear that even in his "a-historical" first period, Schelling was laying the foundations for the type of historical construction which characterized his philosophy from 1809 on.

## I. The Character of History

While Schelling's philosophy as a whole developed considerably during his first period, his views on the philosophy of history display a remarkable consistency. From the very beginning he sought to differentiate nature and history and to set forth the characteristics which mark off history as a unique field of investigation. The basic distinction between nature and history is that in the former, events occur "according to necessary laws,"[1] while in the latter such necessity does not occur. For "by etymology, history is knowledge of what has happened (*"Geschehen"*). Hence as object it does not have the *permanent*, the *constant*, but the *changeable*, that which is *progressing in time.*"[2] Thus nature and history are mutually exclusive realms. The events of nature can be calculated *a priori*. The mechanism which natural phenomena display makes it possible to predict with accuracy the pattern which such phenomena will form. But "there is history in the... truest sense only where it is absolutely... impossible to determine the direction of a free activity *a priori*."[3] Schelling is most emphatic on this point. He insists that;

> "...in general everything which follows according to a determined mechanism, or has a theory *a priori*, can by no means be an object of history. Theory and history are absolutely opposed. Man has a history only to the extent that what he does permits of no reckoning in advance according to any theory. Spontaneity is... the goddess of history."[4]

If this is the case, then it would seem that a philosophy of history is an impossibility. And as a matter of fact, this was precisely the conclusion which Schelling drew in his earliest period. In an article appearing in the *Philosophical Journal* of 1797–98,[5] Schelling argued that no philosophy of history is possible, at least not in the sense in

---

[1] I, 1, 467.    [2] *Ibid.*, p. 466.    [3] *Ibid.*, p. 470.    [4] I, 3, 589.
[5] "Allgemeinen Übersicht der neuesten philosophischen Literatur", S. W. I, 1, p. 465–73.

which a philosophy of nature is possible. For since "only what has *no* theory *a priori* has history",[1] and only that which *has* a theory *a priori* is science, history is excluded from being a science. Thus "if philosophy of history is the same as science of history *a priori*... a philosophy of history is impossible."[2]

The only way of avoiding such a conclusion, obviously, is by a redefinition of the philosophy of history. And in his later writings, Schelling proceeds to this task. He does not abandon the general distinction which he has made between nature and history, but continues, rather, with an elaboration of it, at the same time giving the concept of history greater depth. It should be noted, too, that to deny that history is calculable *a priori* is not to deny that history as such has significance. What that significance is and how it may be known were to become apparent to Schelling as he proceeded. It was necessary first, however, to guard against the conclusion which was equally as erroneous as the conclusion that history can be calculated *a priori*: the conclusion, namely, that history is a completely arbitrary succession of events, with no meaning whatsoever. Rather, says Schelling, we must realize "that an absolutely lawless series of events as little deserves the name of history as does an absolutely law-abiding series."[3] History cannot be "a series of events without end or purpose."[4] It must have a goal toward which its events tend and in view of which the events themselves acquire significance. In other words, the movement of history is teleological.

In determining more precisely the character of history, Schelling calls attention to a feature of it which was originally pointed out by Kant in his *Idea of a Universal History*. Since the events of history do not repeat themselves in the way that those of nature do—since, in fact, the events of history do not periodically recur and thus cannot be calculated *a priori*—the occurrence of any specific historical event cannot be foreseen. There remains, therefore, only one alternative if history is to have a meaningful structure. It must possess the unity and homogeneity of a species, so that while any particular event, as such, remains meaningless, the species itself, or the actions of its members taken collectively, will possess a law-abiding character. Thus, strictly speaking, history pertains only to the race: "history in general is possible only of beings which express the character of a species."[3] The events which characterize the movement of

---

[1] I, 1, 471.    [2] *Ibid.*, p. 473.    [3] I, 3, 589.    [3] *Ibid.*, p. 590.

the species must be assumed to be tending toward a goal; and no matter how far short any individual or group may fall of that goal, the race as a whole is measured by its tendency toward or away from it. As Schelling expressed it, "there is history in general only where there is an ideal and infinitely many deviations from that ideal in particular [instances], at the same time that there is complete congruence with that ideal on the whole..."[1] Thus "history consists neither in absolute conformity to law nor in absolute freedom."[2] Rather we must recognize that "only freedom and conformity to law together, or the gradual realization of a never completely lost ideal by an entire species of beings, constitutes the characteristic of history."[3]

To maintain that freedom characterizes the events of history thus implies that the individual events, as such, are undetermined, while the pattern into which they fall is fixed. But now the question arises as to how such freedom is possible, and how the events which are designated as free are connected with one another and with the totality of events which make up the universe. In other words, the problem is to account metaphysically for the characteristics which history displays.

## The Metaphysics of History

Basic to Schelling's whole metaphysical conception is the assumption that no part of reality is separated from the whole in any ultimate sense. Thus history—which is explicitly denied the status of mere fantasy[4]—must be given a definite position within the context of the all. So far we have noted that Schelling distinguished history from nature primarily by the indeterminate character of history's events. But this is basically a negative definition and does not serve to fix the positive nature of this subject-matter. It goes almost without saying, however, that history deals with the activities of man and that therefore it is man and his institutions which the philosopher of history seeks to comprehend.

It makes little difference, for our purposes, which of the various points of view embraced by Schelling during his first period is adopted for an account of his evaluation of history. But since he himself regarded his philosophy of identity as a synthesis of his earlier po-

---

[1] I, 1, 469.  [2] *Ibid.*  [3] I, 3, 588.  [4] *Ibid.*, p. 589.

sitions, we may use this as our guide at this point. From this stand-point, that feature of history which we have already remarked in Schelling's philosophy, viz. the unpredictability of its individual events and its teleology as a whole, is to be understood metaphysical-ly not as a realm apart but as one form of the Absolute itself: "history as a whole is a progressing, gradual revelation of the Abso-lute..."[1] For this reason, it should not be assumed that nature and history are two entirely different fields, To be sure, the events of nature are calculable *a priori* while those of history are not, but the same story is told in both. The one Absolute Identity of real and ideal is contained in both nature and history, the difference being that the Absolute appears in nature under the potency, or form, of the *real*, while it appears in history under the potency of the *ideal*:

> History is the higher potency of nature, in so far as it expresses in the ideal what the latter expresses in the real; but in essence the same thing is in both, only altered by the determination or potency under which it is placed. If the pure essence could be seen in both, we would recognize the same thing which is represented in history as ideal, represented in nature as real.[2]

For nature is the sphere of the finite; it is what it is by necessity.[3] But in history, freedom makes its appearance. Man who is not de-termined as are the events of nature, but who frees himself from nature by making both nature and himself his objects, thus manifests ideality as a characteristic which nature lacks. Hence "man, the rational being in general, is so placed as to be a supplement to the world of appearance,"[4] since, from the point of view of the Absolute, he contributes self-consciousness to the over-all picture which the Absolute eventually reveals.

The appearance of freedom is therefore a necessary stage in the Absolute's self-expression. Its ultimate meaning may be variously designated, depending upon the angle from which it is approached. If freedom is understood as equivalent to self-consciousness—i.e. as freedom *from* the world of appearance—then its emergence is to be seen as that stage "when intelligence egresses from the absolute situation... and becomes conscious of itself (differentiates itself), which takes place in that its activity becomes objective to it." At this point "the free and necessary therein separate themselves."[5] This is the stage at which the theoretical philosophy achieves full ex-

---

[1] I, 1, 439.    [2] I, 3, 603.    [3] I, 5, 306.    [4] I, 5, 218.    [5] *Ibid.*

pression; and since, during the period of his formulation of the system of transcendental idealism, Schelling regarded philosophy as "a history of self-consciousness,"[1] his characterization of freedom in this way served to lend emphasis to his view that man's primarily philosophical activities are an integral part of the Absolute's activities. From a theoretical point of view, or from the angle of man's role in the Absolute's revelation of itself as ultimate identity of knower and known, history is indeed "none other than the history of the various situations through which Mind arrives at the intuition of itself, a pure self-consciousness."[2]

However, freedom can also be understood, transcendentally, from a practical point of view, and it is this which ulitmately serves to fix the significance of history most conclusively. For here the moral, political and religious problems come to the fore, and it is these with which the philosopher of history is primarily engaged. Practical philosophy regards the Absolute, as it reveals itself in history, as a progressive realization of a moral order which, objectively regarded, "can be only the gradual emergence of the constitution for world-citizenship."[3] In fact, it is such a world government which Schelling declares to be the "the sole ground of history."[4] Freedom appears at this level, accordingly, as the instrument by which the movement of history toward this goal is to be realized. But when the word "freedom" is used in this context, it means something more than the freedom of the knowing subject in relation to objectivity. For in that the freedom of the empirical ego is expressed by its freeing of itself from the determination of the Absolute and its progressive achievement of *self*-determination[5]—the highest expression of which is full self-consciousness—it thereby acquires the ability to will independently of the Absolute. Such freedom, which is "freedom to choose,"[6] is the freedom of historical man which is denoted as "spontaneity." It is such spontaneity which distinguishes the activities of man in history. In fact, it is the appearance of spontaneity which, mythologically, is regarded as "the loss of the Golden Age, of the Fall,"[7] when man took

---

[1] I, 3, 602.
[2] I, 3, 399. See above, p. 64v. Such an expression, however, characterizes Schelling's philosophical point of view as a whole.
[3] I, 1, 382.
[4] I, 3, 592.
[5] *Ibid.*, Cf. I, 5, 283, 307, 312.
[6] Cf. I, 3, 524v.
[7] I, 1, 440.

his first step beyond the control of instinct, when lawlessness made its appearance. By an extension of this point of view, "in the ideas of philosophers, history ends with the reign of reason, i.e. with the Golden Age of legality, when all spontaneity has disappeared from the earth, and man through freedom will have returned to the same point at which nature originally placed him, and which he left when history began."[1]

The teleology of history may now receive more precise definition. The spontaneity which is "the goddess of history"[2] is, after all, only one side of the picture which history presents. If there were not some kind of necessity in the movement of history as a whole, history would be reduced, if not to sheer chaos, at least to a mere empirical description of what has happened. But the philosopher of history seeks a meaning in history as a whole. If, as a philosopher of history, I maintain that "all of my activities proceed as regards their final goal toward something which is realizable not by the individual alone but *only by the whole race*," then "I require something absolutely objective which, absolutely independent of my *freedom*, guarantees… the success of the activity [of the race] for the highest goal."[3] This conclusion is unavoidable, "for only when in the spontaneous i.e. completely lawless, activities of man an unconscious conformity to law rules can I think of a finite union of all activities in a common goal."[4]

The outcome of history, therefore, does not depend upon the wills of the individual actors. My activity may be directed toward purely private ends; yet "through freedom itself, in that I believe myself free to act, there shall arise unconsciously, i.e. without my assistance, that which I did not intend…"[5] Thus the philosopher of history must accept the presupposition "that man be free in regard to that with which activity is concerned; but as regards the result of his activity, it is necessary that man be dependent on a necessity which is above him and which itself has a hand in the play of his freedom…"[6] This "concealed necessity" in history…" by virtue of which man through his free activity itself and even against his will must become the cause of something which he never willed"[7]—has been called Fate or Providence. The philosopher, however, gives the same thing a different name by reason of the perspective from which he sees all reality

---

[1] I, 3, 589; cf. I, 1, 439.     [2] *Ibid.*     [3] *Ibid.*     [4] I, 3, 596–7.
[5] I, 3, 597.          [6] I, 3, 594.     [7] I, 3, 594.

in terms of the Absolute and its activities. He sees all intelligence in its finite state as having egressed from the Absolute; and by the same token, that which is objective in history, by which its "concealed necessity" operates, is acribed by the philosopher to "an absolute synthesis of all the intelligences together, in which [synthesis] all contradictions are resolved and suspended in advance." In this way the philosopher accounts for the predetermination of the whole of history; and for him "the development of the absolute synthesis in various sequences is history."[1]

Ultimately the specifications of the philosophy of identity are invoked to give the character of history its final delineation. The objective of predetermination of all human activity in history—history's necessity—is explained by the absolute synthesis of all intelligences; but "this does not explain... how the freedom of activity itself corresponds with this objective predetermination."[2] The objective in history actually represents the nature side of history, and thus must be conformable to law. But the "coexistence of lawlessness, i.e. of freedom, with conformity to law... still leaves unexplained... the harmony between the objective and the freely-determinative."[3] This pre-established harmony between the ideal and the real, subjective and objective, "is conceivable only through something which is above both, which hence is neither intelligence nor free but rather is the common source of both..."[4] This which is neither subject nor object, nor both together, can be "only the *Absolute Identity* in which there is no duplicity whatsoever, and which for this reason, since the condition of all consciousness is duplicity, can never achieve consciousness."[5] And since it is also beyond objectivity, and can never be an object of knowledge, it can only be an object of "faith."[6]

The various points of view in regard to history can thus be understood from within the context of the philosophy of identity. The view that history is completely determined, which is the view of fatalism, has arisen from devoting exclusive attention to the unconscious or objective in history. Atheism, on the other hand, has arisen from the opposite error of directing attention exclusively to the subjective or lawless in history. But when reflection has been directed to the presupposition that it is the Absolute which manifests itself in

---

[1] I, 3, 598.    [2] I, 3, 599.    [3] *Ibid.*    [4] *Ibid.*    [5] I, 3, 600.
[6] *Ibid.*

history, and that it is Providence rather than Fate which rules the activities of man, there has arisen "religion in the only true meaning of the word."[1]

This view of history must, of course, deny that the Absolute or God has ever completely revealed itself in history. For the *complete* revelation of God could occur only through the suspension of freedom and with it the suspension of history itself. Such a complete revelation, when all spontaneity has disappeared from the earth, is the Golden Age at the end of history when God shall be "all in all." As the situation of history now stands, "God *is* not... if He *were*, we would not be; but He *reveals* Himself continually. Man bears through his history a progressive proof of the existence of God—a proof which, however, can be completed only through the whole of history..."[2]

> If we think of history as a drama in which everyone who has a part in it plays his role with complete freedom and at his own discretion, than a rational development of this confused play can be conceived only if it is one Spirit which composes in all, and if the poet, to whom the individual actors are mere fragments (*disjecti membra poëtae*), has so harmoniously arranged in advance the objective outcome of the whole with the free play of all the individuals that at the end something actually rational must result. But if the poet *were* independent of his drama, we would be only the players who execute what he has composed. But if he *is* not independent of us, but reveals and discloses himself only successively through the play of our freedom itself, so that without this freedom he himself *would* not be, then we are fellow-poets of the whole and our own designers of the roles we play.[3]

## II. The Content of History

The content of history, from a philosophical point of view, has largely been indicated in the foregoing. It is still necessary, however, to make explicit the different positions from which history may be regarded and which alter, accordingly, the estimate of its significance. Schelling maintains that there are "various standpoints from which history may be regarded,"[4] and that any particular standpoint inevitably furnishes the one who occupies it with a unique understanding of what history contains. In other words, from Schelling's

---

[1] *Ibid.*    [2] I, 3, 601.    [3] I, 3, 603.    [4] I, 3, 602.

point of view, there are what might be termed levels of knowledge which act as determinants of the content of history. But we must hasten to add that Schelling does not hereby commit himself to a relativistic interpretation of history. It should become evident as our exposition proceeds that just as there are levels of knowledge from which the Absolute may in general be regarded, ranging from that of naive realism to that of the transcendental intuition, so history, as one form of the appearance of the Absolute, may be variously interpreted, depending upon the epistemological orientation of the observer. For Schelling, all knowledge is ultimately knowledge of the Absolute, even though the conditioned forms of knowledge provide a variety of interpretations of its content.

The nature of the subject-matter which is denoted as history should now be manifest. In sum: "history is neither that which is purely lawful in terms of the understanding, subordinated to the concept, nor the purely lawless, but rather that which joins together necessity in the whole with the appearance of freedom in particular."[1] In general, it is the element of freedom which distinguishes history from nature. But such a characterization of history is delivered from a philosophical standpoint, and the question remains whether history may not be something different for the historian and/or the historical researcher. To be sure, both philosopher and historian are engaged in an interpretation of human events, but their appraisal of those events may differ widely.

Historiography in general is occupied with the empirical content of history. Its attention is directed primarily to the events themselves, and only secondarily, if at all, is it concerned with the overall context within which those events appear. There are three sides to the empirical standpoint—or three possibilities of expression for the historiographer—corresponding to the real, the ideal and their synthesis. To the extent that emphasis is placed upon the real, i.e. the events themselves, or the ideal, i.e. the subjective evaluation of the events, historiography has not achieved its fullest expression. It is only when a synthesis of the real and the ideal is attained, as it is in what Schelling calls "historical art",[2] that "true history" emerges. As we shall see, most historiography, when measured by the standard proposed for it by Schelling, falls far short of its optimum achievement.

---

[1] I, 5, 307.      [2] I, 5, 280.

The least significant type of historiography, in Schelling's view, is that which is concerned with "the pure appraisal and ascertainment of what has happened."[1] Here emphasis is placed primarily upon the real, the "bare facts" of history. This is the task of the historical researcher; and while no doubt such a task has problems of its own, it cannot be claimed that the mere narration or chronicling of human events, in itself, is of great significance. The researcher supplies the raw material upon which the historian works. But the task of the researcher, taken by itself, is comparable to the mere gathering of information by the reporters who supply the natural scientist with the data for his analysis and interpretation.

The next higher standpoint from which history may be regarded— higher because it embodies a large element of interpretation—is that of "the arrangement [of events] according to an end designated by the subject."[2] This kind of historiography "requires an accurate and empirically grounded connection of events,"[3] so that the events themselves possess the necessity which the categories of the understanding guarantee for the empirical world in general. But the *connection* of the events, the sequence of their occurrence according to some plan or purpose, is supplied more or less arbitrarily by the historian himself, usually in terms of some lesson that history is supposed to teach. This treatment of history, "in virtue of the meaning firmly established of old, is called the pragmatic."[4] Polybius, for example, wrote with the express purpose of making his history a technical study of the science of warfare. Tacitus, too, wrote a history which is properly called pragmatic, since "he represents the operation of immorality and despotism on the decline of the Roman Empire."[5]

Such historiography is occasioned by the circumstances surrounding the knowledge of history as a part of the empirical world in general. The understanding ("*Verstand*") requires, and supplies, necessity for its representations. But by itself, the understanding cannot account for the continuity of the events or the purpose which their appearance serves. Reason ("*Vernunft*") must come to the rescue of the understanding and propose "ideas" which function so as to provide the universality which completion for the empirical representations requires. But it is precisely at this point that pragmatic is to be distinguished from truly universal history. For the

---

[1] I, 5, 310.    [2] I, 5, 307.    [3] I, 5, 308.    [4] I, 5, 309.    [5] I, 5, 308.

pragmatic historian selects a limited goal for history, in keeping with his didactic or political interests, so that "the pragmatic goal of history excludes universality from itself and necessarily demands a circumscribed object."[1] Pragmatic history is biased history. It designates some particular goal, such as the advancement of science, the extension of means of communication or something similar; but, in every case, instead of deriving history's goal from the nature of history itself, it supplies a goal which the individuals' interests or taste dictates. Thus "it is precisely because of their subjective bent" that "no one with any sense places either Polybius or Tacitus in the first rank of history."[2]

Interestingly enough, it is precisely at this point that Schelling attacks Kant's construction of history as it appears in his *Idee zu einer allgemeinen Geschichte der Menschheit*. For in that "Kant's plan for a history in a cosmopolitan sense foresees a mere conformity to the laws of the understanding,"[3] which is the same as assuming the existence of mere *natural* necessity in history, it falls short of the universality which true history requires. Kant's program for history is but an "empirical reflection of the true [i.e. transcendental] necessity," and as such it must be called "not so much a cosmopolitan as a provincial history."[4] The pragmatic character of Kant's plan of history becomes evident as soon as one sees that he has gauged the progress of mankind by its approximation, through the eventual emergence of a legal constitution, to the goal of peaceful commercial relations, and thereby representing this "as the highest fruits of man's life and endeavors."[5] Even though the modern world has come to regard such pragmatic history as the highest expression of historical writing, it has, in Schelling's view, "acquired a status similar to that of the amanuensis in Goethe's *Faust*: 'What you call the spirit of the times is your own spirit in which the times mirror themselves'."[6]

The highest form of historiography, according to Schelling, is achieved only when history has been freed of all subjective reference. The empirical standpoint, or pragmatic history, is by its very nature incapable of such objectivity. True history appears only when the actual events disclosed by historical research (the real) are interpreted and connected according to the supra-empirical necessity (the ideal) which governs their occurrence, independently of all subjective bias. This synthesis of the real and the ideal "is possible nowhere but

---

[1] Ibid.     [2] *Ibid.*     [3] *Ibid.*     [4] I, 5, 309.     [5] *Ibid.*     [6] *Ibid.*

in art, which lets reality remain as it is, just as the stage represents real events or happenings, but in a completeness and unity by which they become an expression of the highest ideas."[1] Thus true history emerges when "the third and absolute standpoint of history" is achieved: "that of historical art."[2]

Empirical history is limited by the subjectivity of its point of view. It satifies the understanding, to be sure, but it leaves reason's demands unfulfilled. But the historian who achieves the level of historical art provides the necessary link for the comprehension of history's true meaning. Schelling is anxious, however, that his espousing of the ideal of artistic production for historiography should not lead to misunderstanding. To deal with historical events as an artist deals with his materials does not mean that the historian alters the materials of history in order to achieve an "artistic," or decorative effect. On the contrary, the historian is bound by all the canons of truth, and can by no means neglect the empirical connections of the events which he portrays. Again, Schelling suggests, the historian is faced with essentially the same situation as the grounding of the action in the drama "wherein the single [events] must follow from the preceding ones, and finally all events must follow from the first synthesis; but the continuity of the events themselves must be conceivable not empirically, but rather from a higher ordering of things."[3] But when this ideal is achieved, history at last is presented in a form which will satisfy the demand of *reason*; for then "the empirical grounds, through which it satisfies the understanding, are used as instruments and means for the appearance of a higher necessity."[4]

Again we see the metaphysical foundation of Schelling's philosophy in general breaking through in his philosophy of history. For even as his philosophy of identity regards the Absolute, from one point of view, as a synthesis of the real and the ideal, so, it would appear, the synthesis of necessity and freedom which "historical art" discloses is itself none other than the Absolute Identity itself. And indeed Schelling himself points out that "this same identity... is the standpoint of philosophy and religion as regards history."[5] But he immediately exempts the historian from allegiance to either a religious or a philosophical viewpoint. It is not the business of the historian to commit himself to any explicit doctrine. Such explication and commitment is the task of the philosopher and the

---

[1] I, 5, 308.    [2] I, 5, 309–10.    [3] I, 5, 310.    [4] *Ibid.*    [5] *Ibid.*

theologian, not of the historian *qua* historian. The true historian merely represents that identity of freedom and necessity in his work. At best he is the instrument by which that identity manifests itself. To define the ultimate meaning of that identity is beyond the scope of his activity as an historian.

Through the work of the historical artist, "history is recognizable only as unconceived and entirely objective identity, as Fate."[1] The historian does not write with the conscious purpose of portraying Fate, but in spite of himself and independently of his activity, Fate appears as the higher necessity running throughout the series of the events which he portrays. In the historical writings of Herodotus, for example, "Destiny and Recompense proceed as invisible and omnipotent divinities."[2] And in the still more exalted, though independent, style of Thucydides,—who also makes use of the dramatic device of introducing speeches into his narrative—the same identity is brought to objective presentation. In comparison with such sublime historiography, Schelling regards "the so-called universal histories" of modern times as mere "compendiums in which everything particular and significant is obliterated."[3] True universal history must be composed in the epic style, which is the style of Herodotus. Classical tragedy is also a model for the historical artist. But outside of these, the would-be historian might turn to the naive simplicity of the ancient chronicles "which make no pretentious character sketches, or psychologically motivate."[4] Modern history is cursed with the subjectivity of the modern age, and has lost the feeling for the objectivity which was the blessing of the ancients.

Historiography, as such, is not concerned with the interpretation of history. Pragmatic history, indeed, may seem to be an exception to this judgment, but Schelling is unequivocal in his condemnation of the pretense of empirical history to furnish an explanation of the events which it purports to describe. In fact, it is precisely the confusion, introduced by the pragmatic historian, between the objective presentation of events and the biased interpretation of them which Schelling tried so strenuously to remove. For even the true historical artist, according to Schelling, must guard himself against the temptation to pass judgment on the nature of the connection of the events which he portrays.

---

[1] *Ibid.*      [2] I, 5. 311.      [3] *Ibid.*      [4] *Ibid.*

It is the "higher necessity" in history, revealed in the writings of the historical artist, which must be elucidated by him who would achieve the fullest understanding of history's content. In general, Schelling recognizes two standpoints, the theological and the philosophical, from which this higher necessity may be adequately illuminated. In his earlier writings, when philosophy itself represented for him the highest expression of the Absolute, Schelling confined his explication of history for the most part to the categories which philosophy alone employs. But as he progressed, theological interests emerged more and more strongly, until finally his whole thought was molded around the language and problems of religious concern. In his first period, however, he recognizes both points of view, although inclining somewhat toward a religious interpretation.

Accordingly, as he expressed it in his *Lectures on the Method of Academic Studies*, "the highest [standpoint from which history may be regarded] is the religious, or that in which the whole of history is conceived as the work of Providence."[1] Schelling denies, however, that the religious interpretation is essentially different from the philosophical. It is not a matter of choosing between the true and the false. For "by itself the religious construction belongs to theology, the philosophical construction belongs to philosophy," and each in its own way has something valuable to contribute.[2] The main difference between the religious and the philosophical construction is that the latter provides a narrower view of history. The philosophy of history is, after all, but one branch of philosophy as a whole, whereas theology "is, in general, the highest synthesis of philosophical and historical knowledge."[3] In Christianity, "the universe as a whole is regarded as history,"[4] while the philosophy of history is "that which objectivates the ideal side of philosophy,"[5] in contrast to the philosophy of nature which represents the real side of philosophy. Thus of the two points of view, the theological and the philosophical, which may be selected to account for the connection of historical events, it is the former which provides the most comprehensive construction.

The philosophical construction of history has been investigated at some length in much of what has preceded.[6] Here it may be sufficient to summarize what we have already noted in order that this view-

---

[1] *Ibid.*     [2] I, 5, 307.     [3] *Ibid.*     [4] I, 5, 286.     [5] I, 5, 287.
[6] I, 5, 283.

point may be placed in its proper perspective. The "higher necessity" of history which the historical artist reveals is to be understood, from the philosophical standpoint, as the Absolute Identity.[1] The content of history is defined by the philosopher as freedom. It is, more precisely, the freedom of man by which the Absolute separates itself from objective necessity. It is freedom understood as "spontaneity", as freedom to choose, or the ability to act irrationally.[2] Such freedom, in mythological language, inaugurated the "Fall", and it will end with the Golden Age of legality, the complete reign of reason, when all spontaneity has disappeared. As the object of history in this more limited sense, the philosopher posits "the erection of an objective organism of freedom, or the State,"[3] The movement of history is conceived as guided by the "construction of the legal constitution,"[4] by means of which the State, as representing the synthesis of necessity and freedom, would emerge as an end in itself —not, as in Kant's view, as a means to the achievement of security for commercial relations.[5] From this standpoint, the State must be seen as "by nature absolute," for thus at the end of history it will become "the immediate and visible form of the Absolute Life."[6] In that the State is represented from the philosophical point of view as the objectivation of the Absolute itself, it stands as the goal to which all human history moves, as the expression of complete harmony of freedom and necessity, and as the achievement by mankind of complete rationality. The "higher necessity" of history is thus interpreted by the philosopher as the activity of the Absolute itself in its gradual self-realization by which, through the appearance of freedom for the individual, there is eventually secured conformity to law for the whole.

It is the construction of history from the religious point of view, however, which most engages Schelling's enthusiasm. The religious construction of the "higher necessity" in history is dependent, though, upon the insights of a particular religion, viz. the Christian. For not all religions deliver the same judgment as Christianity upon the significance of history. In fact, Christianity is distinguished from other religions by virtue of its view that the universe as a whole is historical in character. Moreover, "Christianity in its innermost nature and in the highest sense is historical."[7] When, now, the in-

---

[1] See, e.g. pp. 78–82 and (earlier pages).
[2] I, 5, 310.          [3] I, 3, 589.      [4] I, 5, 312.      [5] I, 5, 283.
[6] *Supra*, pp. 85–6.      [7] I, 5, 316.

sights of Christianity in regard to history are combined with the philosophical elaboration of it which Schelling's system provides, the result is a theology which has as its foundation the religious interpretation of history. In brief, Schelling's most comprehensive interpretation of the content of history finally emerges as a synthesis of the historical construction of Christianity and the religious construction of the whole of history. When, in Schelling's view, philosophy, "which elevates itself above the empirical enchainment of things," is recognized as "the true organ of theology as science," a construction of history is possible wherein "the highest ideas of the Divine Essence... become objective."[1]

The historical construction of Christianity, when aided by philosophy, provides a unique conception, not only of human history *per se*, but of the universe as a whole. From the point of view of Christianity alone, "the ruling intuition of the universe is the intuition of it as history and as a world of Providence."[2] At no point does this appear more clearly than in the contrast between Christianity and the religion of the ancient Greeks. If it is acknowledged that "nature and history in general are related as real and ideal unity,[3] then it should also be seen that the religion of the Greek world and the religion of the Christian world are related in the same way. Greek religion is a religion of nature; that is to say, the Divine revealed itself to the Greeks through natural objects and as beings which are continuous with natural phenomena. But in Christianity, "the Divine has ceased to reveal itself in nature and is knowable only in history."[4] The real world, the world of nature and of closed forms, the finite, is superseded by the ideal world, the world of history and of "fleeting" forms, the infinite. Among the Greeks, the gods are represented "as beings of a higher nature, abiding, unchanging forms."[5] But in Christianity, "the forms are not abiding but appearing; not eternal, natural beings but historical forms in which the Divine reveals itself only in passing, and whose fleeting appearance can be held fast only by faith, but never changed into an absolute present."[6]

This distinction between the ancient Greek world and the Christian world is, however, of more than passing interest to the philosopher of history. For when it is seen that Christianity is by nature historical,

---

[1] I, 5, 288.    [2] I, 5, 299.    [3] I, 5, 290.    [4] I, 5, 289.    [5] *Ibid.*
[6] I, 5, 288.

and this historical orientation of Christianity is joined with the higher philosophical view of history itself "as an efflux of the eternal necessity,"[1] then there is also provided therewith the possibility of viewing history itself as *both* "a Divine *and* an Absolute appearance," and thus we arrive at "a truly historical science of religion, or theology,"[2] or a philosophical exposition of Christianity.

Thus Schelling proceeds in his theology—which has now become a philosophical exposition of history from within the framework of the Christian faith—to an elaboration of the various aspects of human history. Earlier, in his *System of Transcendental Idealism*,[3] Schelling had distinguished three periods of history, those of Nature, Fate and Providence. Now, in his *Methods of Academic Studies*,[4] he continues with a description of these periods. As God or the Absolute reveals Himself in the dimension of history, which is to be understood philosophically as "the higher potency [or form] of Nature,"[5] this one Divine Essence is to be seen again under one or the other of two potencies. In other words, "Fate is also Providence, but recognized in the real, just as Providence is Fate, but intuited in the ideal."[6] During the time of identity of the one Eternal Necessity, when the conflict of infinite and finite had not emerged and the Eternal remained enclosed within the finite, the Absolute revealed itself as nature. This was the period of "the most beautiful flowering of Greek religion and poetry,"[7] the classical period of Greek civilization. When man began to move away from this identity, when freedom began to express itself, there took place a conflict between the freedom of the subject and the ancient Necessity, which then revealed itself as Fate. This transition represents the end of the ancient world, and Schelling regards its history as a whole as the tragic period of human history. The modern world begins when man breaks away from nature and becomes conscious of his separation from the Absolute. There arises, accordingly, the demand for a conscious reconciliation to take the place of the original unconscious identity; and as a substitute for the former unconscious identity with nature, and in order to heal the "split" between man and God, experienced as sin, unity is sought on the higher stage of Providence.

A closer scrutiny of the characteristics of these periods reveals several significant contrasts. The ancient world is the "nature side of

---

[1] *Ibid.*    [2] I, 5, 295.    [3] *Ibid.*    [4] I, 3, 603–4.    [5] I, 5, 290.
[6] I, 5, 306.    [7] I, 5, 290.

history."[1] In it the dominant idea is the inclusion of the infinite in the finite, and accordingly its mythology is "symbolic of the Infinite."[2] Christianity, on the contrary, strives "to take up the finite into the infinite, i.e. to make it an allegory of the infinite."[3] In Greek thought, the finite, nature, is a self-contained world; and since its gods were merely higher powers of nature, nature itself was regarded as symbolizing the character of the gods: eternal, unchanging and complete in themselves. But in Christian thought, where the infinite is regarded as the ultimate, nature is valued merely as indicating the infinite and is regarded as quite subordinate to the infinite. Furthermore, "where the infinite itself can become finite it can also become multiplicity; it is capable of polytheism: where it is only indicated through the finite, it necessarily remains one, and no polytheism as a simultaneity of divine forms is possible."[4] The polytheism of Greek religion is a result of the view that Divinity itself is a self-contained reality, so that each appearance must be regarded as independent of every other. The monotheism of Christianity, on the other hand, is safeguarded by the tendency to regard finitude as a mere instrument or token of Divinity which itself is removed from dependence upon the finite.

The result of Christianity's orientation is a reversal of the relationship which had been assumed between nature and the ideal world. Nature was no mystery to the Greeks. It was rational, ordered and self-sufficient. Its gods were not extra- or supra-natural, since they were seen as a part of nature itself. As a result, the pagans were not excited to investigate such phenomena as electricity and the chemical changes of bodies. For these excited no awe in themselves. But the modern world, under the influence of Christian thinking, regarded nature as a mystery and a secret, for it looked upon nature not as a self-contained world, but rather "as a likeness of the invisible and spiritual world."[5] For this reason, "nature" has meant two different things to pagans and Christians.

Again we may note a contrast between Christianity and paganism in terms of reliance upon tradition. Even as nature, once understood, repeats the same story without change, so a religion, such as that of the Greeks', which is based upon nature has no need of an historical basis. But in Christianity, "where the Divine does not live in enduring forms, but passes away in fleeting appearances, it has need of holding

---

[1] *Ibid.*     [2] I, 5, 292.     [3] I, 5, 430.     [4] *Ibid.*     [5] I, 5, 288.

it fast and eternalizing it through tradition."[1] Greek religion makes the finite the medium for the intuition of Divinity and as a result its ideas of divinity must be expressed in terms of being. But in Christianity the Divine becomes objective only through activity, which is characteristic of history. And since history is itself endless, unlimited, some limited entity must be called upon to represent the manifestation of Divinity. Its limited character, however, is incidental to its true significance, which is the manifestation within it of the Divine. Such is the Church in Christianity. Its essence "is not itself real, like the State, but ideal"; and thus it is able to represent "the unity of all in the Spirit."[2]

Hence the contrast between the Church and State is based directly upon the antithesis between the Christian and Greek worlds. The harmony of necessity and freedom, which is understood by Schelling as the goal toward which history moves, can be represented either in the real or in the ideal. That is to say: if the real, or finite, is regarded as primary, as it was among the Greeks, then the goal of human activity would be envisioned as the ultimate subordination of all freedom, or caprice, to the finite entity, the State. Thus Plato's *Republic* stands as the definitive statement of the Greek vision of the good life—a life which finds its culmination in the complete organization of the public life in terms of an objective, but finite, harmony. In Christianity, on the other hand, the ideal and infinite is regarded as primary, and no finite entity can represent the ultimate goal for human activity. Hence, in place of the objective harmony of necessity and freedom envisioned by the Greeks, Christianity proposes a subjective harmony "in an ideal unity which is the Church,"[3] But the Church, as a finite entity, is not an end in itself. It is merely the means by which an ultimately subjective unity through the infinite activity of the Spirit is made possible.

But if any single feature serves to set off Christianity from paganism, it is the presence in the former of mysticism. Greek religion is essentially symbolic in character; i.e. it regards natural forms as representative of the character of the gods. But Christianity has a symbolism of its own which serves uniquely to differentiate it as a religion from paganism. In order to see this contrast more distinctly, however, it is necessary to differentiate symbolism and mysticism more carefully. Schelling maintains that "just as the activity which

---

[1] I, 5, 289.    [2] I, 5, 293.    [3] I, 5, 314

expresses externally the unity of the infinite and the finite can be called symbolic, it can also be called, internally, mystic, and mysticism in general a subjective symbolism."[1] Thus Schelling regards the Greek representations of the gods as a symbolic activity since it not only pictures the unity of the infinite and the finite in terms of the finite but also regards this representation externally, or objectively. In Christianity, however, this unity can be conceived only in terms of the infinite; and since the infinite reveals itself only in passing, the desired identity can never be achieved "here and now." The historical character of Christianity precludes, as such, any temporal realization, in a complete sense, of union with God. Nevertheless "mysticism is the necessary manner of intuition prescribed by the innermost spirit of Christianity."[2] For every attempt to express exoterically the ultimate significance of the Christian apprehension of the Divine is basically an attempt to make an object of faith into an object of rational sight. The contradictions involved in such attempts have led frequently to atheism, which is a subjective (and thus complete) affirmation of the contradiction which, objectively, is maintained by faith. Christian mystics, however, "have wished faith turned into a perception, and the fruit of time which was not yet ripe to appear in advance."[3] Mysticism has thus become the source of heresy in Christianity. But Christianity as a whole has mysticism as an innate tendency, in contrast to Greek religion which is essentially free from all mysticism.

Nevertheless, Christianity is not content to maintain itself in the situation of faith completely. As Schelling himself discovered, its dogmas have a high degree of speculative significance. To render its theology explicit is not contrary to a tendency which has frequently manifested itself among the ranks of believing Christians. As Schelling notes, Lessing's *Education of the Human Race* is itself an attempt "to disclose the philosophical significance" of the doctrine of the Trinity, which Schelling viewed as an "absolutely necessary" part of the meaning of Christianity.[4] Schelling criticizes Lessing for failing to relate the idea of the Trinity explicitly to the history of the world, but the speculative attempt in itself is regarded by Schelling as a valuable contribution to the general attempt to make Christian doctrine the basis for a philosophical comprehension of the universe.

When the world is regarded from the perspective of Christian

---

[1] I, 5, 294.  [2] I, 5, 118.  [3] I, Ibid.  [4] I, 5, 294 Cf. *supra* pp. 19-21 on Lessing

theology alone, its unique orientation provides a framework within which the whole of history can be placed. The infinite is its ruling principle, and it witnesses to "the coming of the true infinite into the finite, not in order to deify [the finite] but in order to sacrifice it in its own being to God and thus to reconcile it to Him."[1] Accordingly the primary idea of Christianity "is necessarily the God-become-man, Christ as the pinnacle and end of the old world of gods."[2] As the highest appearance of Divinity within finitude—by virtue of which His attractive power to the pagans is guaranteed—Christ is also the final appearance of the Divine within history. He Himself withdraws into the infinite, but sends His "principle," the Spirit, as the in-dwelling of the infinite in the finite. The Spirit itself, however, is not a real but an ideal principle, hence the means by which the finite is carried back into the infinite, and appears here as "the light of the New World."[3] Such, in outline, is the speculative significance of the Trinity, but related by Schelling—as Lessing's interpretation was not—to the general history of the world.

An interesting aspect of Christianity's "idea", however, is that, in Schelling's view, it is much older than the Christian religion itself. As far back as records extend, he maintains, there are two distinct and opposed streams of religion and poetry. The first is to be found in the religious tradition of ancient India from which was transmitted the oldest system of idealism throughout the Orient until it "found its permanent bed in Christianity."[4] The other stream is the system of realism which came to fullest expression in Greek philosophy—al-though, Schelling believes, Greek mythology itself derives from the idealistic tradition, which was the reason why mythology and poetry were so strenuously opposed by Plato. But the fact that Christianity has existed prior to and outside of its full historical expression proves, according to Schelling, the necessity of its idea. When Christian missionaries went to India and expected to proclaim something quite unheard of in teaching that God had become man in Christ, they were astonished, says Schelling, that the natives by no means dis-puted their report but rather found it singular that for the Christians there had taken place only once what frequently and in steady repe-tition occurred for them—whence once cannot deny that the natives of India "had more understanding of their religion than the Christian

---

[1] I, 5, 292.
[2] *Ibid.*   [3] *Ibid.*   [4] I, 5, 29.8

missionaries had of theirs."[1] But even more to the point is the need, in Schelling's view, to construct Christianity historically against the religious construction of the whole of history.

It was because Christianity brought to the general consciousness this unique orientation that its success was assured. Passages from the *Philosophy of Art* describe Schelling's conception of the situation at the time of the introduction of Christianity to the pagan world. Here, at the beginning of the modern era, "man tears himself free from nature."[2] The Greek spirit had exhausted itself in a futile attempt, during the hegemony of Rome, to embrace everything objective. A feeling of satiety with the real and a longing for the ideal "lay like a sultry air... upon the world of that time, and a general presentiment seemed to draw all thoughts to the Orient as if the Savior would come from there, traces of which [presentiment] lie in the reports of Tacitus and Suetonius."[3] At this point the "eternal necessity" which had revealed itself to the Greeks as Nature was manifested as Fate, dealing bitter, powerful blows, to escape from which there was only one recourse: "to throw oneself into the arms of Providence."[4] It was into this situation that Christianity came, "in the fullness of time," with its proclamation of "good news." Thus was inaugurated the last great age of world history, tending toward the final completion when the identity which is foreseen ideally in terms of faith shall be realized in the harmony of necessity and freedom, when God shall be "all in all." Then, when the "successivity" ['*Nacheinander*'] of the modern world has been changed into an *all-at-once* ['*Zumal*'],[5] and the world which has fallen away through freedom shall again be reconciled to God, the great history of the universe shall have run its course.

In order to complete our picture of Schelling's philosophy of history during his first period, notice should here be taken of one of Schelling's writings, his *Philosophy and Religion* (1804), which is decisive in the shaping of the character of his philosophy from 1809 on, but which is no less important, in the opinion of the present writer, as indicating the influence of a fundamentally historical orientation upon Schelling's thought as a whole. We have already had occasion to note[6] that from the standpoint of Schelling's philosophy of identity, history as a whole has no ultimate significance. The

---

[1] I, 5, 298–9.    [2] I, 5, 427.    [3] I, 5, 427–8.    [4] I, 5, 429.
[5] *Ibid.*    [6] *Supra*, pp. 60–61.

mysticism of the intellectual intuition, which pierces beyond the relative viewpoint wherein history is seen as a mere potency of the Absolute, is valued by Schelling, during this period, as the highest means to knowledge and is regarded by him as the final achievement of consciousness in its journey toward the suspension of the dualism of subjective and objective. In fact, to the extent that under the potency of the ideal the Absolute is conceived as moving toward ever higher syntheses from knowledge to activity (moral) and finally to artistic production, the *history* pertaining to any of these stages is but a stage of transition which is necessary to the appearance of the Absolute, but which is destined to be transcended when finally all oppositions are swallowed up in the One. Nevertheless in the *Philosophy and Religion*, the finite itself, and with it space, time and the categories, are given an independent status, primarily—it is here contended—in order to provide a more adequare metaphysics for the historical construction of reality. The transition from the point of view adopted in this work to that expressed in *Of Human Freedom* (1809) is but a minor one. And as we shall see, the orientation of all of Schelling's philosophy from 1809 on is historical.

What in large measure is lacking in Schelling's philosophy up to this point is a metaphysics which will make the world of history significant in itself. This defect is to some extent remedied by the *Philosophy and Religion*. To the question, how comes there to be a world of finitude, a world of particular things which are not only rationally comprehended but also sensed, Schelling answers with the old doctrine of the "Fall" of the world of sense. At once Schelling repudiates what had no doubt been strongly suggested in many of his earlier writings, viz. the theory of emanation, "according to which the efflux of the divinity, in a gradual gradation and separation from the source, loses the divine perfection, and so finally passes over into the opposite (matter, privation), just as light is finally limited by darkness".[1] On the contrary, Schelling maintains, "there is no steady transition from the Absolute to the actual; the origin of the world of sense is to be conceived only as a complete break from the Absolute, as a leap".[2] Thus, while finitude is still regarded as a lower form of being, its appearance is such that a genuine history which will effect reconciliation with the Absolute is now made a part of the total significance of the universe.

---

[1] I, 6, 35–6.     [2] I, 6, 38.

The eventual appearance of the finite is the result of a somewhat complicated evolvement from the original Absolute. The Absolute itself is pute ideality. But as a result of its self-knowledge, it converts its ideality into reality, and thereby produces "a counter-image which is at the same time, by itself, truly *another Absolute*... an intuition of itself in the real..."[1] Strictly speaking, of course, there is only one Absolute. But to the extent that the Absolute has knowledge of itself, this must be expressed by means of a real image, and hence the second Absolute. But this second Absolute, the real image of the original, is itself an *independently* real being; for "the exclusive characteristic of the Absolute is that it endows its counter-image with the essence of itself,... with independence, hence... *freedom*".[2] It is from this freedom, or self-determination, with which the counter-image is endowed that the world of appearance derives its autonomy. For the eternal ideas which are contained within the counter-image share the independence of the counter-image itself and are, in fact, an expression of this independence. It is this self-objectivation of the Absolute which thus grounds the *possibility* of the Fall, although the *actuality* of the Fall of the ideas "lies entirely within the fallen itself which thus only *through and for itself* produces the nothingness of sensible things".[3] The Fall itself is outside of all time and is, rather, the occasion of the appearance of things in time. But the Fall marks the inauguration of a double life for the world of ideas: "one [life] in itself, by which, however, it obligates itself to finitude and which... is an appearance of life; the other life is in the Absolute, which is its true life".[4] It is the former kind of life, the life in itself in separation from the Absolute, which is characteristic of finitude and of the world of sensible things.

No one will deny that Schelling has not yet, at this point, made a complete break with the rationalism of his earlier period. Nevertheless, he has provided himself with a better conceptual scheme for the evaluation of history. For now he is able to say that the life in itself of finite things "expresses itself in its highest potency as *egoity*".[5] And since "egoity is the general principle of finitude", and as such represents "the point of farthest distance from God", the rationale of finitude is expressed in a "return to the Absolute, the re-assumption into the Ideal".[6] In other words, the movement of finitude as a whole,

---

[1] I, 6, 34.    [2] I, 6, 39.    [3] I, 6, 40·    [4] I, 6, 41.    [5] I, 6, 42.
[6] *Ibid*.

"the great design of the universe and of its history, is none other than
the perfected reconciliation and resolution in Absoluteness".[1] The
world is not separated from God in any ultimate sense. Nevertheless
egoity is separation, and as such sinful. Its sinfulness is occasioned
by the endowment of it with freedom, and this freedom itself must
be overcome, gradually but nevertheless completely, in a final sur-
render to God. The philosophy of history is now to be understood not
only in terms of the movement of mankind throughout various
stages within time. Rather time itself becomes a part of the "eternal
history of God:

> History is an epic composed in the mind of God; its major parts
> are: that which represents the going-forth of mankind from its
> center to its greatest distance from Him, the other which represents
> the return. The former is the Iliad, the latter the Odyssey, of
> history. In the former, the direction was centrifugal, in the latter
> it is centripetal. The great design of the entire appearance of the
> world expresses itself in this manner in history. The ideas, the
> spirits, had to fall away from their center and enter into nature,
> the general sphere of the Fall, into particularity, in order that after-
> wards they might, as particulars, return into the indifference, be
> reconciled to it, and be in it without disturbing it.[2]

## III. SCHELLING AND HEGEL

The affinities between many aspects of Schelling's philosophy of
history and Hegel's will already have become evident to anyone who
is acquainted with the larger circle of thought represented by German
Idealism. That such affinities are not accidental will also be evident
to anyone similarly acquainted with the personal relations between
these two philosophers. Hegel had affiliated himself with Schelling at
an early age and had, apparently, looked up to Schelling as his intellectual leader, even though Schelling was five years younger than
himself. Hegels' thought matured much more slowly than did Schelling's, and it wasn't until 1806 that Hegel finally embraced a position which placed him at odds with Schelling. While both Schelling
and Hegel were at Jena, they edited together the *Kritische Journal
für Philosophie*; and "the fact that a dispute could arise concerning
the authorship of one of the articles appearing in the *Journal* proves

---

[1] I, 6, 43.     [2] I, 6, 37.

how much the two men were in agreement with one another".[1] But when Hegel's *Phänomenologie des Geistes* appeared in 1806 with its reference to Schelling's Absolute, as it appeared in his philosophy of identity, as "the night in which, as we say, all cows are black",[2] their amicable relations were permanently at an end. Not only did Schelling accuse Hegel of having plagiarized his system but he never lost an opportunity to point out the differences between his later philosophy and Hegel's.

The evidence would seem to indicate that Hegel was strongly influenced by Schelling, and particularly by the latter's philosophy of history as this was developed in *The Methods of Academic Studies*. A comparison of the divisions of history together with the methods appropriate for their treatment as set forth by Schelling in this work, and the similar catalogue made by Hegel in his Introduction to his *Lectures on the Philosophy of History*, serves to bring out rather clearly the dependence of Hegel upon the suggestions (if not the exact pattern) proposed by his former colleague.

We have already noted[3] that Schelling is careful to differentiate between historiography and the philosophic interpretation of history. The former is concerned solely with the narration of what has happened, and allows of no interpretation on the part of the historian. Where such interpretation enters in, as it does in "pragmatic" history, the result is a distorted version of history which falls far short of the excellence attained by "historical art", where the historian, such as Herodotus, allows the "higher necessity" of history to appear without attempting to analyze it. The philosophic interpretation, on the other hand, delivers a judgment upon the "higher necessity", seeking to provide a metaphysical explanation for that which is variously designated as Fate or Providence. And as we have noted, Schelling was convinced that a synthesis of philosophy and religion—or what amounts to a philosophical theology—is the most adequate instrument for the interpretation of the content of history.

With several important exceptions, Hegel's prescriptions for the treatment of history parallel those of Schelling. Hegel notes three major methods by which history may be treated, and corresponding

---

[1] J. E. Erdmann, *A History of Philosophy*, tr. by W. S. Hough. (New York: The Macmillan Co., 1909), Vol. II, p. 682.

[2] Introduction to *The Phenomenology of Mind*, tr. by J. B. Baillie in *Hegel Selections*, ed. J. Loewenberg, (Charles Scribner's Sons, 1929), p. 14.

[3] *Supra*, p 75.

to these methods, three kinds of history which result: original, reflective, and philosophical history. The first type, original history, invites comparison with the kind of historiography which Schelling denoted as being concerned primarily with the real, the events themselves, exclusive of their reference to the context in which they appear.[1] It is the chronicler who, according to Hegel, has as his aim "nothing more than the presentation to posterity of an image of events as clear as that which he himself possessed in virtue of personal observations, or life-like descriptions".[2] It should be noted that Hegel places in the category of original history only that which "is present and living" in the environment of its authors,[3] while Schelling would seem to include under this heading information obtained about events of the past. But both Schelling and Hegel agree that the "original" historian is not concerned with reflections "for he lives in the spirit of his subject; he has not attained an elevation above it".[4]

The second type of historiography noted by Hegel is what he calls "reflective history", so-called, apparently, beause it is history "whose mode of representation is not really confined by the limits of the time to which it relates, but whose spirit transcends the present".[5] This is a somewhat broader category than that suggested by Schelling in his second classification, "pragmatic" history, which appears for Hegel as one species of "reflective" history. Its aim is "to gain a view of the entire history of a people or a country, or of the world".[6] Livy is an example of a historian who pursued this aim. Its weakness, according to Hegel, lies in "that the individuality of tone which most characterizes a writer belonging to a different culture is not modified in accordance with the periods such a record must traverse".[7] As a result, the view of the past is frequently distorted so as to match the presuppositions of the historian.

The second species of reflective history is "pragmatic", and here the close connection with Schelling seems more evident. For both Schelling and Hegel, pragmatic history is didactic history, and its aim is not so much the objective presentation of the past as it is the

---

[1] S. W. I, 5, 307.
[2] G. W. F. Hegel, *Lectures on the Philosophy of History*, tr. from third German edition by J. Sibree, (London, 1894), p. 2.
[3] *Ibid.*
[4] *Ibid.*
[5] *Ibid.*, p. 4.
[6] *Ibid.*
[7] *Ibid*, p. 5.

use of the past to illustrate some general principle which will be applicable to the present. It is reflective history, to be sure, since there is a large element of interpretation in it. But it does not escape the arbitrariness which the historian's individual interests dictate. It selects some limited goal as that toward which the course of history is supposed to be tending, and ignores the general purpose, the "higher necessity", of history. As Hegel notes, pragmatic history frequently claims to extract a moral teaching from history; hence "rulers, statesmen, nations, are wont to be emphatically commended to the teaching which experience offers in history. But what experience and history teach is this—that peoples and governments never have learned anything from history, or acted upon principles deduced from it".[1]

The third and fourth species of reflective history distinguished by Hegel are really but an elaboration of what Schelling understood by pragmatic history. The third variety, "critical" history, is really a history of history, or "a criticism of historical narratives and an investigation of their truth and credibility".[2] It stems from the so-called "higher criticism" of philology, whence its peculiar aim of extorting from the records something other than the matter recorded. Its virtue is limited only by the imagination of the historian. The critical historian makes the past a living reality by "putting subjective fancies in the place of historical data".[3] The specialized history which, fourthly, is regarded by Hegel as a species of reflective history is the kind of history which takes general points of view, such as history of law, of art, and of religion. The generality of its point of view enables it to form "a transition to the philosophical history of the world."[4] But since it is fragmentary rather than truly universal history, it does not achieve the fullness of view which Hegel demands of philosophical history. Thus Hegel would deny that the religious is the highest point of view from which history may be surveyed. Schelling's philosophical theology would appear to him as a compromise which must be transcended in order that the true (i.e. that most general) interpretation of history could be given.

It would seem indisputable, however, that Hegel followed Schelling closely in setting up the divisions of history and in specifying the methods appropriate to each. Some finer distinctions are made by Hegel, to be sure, especially in the varieties of "reflective" history he distinguished, while Schelling was content to specify the general

---

[1] *Ibid.*, p. 6.      [2] *Ibid.*, p. 7.      [3] *Ibid.*, p. 8.      [4] *Ibid.*,

character of "pragmatic" history as that which—for both himself and Hegel—is a bastard form of historiography, primarily because of the subjectivity of its treatment. The widest divergence between Schelling and Hegel would seem to be found in Schelling's conception of "historical art"—a category which Hegel entirely ignores, preferring, instead, the less definite category of "original" history. No doubt this divergence stems from Hegel's much lower estimation of art and artistic production.

It would scarcely seem necessary to point out in detail the affinities between Schelling's and Hegel's views of the content of history from the perspective of philosophy. Both regard history as a realm in which the Absolute comes to expression. Hegel regards universal history as the stage where "Spirit displays itself in its most concrete reality,"[1] while Schelling, during his first period, views history as merely a "potency" of the Absolute, and hence as a less valuable medium than that which the philosopher has at hand in the "intellectual intuition." Thus history does not achieve the status in Schelling's philosophy at this time that it did for both him and Hegel later on. We shall have occasion to refer to Hegel again in considering Schelling's philosophy of history during his second period. But it would appear evident, at this point, that Hegel's interpretation of history follows closely many of the distinctions and definitions which were originally proposed by Schelling.

---

[1] *Ibid.*, p. 17.

CHAPTER FOUR

# THE ROLE OF HISTORY IN THE POSITIVE PHILOSOPHY

## I. Schelling's Criticism of Rationalism

Schelling developed his philosophy of history from 1809 on in connection with a thorough criticism of rationalism and the erection, at the same time, of what he called a "positive" philosophy. The significance of this re-orientation of Schelling's thought has been noted by others, but usually in a somewhat restricted context. It is true that the later Schelling sought to effect a synthesis between essence and existence, thought and being, after pointing out the distinction between the two which had been obscured by traditional rationalistic philosophies, notably Hegel's. But the positive philosophy which Schelling erected is also to be understood as motivated primarily by the conviction which had been growing with him for some time that reality as a whole is essentially historical in character, that the static metaphysics of traditional philosophy is incapable of explaining the historical nature of being, and that the history of the universe has been most adequately set forth in the religious tradition of mankind, especially as this reaches its culmination in Christianity. It is from the point of view of this conviction that Schelling's contributions to metaphysics, epistemology and philosophical method during his later period are to be evaluated.

The problem which is central to Schelling's philosophizing during this period is to account metaphysically for man. As he expressed it in his *Introduction to the Philosophy of Revelation*, "Just he, man, impelled me to the final imponderable question: Why is there anything? Why not Nothing?"[1] Such a question, which may seem somewhat ambiguous at first glance, is nevertheless the crux of the philosophic enterprize. For it is the ultimate question which is posed to the human understanding. Essentially it is a question which is put to metaphysics, for it gropes toward the universal context within which existence itself is to be placed. Schelling does not hereby devi-

---

[1] S. W. II, 3, 7.

ate from the view of the nature of metaphysics which had guided his own earlier philosophizing and which had been explicitly defined by Kant. It was Kant who had first clearly recognized that in metaphysics reason leads one "to the objective boundary of experience, viz., to the reference to something which is not itself an object of experience, but is the ground of all experience."[1] The difference between Kant and Schelling on this point is not in respect to the nature of the metaphysical enterprize but in respect to the chances of its success. For Schelling believed that he had constructed a philosophic method which would surmount the objections of Kant and deliver positive answers to the questions which metaphysics raises.

Philosophy deals essentially, according to Schelling, with the ultimate questions of metaphysics. When it turns its attention to nature alone, it does not find it difficult to discover a solution to the questions which are raised in this field. Nature *can* be interpreted teleologically (and hence metaphysically) in terms of principles basic to its own operations. Or man himself may be represented as the goal of nature, as the highest pinnacle of its achievements and the end toward which the realization of all its potentialities tends. But the true end of man is not so easily discerned. If I as an observer who would understand nature *and* man turn my gaze toward *history* wherein man's activities, stemming from his freedom, are to be observed, I find that "this world of *history* presents such an unreliable drama that I may well doubt that there is a goal and hence a true ground of the world." For while every other natural being has its place and fulfills its purpose, man appears, at least to himself, without purpose. History as such seems to confirm the judgment that "all is vanity," for "even though man and his activity make the world comprehensible, he himself is the most incomprehensible of all."[2] As a result, "since [man] should be the goal of everything else, because of him everything else again become purposeless."[3] Only if man himself has a well-defined goal can existence as a whole, through him its highest expression, be endowed with meaning. This is the reason why man himself impels one to the question, Why anything, why not nothing?

This question, which Schelling now considers the metaphysical

---

[1] Kant's *Prolegomena to any Future Metaphysics*, edited in English by Dr. Paul Carus. (Chicago: The Open Court Publishing Company, 1933), p. 134.
[2] S. W. II, 3, 7.     [3] *Ibid.*

question *par excellence*, can be asked in a variety of ways. But however it be asked, it resolves itself eventually into a question as to the
basic structure of human nature and accordingly of the context
within which that human nature is to be placed. This is the question
which philosophy seeks to answer, and in one form or other, has
sought to answer from the beginning. Until the critical investigations
of Kant, metaphysics was generally recognized as "the science which
concerns itself especially with the supra-natural and the supra-
sensible."[1] Its content was God and His relation to the world, man as
a link between the physical and the supra-physical worlds, the nature
and origin of good and evil, and the immortality of the human soul.
In limiting knowledge to objects of possible experience, however,
Kant destroyed the ancient metaphysics and with it, presumably,
the possibility of representing an ultimate context for human
experience. But at the same time that Kant destroyed the ancient
metaphysics he became the founder of a new science which claimed
to present "a complete and exhaustive theory of the faculty of
human knowledge."[2] Thus, through his *Critique of Pure Reason*, Kant
laid a basis for a science which could at least account for the quest on
the part of reason for its own presuppositions.

On the other hand, according to Schelling, Kant's theory of knowledge produced a negative conclusion in regard to the possibility of
knowing real things:

> Kant maintained that there is a knowledge of things *a priori*;
> but from this knowledge *a priori* he extracted just that which is the
> important thing, namely the existing itself, the essence, the nature
> of the thing, that which actually *is* in it; for that which appears in
> things by virtue of the alleged determinations of our knowing
> faculty is not actually in them—but what is that which is in them,
> in the last analysis, independently of the determinations of our
> knowing faculty? To this Kant has no answer.[3]

The obvious step beyond this position was that which was actually
taken, first, by Fichte. If all our knowledge is *a priori*, but at the
same time *genuine* knowledge, we must assume that existence itself
may be known in this fashion and that, accordingly, not only the
form but also the content of what is known have the same basic
origin. In deriving all reality from the Ego, Fichte erected a system

---

[1] S. W. II, 3, 33.    [2] S. W. II, 3, 46.    [3] S. W. II, 3, 50.

of absolute idealism in which "the entire so-called objective world has no actual objective existence, but rather exists only in the necessary representations of the Ego."[1] Thus the way beyond the limitations upon knowledge imposed by Kant is pointed out in the science of knowledge which Fichte constructed on the basis of Kantian insights. For the transcendental, i.e. supra-empirical, science which Kant founded is extended by Fichte so as to become, in effect, a metaphysics. The a-temporal activity of the Ego becomes the ground of all the determinations attributed to existence. All that was needed, in order to arrive at the position achieved by succeeding idealistic philosophies, was the removal of that limitation by which the Ego was regarded merely as the Ego of *human* consciousness. When this was achieved, philosophy again found the way to that absolute Prius which Kant had previously described. In this way an ultimate context was again supplied for the understanding of man and his works.

But now, according to Schelling, the point has been reached where a fundamental re-orientation must be introduced into the metaphysical and epistemological assumptions which had guided German philosophy hitherto. Epistemologically, the distinction must be made between the form and the content of knowledge, while at the same time the metaphysical assumption that Reason is ultimate reality must be brought under scrutiny. Idealism as a whole is characterized by the presupposition that Reason has itself as content, and that to the extent that it makes itself its own object it finds the absolute Prius in itself, and thereby it is able to achieve an *a priori* knowledge of all being. This had been the position taken by Schelling himself in his earlier period, and it was the position which both Fichte and Hegel had extended in various directions. But the question remains whether, in making such an assumption, philosophy had arrived at the true Prius of being. For, as Schelling observes:

> there are two quite different things involved in knowing what a being is, *quid sit*, and that it is, *quod sit*. The former—the answer to the question: *what* it is—provides me insight into the *essence* of the thing, or it provides that I understand the thing, that I have an understanding or a concept of it, or that I have *it itself* in concept. But the other, the insight *that* it is, does not provide me with the mere concept, but with something transcending the mere concept, which is *existence*.[2]

---

[1] *Ibid.*, p. 51.     [2] *Ibid.*, p. 57–8.

In brief, what Schelling is objecting to is the idealistic-rationalistic assumption that reason can be its own content. To have a knowledge of *existence* it is not sufficient to have conceptual knowledge. Concepts are *instruments* for the ordering of existence, but they do not by themselves provide knowledge of existence. One must get beyond essence to existence if one is to have true knowledge of the ultimate Prius of reality. Furthermore, an *a priori* knowledge by itself can no longer be regarded as sufficient. For knowledge of existence can be given only by *experience*. The limitations of pure rationalism are seen as soon as it is realized that "to the extent that the question concerns the *what*, this question directs itself to the *reason*, in contrast to which... *that* this *is*, that it exists, only experience can teach."[1]

Schelling's criticism of rationalism thus takes the form of an "existentialist" orientation toward reality. The unfortunate connotations suggested by this term to many modern minds should not blind one, however, to the positive contribution Schelling hereby makes not only to the post-Hegelian development of philosophy in general, but also to the formulation of an adequate metaphysics for the philosophy of history. Schelling was searching for a means of expressing philosophically the context within which man and his institutions could be adequately represented, and it is primarily from this point of view that he criticizes idealism. This type of philosophy assumes as a first principle precisely that which demands explanation. In making reason ultimate, it has no way of accounting for reason, and it is just this which must be accounted for if man—who, of all beings, exhibits rationality—is to be metaphysically understood. When this impulse of Schelling's is taken into account, his raising of the question, "...why *is* there reason, why not unreason?"[2] can easily be appreciated. It is just this question which philosophy, perhaps understandably, has ignored. "Indeed", as Schelling observes:

> at first glance it is quite proper... to posit reason as universal substance, as that which *necessarily is*. But the existence of reason itself is much rather something conditioned, positive. For, absolutely expressed, why should not the opposite be just as possible?[3]

Hegel's philosophy, in Schelling's view, is the outstanding example of the failure of reason to ask for its own presuppositions. Hegel's is a pure "rational science," and as such it "concerns itself only with the

---

[1] *Ibid.*, p. 58.     [2] I, 10, 252.     [3] *Ibid.*, cf. II, 3, 247–8.

what of things, their essence."[1] It is based on "a falsely conceived identity... of thought and being"[2] and thus makes a spurious claim to be representative of existence itself. The Hegelian logic has as its content "mere concepts."[3] Among these concepts, to be sure, there is to be found the concept of the actual, deduced as a necessary form of the Absolute's self-determination. But "precisely therein, that the science of reason deduces the content of thought... lies the illusion that it has grasped not only *the* actual but also actuality, or that the actual has arisen in this manner; that that merely logical process is also that of actual becoming."[4] In other words, Hegel has assumed but has not proved that logical process is identical with real, or existential, process. Such may well be the case, but empirical verification of that assumption is by no means forthcoming from Hegel's system as such.

Rightly understood, Hegel's philosophy is nothing but an extended and elaborated form of the old ontological argument. According to Hegel, existence is a necessary predicate of the Absolute, at least to the extent that it achieves full self-expression. But this is also the contention of the ontological argument. From the *concept* of God His existence is asserted as a necessary attribute of His nature. What holds, therefore, in criticism of the ontological argument may be applied with equal force to the Hegelian system: "God... *if* he exists, *can* be only the necessarily existing."[5] But the hypothetical element still remains. Such an argument does not prove that God necessarily exists, but only that necessary existence distinguishes the nature of God from the nature of other existence. There still remains the question of whether God exists otherwise than in concept.

The ontological question remains as much of a question as ever. And as a matter of fact, Schelling maintains, the irrational, or suprarational, aspect of being seems to be more ultimate than rationality. As opposed to the Hegelian identification of reality and rationality, Schelling would point out that "order and form nowhere appear to have been original, but [rather that] what had initially been unruly had been brought to order."[6] Sheer existence displays an "incomprehensible basis," an "irreducible remainder which cannot be resolved into reason by the greatest exertion, but always remains in the

---

[1] II, 3, 60.    [2] II, 3, 59.    [3] II, 3, 65.    [4] *Ibid.*    [5] II, 3, 159.
[6] I, 7, 359: *Of Human Freedom*, trans. by James Gutmann. (Chicago: The Open Court Publishing Company, 1936), p. 34.

depths."[1] Rather than assuming that thought and being are by nature identical or even compatible, we should recognize the resistance which being offered to thought. In spite of the attempts of philosophers to reduce existence to conceptual order:

> ...being always stood opposite thought... as something unconquerable, so that philosophy, which would explain everything, found nothing more difficult than to give an explanation of just this being. It had to accept as explanation precisely this incomprehensibility, this active opposition toward all thought, this dynamic darkness, this positive inclination to obscurity.[2]

In other words, existence is not only more than conceptualization represents it as being, but it is also fundamentally "resistant" to rational delineation.

Such expressions as "the extra-logical nature of existence" and "the irrational aspect of being"—especially the latter—might lead some to suppose that Schelling has committed himself to the type of anti-rationalistic obscurantism which has become a feature of much of modern thought. But, seen against the context within which Schelling philosophized at this time, it will impress one, rather, that Schelling is merely trying to establish an epistemological position which will overcome what seem to him, in this period, as grave defects of German idealism. The term "irrational" does not have the same connotations for Schelling as it may have for the English reader. What he meant, apparently, by expressing himself thus was that reality must be recognized as being *more than* rational; that reason alone cannot determine existence; that besides the purely logical aspect of reality there is also the "extra-logical," or experiential, aspect; that this non-rational, experiential aspect precludes the possibility of proceeding purely deductively, as rationalism had, at least from the time of Anselm, from the elucidation of concepts alone in order to establish the existence of the world and its contents. In this respect, at least, it would seem that Schelling made a genuine advance over his idealistic predecessors. For it now seems to be quite generally recognized that, from the point of view of purely formal logic, existence cannot be asserted without appeal to some kind of experience. Formal logic—what Schelling terms "essence"—is, as far

---

[1] *Ibid.*, (S. W. I, 7, 360).
[2] I, 8, 212: *The Ages of the World*, trans. by F. de W. Bolman. (New York, Columbia University Press, 1942), p. 98.

as the denotation of its objects is concerned, entirely hypothetical. We cannot, in other words, pass immediately from definition to description. In the words of the eminent modern logician, Bertrand Russell—to cite only one of several who share this point of view:

> The ontological proof of the existence of God, if it were valid, would establish the logical necessity of at least one individual. But it is generally recognized as invalid, and in fact rests upon a mistaken view of existence—i.e. it fails to realize that existence can only be asserted of something described, not of something named, so that it is meaningless to argue from 'this is the so-and-so' and 'The so-and-so exists' to 'This exists.' If we reject the ontological argument, we seem driven to conclude that the existence of a world is an accident—i.e. it is not logically necessary. If that be so, no principle of logic can assert 'existence' except under a hypothesis, i.e. none can be of the form 'the propositional function so-and-so is sometimes true.'[1]

Schelling offers such a criticism of rationalism in the interest of a philosophical method which will adequately characterize "the extra-logical nature of existence."[2] Furthermore, Schelling believed, the solution to the dilemma posed by the criticism he made is to be found in a return to the epistemological position of Kant. It was Kant who had first clearly differentiated between the form and content of knowledge, between knowledge of the "what" which the form supplies and knowledge of the "that" which the content supplies. To the former belongs the conceptual aspect of reality, and to the latter the experiential element. To be sure, Kant himself had sought, through this distinction, to limit knowledge of objects of possible experience, and "he believed to have made an end forever of *all* knowledge of the supersensible by his critique." But the abiding result—which Kant himself did not appreciate—was "that the negative and the positive had to be separated in philosophy."[3] Kant had nothing to say as to the character of that which is in things independently of their formal, i.e. *a priori*, determinations. But the answer to this question is to be sought not in a denial of any genuine difference between the form and content of knowledge, but rather in a delineation of the negative and positive elements and an attempt to gain insight into the existential content.

---

[1] Bertrand Russell, *Introduction to Mathematical Philosophy* (New York and London, 1919), pp. 203–204.

[2] II, 3, 95.

[3] I, 10, 74. Quoted by Bolman, *op. cit.*, p. 40.

What is needed, therefore, if philosophy is to become truly aware of its own bases, is that it open itself, become receptive, and recognize its true function of giving form to a pre-existent content. One does not abandon the *a priori* and seek to reduce everything to sheer existential content. To do so would be to commit as grievous an error in this direction as Hegel committed in the opposite direction. Nevertheless cognizance must be taken of "the extra-logical nature of existence," and accordingly provision must be made for its incorporation into a philosophical system. The result will be a division of philosophy into two branches corresponding to the distinction between form and content or, in Schelling's words, "negative" and "positive." This does not involve the erection of two different philosophies, but rather the formulation of "two sides of one and the same philosophy, the one philosophy in two different but necessarily connected sciences."[1] The result will be "one science which explains the actual existence of things..."[2] Both the "what" and the "that" will thus receive philosophical expression.

To the rational is opposed the empirical, and it is the empirical which the positive side of philosophy must relate. Reason by itself "can discern or prove outside of *itself* no actual, true being..."[3] By "actual being" Schelling means existence—that which is non-rational in nature and which, accordingly, is other than conceptual being. Thus that which the positive science concerns itself with is "that which cannot be investigated by the mere *nature* of things, hence by reason."[4] Existing things are individual things, such as this plant, this tree, or this man. The *here* existing individual, at a definite point in space and time, can never be determined as such by reason alone, for "everything which relates itself to existence is more than what permits knowledge according to its mere nature."[5] And yet it cannot be denied that the discernment of what so relates itself furnishes us with knowledge. Such knowledge, however, is necessary if conceptual knowledge is to be recognized as authoritative, and just this authoritative element is what mere conceptual knowledge lacks. As Schelling notes, Thomas Aquinas, in a somewhat different context, had similarly distinguished between what does and what does not permit knowledge according to the mere nature of things. For Thomas, divine things are *ea quae divina autoritate traduntur*. Such things are "also *supra naturam*, i.e. they are *more* than permits insight of them

---

[1] II, 3, 94.    [2] II, 3, 95.    [3] II, 3, 171.    [4] *Ibid.*    [5] II, 3, 172.

by their mere nature, according to mere conceptual necessity."[1]

The authority which the positive, or empirical, science is called upon to furnish for the concepts of the negative philosophy has frequently been that of sense experience. When so regarded, the appeal to the testimony of sense becomes an act of faith, for "through faith (viz. on mere authority of our senses, not by reason) we know that things *exist* outside of us..."[2] But Schelling deplores the restriction which earlier empirical philosophies have laid upon themselves in assuming that "*everything* capable of being experienced can be found only in the external or inner sensible world."[3] If that which is real is to be defined by that which is experienced, and that which is experienced is limited to what is sensibly experienced, then reality is denied to everything which lies, either in fact or in principle, beyond the range of sense experience. At this point in his thinking, Schelling has, as we have noted, already committed himself to the proposition that knowledge of existence, and accordingly knowledge of reality, can be given only by experience. But he cannot admit that existence is to be restricted to what is sensibly experienced. As examples of things wich are experienced otherwise than sensibly, he cites "universal and necessary concepts" and "a freely willing and acting intelligence."[4] The reality of such entities cannot be proved by *sense* experience, but nevertheless it is not necessary to conclude that they are unknowable. In the case of knowing a man "in respect to his intellectual and moral character, he is knowable only *a posteriori*, viz. through his utterances and actions."[5] And yet we do have a knowledge of the man as an intelligence—indirectly, to be sure—but certainly without depending exclusively upon our sense experience of him.

But if experience is to have a broader reference than mere sensibility, what will be the character of its ability to apprehend reality? Before answering this question to his own satisfaction, Schelling considered a higher form of empiricism which he denoted as "mystical empiricism"./Such empiricism claims to have the supersensible as an actual object of experience. It is, or claims to be, a direct apprehension

---

[1] *Ibid.*
[2] *Ibid.*
[3] II, 3, 112–3. Quoted by Bolman, *op. cit.*, p. 42.
[4] II, 3, 113.
[5] *Ibid.*
[6] II, 3, 115.

of the supersensible, and accordingly as being in a position to dispense with the mediation of conceptual schema. Theosophy, for example, claims to make the supersensible an object through "a possible rapture of the human being in God, as the result of which a necessary, inerrant vision is attained, not only into the divine essence, but also into the essence of creation and all that preceded it."[1] But the theosophy of Jakob Böhme is no more adequate to the task of representing existence than is the rationalism of Hegel. Even though theosophy *strives* to reach a position beyond rationalism, the knowledge which it achieves is mere substantial knowledge which grasps only essential relationships and for which "nothing can arise through a deed, e.g. through free creation."[2] What Schelling demands at this time is an "historical" content for philosophy, i.e. a content which is non-*a priori* and which, hence, is dependent on empirical rather than rational connections.[3] But "theosophy is by nature no less unhistorical than rationalism."[4]

Two other forms of mystical empiricism noted by Schelling are those which claim contact with the supersensible through feeling, on the one hand, and through revelation on the other. But the reliance on feeling, as expressed, for example, in Jacobi's early philosophy, is based on a repudiation of *all* science, and Schelling was just as anxious to preserve the "negative," or rational, side of philosophy as he was to point out its limits. Furthermore, feeling is a subjective faculty, and its ability to convince one of objective existence is limited to the individual.[5] Nor is the Christian revelation—or revelation in general—to be taken as furnishing an empirical basis for philosophy. For the positive philosophy which Schelling sought to erect:

> Revelation is... not source, not point of departure, as for the so-called Christian philosophy, from which, in this respect, it is *toto coelo* different. Revelation will appear herein in no other sense than that in which nature and the entire history of the human race appear in it...[6]

Revelation is a fact to be explained, not a source of explanation for all else.

---

[1] II, 3, 119.
[2] II, 3, 124.
[3] For this use of the term "historical," see II, 3, 139n. Cf. II, 2, 138.
[4] II, 3, 125.
[5] II, 3, 115f.
[6] II, 3, 133.

Therefore there must remain a form of empiricism which is not subject to the objections which can be brought against the traditional varieties. If one denies that experience must be restricted to sense-experience, and maintains at the same time that reason must have other than itself as object, there remains only one alternative: a "metaphysical empiricism" which delivers authentic knowledge of true existence lying beyond the range of sense-experience.[1] Such an empiricism would, in Schelling's view, take account of precisely that feature of reality which rationalism had been impotent to deal with: "a free deed... an actual event ['*Geschehen*']." For, as Schelling maintains, "it is easy to see: only decision and deed can *ground* a genuine experience."[2]

The answer to this problem, according to Schelling, is to be found in the "positive science" of existence whereby an empirical basis is furnished as a verification for reason's speculations. What is demanded at the same time, however, in order to have a philosophy which is truly metaphysical in character, is a knowledge of the Prius of being, and for this knowledge reason must attempt to achieve rapport with that which is also its own presupposition. This was, in essence, the intention of the ontological argument. But, as we have noted,[3] the ontological argument, according to Schelling, is subject to the futility of all rationalism in trying to arrive at contact with existence on the basis of reason alone. Accordingly, since the positive philosophy cannot proceed from pure thought, "it will proceed from that which is outside of all thought" and from "that which is *absolutely* outside of thought: ...the *completely transcendent being*."[4] This being, the "absolute Prius," cannot be denoted as God except *a posteriori*. Hence the procedure of the positive science of existence is, in effect, a reversal of that rationalism which is based upon the traditional ontological argument.

A comparison of Schelling's procedure in the construction of his metaphysical empiricism with the method of rationalism is perhaps, as Schelling himself indicated, the most instructive approach to an appreciation of what is involved here. According to the Anselmian employment of this, the rationalist argument for the existence of a Highest Being, God is that than which nothing greater can be given, *quo majus non datur*. But the greatest, or highest, would not be such if it did not also exist, for then we could conceive of a being which

---

[1] II, 3, 114.     [2] *Ibid.*     [3] *Supra*, p. 99ff.     [4] II, 3, 126–7.

also existed and which, therefore, would be greater than God. Hence the highest being exists, *if* there exists a highest being in concept. If such is the case, then the proposition that it exists is merely tauto- logical. The Cartesian application of the same argument seeks to im- prove its form and starts, accordingly, with the premise that to exist accidentally contradicts the nature of God, and thus affirms neces- sary existence in respect to God (although, of course, not in respect to things in general.) But, as Schelling points out, what is here "proven" is that God is the necessarily existing being, *if* he exists; it is, however, still undetermined "whether He does or does not exist."[1]

Hence, according to Schelling, what is called for is a reversal of the procedure of the ontological argument. While "I cannot proceed from the *concept* of God in order to prove God's existence,... I can proceed from the concept of that which as such is the indubitably existing... and prove the godhood of the indubitably existing."[2] Here, in embryo, as it were, is the whole of Schelling's later philoso- phy. The philosopher who has denied, as Schelling has, that one can proceed from essence to existence, that rather essence is preceded by existence, must formulate an empirical method by which existence may be conceptually represented. As a philosopher he must begin with the concept, to be sure, but the concept achieves true denotative (and not merely connotative) status through empirical confirmation of that which it implies. The positive science which Schelling pro- posed has as its aim the establishment of that which is the true onto- logical "Prius." But since "the absolute Prius is that which has no prius from the standpoint of which it could be known,"[3] it is "not only *prior* to all existence,... it is *above* all experience,"[4] and thus can be proved to exist only indirectly. The ontological argument had maintained that "God... *if* he exists *can* be only the necessarily existing."[5] In the positive philosophy, on the other hand:

> ...the aboslute Prius *itself* is not to be proved... but rather the *deduction* from it must be proved *factually*, and thereby the *godhood* of that Prius—that it is *God* and hence *God* exists.[6]

Or, to put the matter somewhat more explicitly: the philosopher proceeds from the concept of the Prius, that which is the necessarily existing being, by arguing that if that Prius exists, it can have certain consequences; experience shows that as a matter of fact the

---

[1] *Ibid.*, pp. 157–8.    [2] *Ibid.*, p. 159.    [3] *Ibid.*, p. 129.
[4] *Ibid.*, p. 128–9.    [5] *Ibid.*, 159.    [6] *Ibid.*, p. 129.

deduced consequences exist and the conclusion is drawn that the Prius itself exists and that the circumstances necessary to its manifestation (e.g. that it *will* the existence in the manner ascertained) have also been brought into existence. *What* God is—the question answered by the negative philosophy—is a merely conceptual specification of the nature of God; but *that* God is—the question answered by the positive philosophy—may now receive unequivocal affirmation. Hence the procedure of Schelling's metaphysical empiricism emerges in sharp contrast to rationalism's ontological argument:

> if the necessarily existing is *God*, then this and that consequence ...a, b, c, etc. will be *possible*; but according to our experience, a, b, c, etc. actually exist, hence—the necessary conclusion—the necessarily existing is *actually* God.[1]

It is evident, of course, that, when thus expressed, Schelling's procedure is subject to the charge that he is committing the fallacy of affirming the consequent. Accordingly, his "positive philosophy" appears subject to limitations of which he himself, apparently, was not aware. This is one point, among others, where it would be interesting to speculate as to what Schelling's approach might have been had he been aware of the fallacy in his method, and of the consequences which a recognition of such a fallacy entails. Might he not, perhaps, have discarded his "negative" philosophy entirely and confined himself to an empirical study of mankind's religious tradition? Might he not, therefore, have been less ready to assume so quickly that he had successfully deduced the necessary course of the development of religious history? This is certainly one point at which Schelling displays, in spite of his efforts, his dependence upon a rationalistic tradition. Had he been more successful in freeing himself from that tradition, he might have approached more nearly his ideal of "historical" thinking.

## II. THE NEW METAPHYSICS: REALITY AS HISTORICAL IN CHARACTER

The re-orientation effected in Schelling's whole metaphysics by this elevation of existence to priority over essence produced what was destined to become, both in his own philosophy and in that of those who were influenced by him, a major revolution in the tradition

[1] *Ibid.*, p. 169.

of Western speculation. As A. O. Lovejoy had pointed out, "It is—as has too little been noted by historians—in his introduction of a radical evolutionism into metaphysics and theology, and in the attempt to revise even the principles of logic to make them harmonize with an evolutional conception of reality, that the historical significance of Schelling chiefly consists."[1] But even more significant, perhaps, than the "evolutionism" of Schelling's thought during his later period is the "historism"—of which "evolutionism" is but one phase—which he developed. That the universe evolves, that God at the end is different from God at the beginning, was affirmed repeatedly by Schelling as early as the *System of Transcendental Idealism*.[2] But it is, as Lovejoy notes,[3] with the publication of his reply to Jacobi's attack on his *Of Human Freedom*, in 1812,[4] that Schelling expressed himself unambiguously in favor of a metaphysics which is based on the assumption that God himself has developed from a state of potentially to actuality, and that reality as a whole is through and through historical. For not only does Schelling reverse the whole metaphysical orientation of traditional speculation, according to which the finite, or imperfect, is regarded as a devolution of the Infinite and Perfect, but he also makes human history an integral part of the process by which God achieves complete self-expression.

When we turn to a consideration of the metaphysics which Schelling developed on the basis of his metaphysical empiricism, we see that what is involved is not merely a new method as a means to reinstatement of the old metaphysics, but rather a completely new metaphysics which requires an empirical method. We need merely recall the problem which is central to Schelling's philosophizing from 1809 on, viz. the problem of the existence of man, in order to see the inseparable connection between such a method as will be adequate to the rendering of the Prius intelligible and a metaphysics which will account for man in terms of that Prius. To be sure, Schelling was never interested in representing the history of man and his relation to God without reference to the larger context of reality. On the contrary, as is especially evident in his *Ages of the World*, Schelling

---

[1] *The Great Chain of Being*, (Cambridge: The Harvard University Press, 1936), p. 325.

[2] CF. I, 3, 399.

[3] *Op. Cit.*, p. 322ff.

[4] *Denkmal der Schrift von den göttlichen Dingen—des Herrn Friedrich Heinrich Jacobi*: S. W. I, 8, 19–136.

was equally concerned to trace the development of reality as a whole. But by the same token, "just as man, according to the old and nearly threadbare saying, is the world on a small scale:

> so the processes of human life from the utmost depths to its highest consummation must agree with the processes of universal life. It is certain that whoever could write the history of his own life from its very ground, would have thereby grasped in a brief conspectus the history of the universe.[1]

Schelling's metaphysics has as its aim the statement with full scientific accuracy of the nature of the Primal Existent and its relation to the manifold of existences. Accordingly, "the science which is above all science seeks for the object which is above all objects... and this can only be that of which it can be said only that it is *The Existing*."[2] This, of course, was also the aim of traditional metaphysics. But whereas the old ontology had assumed a Most Perfect Being from which are to be derived deductively in a logical process the series of determinations which the metaphysics of emanation assumes in the ontological process, Schelling posits an imperfect, undeveloped being from which is derived inductively the stages of development leading to the ultimate expression of that being which is God. One cannot assume, according to Schelling, that God *is*—at least not in the sense that simple perfection contains, *ab initio*, the actuality of all the possible predicates of being. For "God himself... is not a system but a life."[3] And even as all life displays development from lower to higher, from simple to complex, from the germ to the adult, so God himself must be assumed to have developed, to have become, to have evolved.[4]

If once this basic drive in Schelling's later thought, to get away from the old emanationist ontology, is clearly understood, the supposedly puzzling character of his speculations vanishes. The old scholastic assumption that the cause is "greater" than the effect, and that thus the Perfect Cause has created an imperfect world, was anathema to Schelling. His celebrated attack on Jacobi was not directed so much against that hapless philosopher personally as against the type of traditional metaphysics which he espoused. The world, for Schelling, is a world which has evolved. It is to be seen as a

---

[1] S. W. I, 8, 207. Bolman, *op. cit.*, pp. 93–4.
[2] II, 1, p. 295.
[3] I, 7, 399. Gutmann, *op. cit.*, p. 78.
[4] Cf. I, 8, 63f.

stage in the process which had its beginning before time, to be sure, but which includes time as an essential part of its evolution. The universe as a whole is a process in which the mighty drama of God's development is played out. It has a beginning, a middle, and an end: and each stage in its development is to be understood as the achievement of a unique contribution to the destiny which guides its restless movements.[1] As Schelling remarks in his *Introduction* to *The Ages of the World*:

> The conception of science hitherto accepted was that it is a mere consequence and development of its own concepts and thoughts. The true conception is that it is the development of a *living*, actual *essence*, which is represented in it.[2]

Hence the philosopher who would render an account of that Being whose life struggles constitute the history of reality must strive to recapture that which to him is past so that he may represent conceptually the pattern of the Divine Becoming. At first, to be sure, he can do no more than construct an hypothesis as to how the Prime Existent has evolved. In keeping with the character of the metaphysical empiricism which he has espoused, Schelling insists that the *proof* of his construction can only be given by an appeal to the facts of nature and history. Such proof can be given only *a posteriori*,[3] and since it "is *never* completed,... this science is only *philo-sophia*."[4] The proof is temporal, and as such it is progressive. Still if there is to be any knowledge of the supra-empirical, philosophy must attempt to characterize that Being which is "prior to and outside of all thought."[5] It must enter into the depths of reality, as it were, and trace the course which God Himself has followed in the process of achieving expression.

The attempt to re-present to consciousness the course pursued and the character possessed by the "primal living reality," the "oldest of all beings,"[6] God, is not, however, a merely capricious exercise of the imagination. For man has within himself "a principle which is outside and above the world."[7] In fáct, according to Schelling's theory

---

[1] Cf. II, 1, 495–7.

[2] I, 8, 199. Bolman, *op. cit.*, p. 83. *Underscoring mine.*

[3] II, 3, 129.

[4] *Ibid.*, p. 131.

[5] *Ibid.*, p. 126.

[6] I, 8, 199, 209. Bolman, *op. cit.*, pp. 83, 85.

[7] I, 8, 200. Bolman, p. 84.

of knowledge, man has two principles, soul ("*Seele*") and spirit ("*Geist*"), the interaction of which produces actual knowledge.[1] The human soul "has a co-knowledge of creation"; it contains "a recollection of all things—their original relationships, their becoming, their significance."[2] In that the soul itself has become, it has participated in and (potentially) embodies the form of all becoming. The knowledge which the soul has, however, is obscured, hidden, and must be awakened by the activity of the spirit wherein also "everything lies... without distinction, that is, as one."[3] It is through its ability to distinguish and interpret in the soul that which is one in itself that the spirit can achieve consciousness of ultimate principles of being. Spirit asks the questions; the soul answers; and "this silent dialogue, this inner art of conversation, the peculiar secret of the philosopher, is that of which the external, therefore called dialectic, is the imitation."[4]

Thus Schelling reinstates the Platonic doctrine of recollection as a means to the formulation of his "negative" philosophy. The innate drive for knowledge which the philosopher experiences is itself an attempt on the part of the soul to come to a conscious recollection of its origins. Even as "what we call knowledge is just striving after conscious recollection"[5] so it is a striving for a discernment of the center which it has left, and at the same time a proof that its true origin is in that center.[6]

However mystical or theosophical such expressions may appear, Schelling himself was anxious to disclaim either for himself or others the ability to achieve genuine knowledge by such means. An immediate vision of divine truth was regarded by him as in itself mute, and as always needing the mediation of dialectic to render it intelligible. Furthermore—and a much more serious shortcoming in Schelling's view—there was always the inability of mysticism to achieve a relationship to objective existence. Hence, in any case, however subjectively certain the philosopher might be that he had truthfully rendered an account of the divine process, it was always necessary for him, ultimately, to turn to concrete facts for verification, either

---

[1] See II, 1, 516–522 and I, 8, 200–1.
[2] I, 8, 200. Bolman, pp. 84–5.
[3] *Ibid.*, p. 201.
[4] *Ibid.*, Bolman, pp. 85–6.
[5] *Ibid.*, Bolman, p. 86.
[6] II, 3, 287–8.

of his "visions" or his conjectures. Existence itself, for Schelling, can be explained only in terms of "a free deed" on the part of its Prius; and this deed always remains something which "can be known... only *a posteriori*."

The schema of becoming, or process, was not fully worked out by Schelling until his *Philosophy of Mythology*. But the basic pattern described by reality's development was present to his mind as early as the writing *Of Human Freedom*. We have already noted[1] that the *Philosophy and Religion* of 1804, with its doctrine of the fall of the world of ideas, provides Schelling with a more adequate metaphysics for the historical construction of reality. It was suggested in our discussion of that work that in endowing the counter-image with freedom, the Absolute is represented as suffering a genuine limitation by virtue of the egoity thereby accorded to finitude; and to the extent that human history is the drama of the reconciliation with the Absolute of that finitude which has fallen away through its freedom,[2] a significance is attributed to history which previously, in Schelling's speculation, had not been possible.

It was the extension of this point of view in Schelling's *Of Human Freedom* in 1809 that marked his definitive break with the rationalistic metaphysics of his earlier period and the inauguration of that dynamic metaphysics which marks the point in his thinking where human history becomes a realm of decisive philosophic significance. The problem here discussed is that of the relation of God and man, and of assigning genuine freedom to human activity. As Schelling notes, traditional schemes had assigned absolute causal power to God, the Highest Being, at the same time that the attempt was made to uphold the belief in man's independence as a freely willing and acting creature. But, Schelling contends, the problem is insoluble in those terms. For if absolute causal power is attributed to God, then "as the sun outshines all the other celestial lights in the firmament, so, but to a greater degree, infinite power extinguishes all finite power."[3] Human freedom is incomprehensible if all creatures are dependent upon the constantly renewed efficacy of God's power. Hence Schelling asks:

> Since freedom is unthinkable in contra-distinction to omnipotence, is there any other escape from this argument than by placing

---

[1] *Supra.*, p. 158ff.
[2] I, 6, 37.
[3] I, 7, 339. Gutmann trans., *op. cit.*, pp. 10–11.

man and his freedom in the divine being, by saying that man exists
not outside God but in God, and that man' activity itself belongs to
God's life?[1]

Indeed, it is the affirmation of the proposition thus suggested that,
with the necessary amplifications, constitutes the substance of Schelling's metaphysics of history from this point on. It contains, in effect,
a renewal of the attack initiated in the *Philosophy and Religion* on
the theory of emanation. For, as Schelling now reiterates, such a doctrine denies genuine freedom, i.e. self-determination, to the creature;
and "no matter how one pictures to oneself the procession of creatures
from God... it cannot be an emanation in which that which has
flowed forth remains the same as its source, thus lacking individuality and independence."[2] The immanence of creatures in God must,
therefore, be such that the freedom, or autonomy, which characterizes the nature of God also characterizes His creatures. Hence both
the autonomy of man and his immanence in God must be affirmed if
genuine freedom is to be attributed to man.

The major difficulty in accounting for human freedom, in Schelling's view, had lain in the conception of a Most Perfect Being, endowed with supreme power, who had created beings supposedly
independent, but whose freedom could, by definition, be only in
contradiction to the omnipotence of Deity itself. If human freedom
is to be made comprehensible, therefore, at the same time that the
affirmation of God's all-embracing reality is upheld, then this freedom must be postulated as a part of the divine life itself. Moreover,
the freedom which is here assigned to man by Schelling is to be understood as self-determination. Pantheism is to be avoided only to the
extent that it be formulated in such a way as to deny the power of
the will to determine itself. The error of Spinoza's system, for example, "is by no means due to the fact that he posits all *things in God*,
but to the fact that they are *things*"; and to the extent that "he
treats the will, too, as a thing," it becomes a part of the system of
determined things, and thereby it is deprived of all autonomy.[3] If
man is to be viewed as possessing freedom, then his will must be undetermined by anything prior to or outside of himself. For in that
"the real and vital conception of freedom is that it is a possibility of
good and evil,"[4] the power of self-determination must be uncon-
ditionally attributed to the human will.

---

[1] *Ibid.*                              [2] I, 7, 346–7. Gutmann, p. 19.
[3] I, 7, 349. Gutmann, p. 22.          [4] I, 7, 352. Gutmann, p. 26.

A comparision of the position here reached with that of the system of identity reveals rather strikingly how much Schelling's thought had moved in the direction of assigning a metaphysical significance to human freedom. Whereas in the earlier work he had made history a mere potency of the absolute, and to that extent human freedom merely an imperfect form of the appearance of the absolute, he effectively removed history from the sphere of genuine philosophic import. At that time he believed that the absolute identity could be apprehended best through the intellectual intuition and that history, accordingly, could afford only a distorted view of the truth.[1] But from 1809 on Schelling could regard human history as itself of primary philosophical importance precisely because unconditioned freedom is assigned to the human will. It is not determined in advance by the will of God or by the structure of reality which God has "previously" ordained, for God himself lives and develops in the life and development of human willing. That which is ultimately realized by the course of human history does not exist, or even subsist, prior to its actual realization. And man's freedom itself is an essential factor in that which shall be brought into being. In this respect, at least, Schelling would seem to have anticipated some of the criticism formulated by the American philosopher, John Dewey, in his strictures against the kind of metaphysics and theology which regards the ideal as inflexibly determined in advance.[2]

The dynamic metaphysics which Schelling now postulates is thus erected largely in response to the conviction that "the concept of becoming is the only one adequate to the nature of things."[3] Furthermore, since he is equally convinced that "there is nothing before or outside of God,"[4] human freedom must be accounted for in terms of the pattern described by the development which God himself undergoes. The famous triad of potencies which Schelling employed for the explication of process in *The Ages of the World* and in his later works is not explicitly referred to in *Of Human Freedom*. Nevertheless he does invoke a trinity of principles which are more often referred to as "nature," "reason" and "spirit." As phases of the life of God, they serve both to render the process of reality intelligible as a whole and

---

[1] *Supra*, pp. 117–18.
[2] See, for example, John Dewey's *A Common Faith*.
[3] I, 7, 358–9. Gutmann, p. 33.
[4] I, 7, 358. Gutmann, p. 32.

to represent the context within which human freedom is to be understood.

It is at this point, as other students of Schelling have pointed out,[1] that Schelling is greatly indebted to the speculations of the German theosophist, Jacob Böhme. While Schelling was, apparently, introduced to Böhme's writings by the poet Ludwig Tieck, it was Franz Baader who, as a student of Böhme, had opened up to Schelling the possibilities of achieving a more adequate grasp of the nature of evil and of the relation of evil to the "life of God." Although Schelling later repudiated mysticism and theosophy as methods of arriving at genuine knowledge, there can be no doubt of the influence of these modes of thought upon Schelling's philosophy from here on. And while it is scarcely necessary to point out in detail Schelling's dependence upon the theosophy of Böhme in his *Of Human Freedom*, as well as in the speculative portions of other writings which followed, it is well for the reader to keep in mind the fact that Schelling, at least in this respect, is not merely a transitional figure from Kant to Hegel, but that he ought also to be linked to a "philosophic tradition which has often passed as theology," viz. the "preoccupations and problems... of Neo-Platonic Christianity in Patristic writings, in the Lutheran Reformation and in traditional Protestant mysticism."[2]

It is necessary first of all, Schelling argues, to distinguish God himself from "the ground of his existence," his "nature,"[3] in order that the separability of things from God may be adequately represented. This, the "dark principle" in God, is "that within *God* which is not *God* himself,"[4] of God as absolutely existing, but rather Will," "primordial Being,"[5] which is the presupposition of God rather than God himself. If anything can be termed the primitive existent, that which precedes understanding, which is itself without understanding, it is will. It is the "irreducible remainder which cannot be resolved into reason... but always remains in the depths."[6] As the blind desire within the depths of the One, the dark principle provokes a response on the part of the One by which "God sees himself in his own image."[7] It is this image which God has of himself in response to the

---

[1] Notably by Gutmann, *op. cit.*, p. xliv ff.
[2] *Ibid.*, p. lii.
[3] I, 7, 358. Gutmann, p. 32.
[4] I, 7, 359. Gutmann, p. 33.
[5] I, 7, 350. Gutmann, p. 24.
[6] I, 7, 360. Gutmann, p. 35.
[7] *Ibid.*, Gutmann, p. 35.

longing of the dark principle which is reason. Reason separates the forces which previously had remained undifferentiated and inchoate within nature. Thus in the "light principle," reason, there is brought about the separation of things, or forces, from God himself, although, of course, within the divine being itself. At this stage, the forces "are divided but not completely separated."[1] They comprise, rather, the material out of which the body will later be constructed. But at the same time the soul is established as "that living nexus which arises, as the center of these forces in their division, from the depths of nature."[2] And since the soul has its origin not in reason but in nature, it remains independent of reason.

In natural objects, according to Schelling, by virtue of the manner of their origin, there is always to be found a double principle—or, more exactly, a duality of aspect—corresponding to their separation from God in God's "nature," on the one hand, and their inclusion in God as forms in God's "reason," on the other. This tension between the rational and the irrational in all things represents the persistence of the "self-will of creatures... insofar as it has not yet risen to complete unity with light... [and thus] stands opposed to reason."[3] So long as this duality remains, even though it be gradually eliminated by the preponderance of rational differentiation at each evolutionary level, nature itself remains "unreconciled" to God.

It is in man alone, however, that the longing of the dark principle is completely fulfilled. Man is the true *imago Dei* in that in him "there exists the whole power of the principle of darkness and, in him too, the whole force of light."[4] Only in man did the response of God to the solicitation of the "ground" provoke a complete image of God. Only in man "is the Word completely articulate, which in all other creatures was held back and left unfinished."[5] And precisely in this *unity*, or equivalence, of the light and dark principles in man, by which the will is raised to complete rational representation, spirit— "the living identity of both principles"[6]—becomes manifest. The dark principle, creatureliness, remains in man, but since it is united with the ideal principle, spirit arises in him. It is spirit, as such, which is selfhood; hence man contains within himself that which is both his greatest glory and his greatest peril.

---

[1] I, 7, 362. Gutmann, p. 37.    [2] *Ibid.*
[3] I, 7, 363. Gutmann, p. 38.    [4] *Ibid.*
[5] I, 7, 364. Gutmann, p. 39.    [6] *Ibid.*

Man, the microcosm, is thus the image of God, except in one important respect: he is a creature. Indeed, "if... that identity of both principles were just as indissoluble in man as in God, there would be no difference—that is, God as spirit would not be revealed."[1] It is, thus, the dissolubility of that identity which involves the possibility of good and evil. The union in man of the light and dark principles to form spirit represents, at the same time, the exaltation to spirituality of that which is other than God, i.e. of the nature in God. Thus "man as an egocentric, particularized being (divorced from God) is spirit."[2] But since selfhood is spirit, man is free—not merely phenomenally, but absolutely, in the sense that as an autonomous creature he acts according to the laws of his own being, and is not determined by anything *ab extra*. Man is a complete being who, though he lives a life in God, and though his life is nothing apart from the life of God, is able to live independently of God to the extent that his life is organized around a center other than God himself. Hence the possibility of evil is contained in man's selfhood, or spirit, which is able to "separate itself from light since it possesses spirit"[3] and thereby elevate the will to a position of pre-eminence. Ideally—in the well-ordered relation—man's self-will is subordinated to the universal will. As such, it is kept in its proper place, subordinated to the light, and thus finds its being in the harmony of creature and Creator. But when selfhood separates itself from light, self-will seeks to leave the center, and thus to make itself the center and create a life of its own in separation from God. What we call evil "is this very exaltation of self-will."[4] The creature is able, thus, to live a life apart from his Creator.

The manifestation of evil, according to Schelling, is thus to be understood not as a mere deprivation, a lack, as in the old emanationist philosophy. Rather must evil "not only be founded on something inherently positive, but rather on the highest positive being which nature contains."[5] Evil has a life of its own, even though it be a false life; and to regard it merely as lack of being is to misconstrue its true character. The most appropriate comparison for evil, according to Schelling, is disease "which is the true counterpart of evil and sin, as it constitutes that disorder which entered nature through a misuse of freedom."[6] Seen in this way, evil may still be

---

[1] *Ibid.*                    [2] *Ibid.*        [3] I, 7, 364. Gutmann, p. 40.
[4] I, 7, 365. Gutmann, p. 41.        [5] I, 7, 369. Gutmann, pp. 44–5.
[6] I, 7, 366. Gutmann, p. 41.

regarded as an illusory life, but it cannot be regarded as unreal. For evil, like disease, "occurs only because some entity whose freedom or life exists only so that it may remain in the whole, strives to exist for itself."[1] Furthermore, the true nature of evil, at the moral level, can be elucidated only by appeal to the conception of personality—a conception which dogmatic philosophy lacks. It is only personality which, in Schelling's view, is capable of expressing fully the positive nature of evil. For true evil can be attributed only to a being which, like man, is possessed of spirit, and which accordingly is an independent whole or unity. The reality of moral evil, or sin, is possible only because man is able to function as an independent unity in whom are found "the identical elements which existed in the unified whole."[2] Hence the positive character of evil manifests itself not in the material—"evil is no more limited or worse than good"[3]—but in the form, i.e. in the fact that it is an individual life lived, parasitically, in opposition to the good.

The reality of evil, in contrast to its mere possibility, as this is explained in *Of Human Freedom*, takes its rise from God's allowing "the will of the basis" to function in opposition to the "will of love."[4] If evil has ultimate reason, it is to be found in God's permitting the division of the principles in order that the will of love might be revealed. The self-will of the creature, endowed with life through the spirituality of its nature, exalts itself so as to provide a means to the actualization of the primal basis of existence. Thereby a conflict is set up within the divine life itself. Previously, in the act of creation, *nature* is brought forth by the elevation of the light principle above the dark basis of existence. As Schelling expresses it, "The birth of light is the realm of nature."[5] With this act, the separation of individual things or forces from the dark basis of existence is accomplished. But it is only with the creation of man that history is inaugurated: "the birth of spirit is the realm of history."[6] And even as it is in man that the dark basis of existence may find spiritual expression, so history is the expression of the actual operation of the will of the basis in opposition to the will of love.

The sketch of the course of history (which is only outlined here and which will be seen as the framework for its fuller exposition in later

---

[1] I, 7, 366. Gutmann, p. 42.      [2] I, 7, 370. Gutmann, p. 46.
[3] *Ibid.*                          [4] I, 7, 375. Gutmann, pp. 51–2.
[5] I, 7, 377. Gutmann, p. 54.      [6] *Ibid.*

writings) is now proposed by Schelling, in *Of Human Freedom*, as the drama of man's work in opposition to God and of God's work in the reconciliation of man to God. The spirituality of man, to the extent that it expresses itself as a being independent of God, consists of an elevation of the dark principle of the basis to a position of prominence in opposition to the light. In that "evil is... nothing other than the primal basis of existence insofar as it strives towards actualization in created beings,"[1] history is a witness to the attempt on the part of the basis to achieve actualization. At first, "evil... remains concealed in the depths, and the age of guilt is preceded by an age of innocence or unconsciousness of sin."[2] For inasmuch as the true God at first did not reveal himself—or, more exactly, since the true aspect of divinity was not immediately revealed—God is worshipped as a plurality of divine beings, and with an unsullied conscience. Hence the "primeval time... commences with the golden age... a period of blessed indifference in which there was neither good nor evil."[3] The golden age is followed by "the age of sovereign gods and heroes, or the omnipotence of nature."[4] The exaltation of nature corresponds to the period of the greatest achievements of the dark principle. Science and art combined to represent the gods in their greatest beauty; and while Schelling does not draw such a comparison here, he obviously has in mind the period of the flowering of Greek, or pagan, civilization as this had been represented earlier by him, among other places, in his *System of Transcendental Idealism*.

The struggle of the dark principle to establish itself as the one omnipotent unity (as Fate?) is abortive. Precisely because it is the false rather than the true unity it is doomed in advance to disintegration. Hence "the time comes in which all this glory dissolves and the beautiful body of the foregoing world decays as through horrible disease, and finally chaos ensues."[5] The gods become evil spirits, false magic appears; and as "the light" approaches, the dark principle is

---

[1] I, 7, 378. Gutmann, p. 55.
[2] *Ibid.*
[3] I, 7, 379. Gutmann, p. 56.
[4] *Ibid.* As Gutmann has pointed out, (*op. cit.*, pp. 108–110), Schelling's periodization of history is here to be compared with his earlier expressions on this theme in the *System of Transcendental Idealism* and the *Philosophy and Religion*. Attention should also be called to his treatment of the periods of history in his *Lectures on the Methods of Academic Studies* (*Supra*, p. 147ff.) and in the Philosophy of Art.
[5] *Ibid.*

revealed in its darkness ever more clearly. It is not as though evil
arose now for the first time, but only that "the contrast is... now
given in which it can appear in its totality and as itself."[1] It is at this
point at which the birth of "the higher light of the spirit" takes place:

> Indeed, in order to encounter personal and spiritual evil, light
> appears in personal and human form, and comes a mediator in
> order to re-establish the relationship between creation and God on
> the highest level. For only personality can make whole what is
> personal, and God must become Man in order that man may be
> brought back to God.[2]

It is no secret, of course, that Schelling here regards the content of
history as synonymous with the Christian drama of salvation. Indeed, as he frankly confesses, his whole philosophic quest, at this
time, is that which was first undertaken by Lessing in his *Education
of the Human Race*.[3] With him, Schelling regards "the development
of the truths of revelation into truths of reason as utterly necessary
if the human race is to be helped thereby."[4] And as Schelling proceeds with his sketch of human history, it is ever more evident that
this is his main purpose. The "second creation" which is inaugurated
by God's becoming Man has not only the aim of representing sin, or
self-will, as it really is but also, finally, of reconciling the good with
God and casting out evil "eternally into non-being."[5] But in that
such a reconciliation takes time, and since God, like all life, "has a
destiny and is subject to suffering and development,"[6] the drama of
salvation must run its course. The dark principle must actualize itself in creation so that the good may be perfectly revealed in contrast.
At the end, God shall be "all in all," and even spirit shall be superseded by love: that which "unites such beings as could each exist in
itself, and nonetheless neither is nor can be without the other."[7]

But Schelling insists, finally, that the struggle of the opposed
principles does not signify a dualism of good and evil nor the activity
of beings *outside* of God. For prior to the distinction of the light and
dark principles, there must be presupposed "a being *before* all basis
and *before* all existence, that is, before any duality at all."[8] Even as
we distinguish God's nature from God himself, or any other attributes of God from that which is God in himself, so we must assume a

---

[1] I, 7, 380. Gutmann, p. 57.      [2] *Ibid.*
[3] *Supra*, p. 19ff.                [4] I, 7, 412. Gutmann, p. 94.
[5] I, 7, 404. Gutmann, p. 85.      [6] I, 7, 403. Gutmann, p. 84.
[7] I, 7, 408. Gutmann, p. 89.      [8] I, 7, 406. Gutmann, p. 87.

"primal ground," or that which, as God, is "groundless."[1] As such, God is "indifferent" to the antitheses which are predicated of him. As we shall see, God so considered is $A^0$, in contrast to $A^1$, $A^2$ and $A^3$. However cryptic this may appear at this point, it is only intended to express Schelling's reiterated contention that:

> In this system there is one principle for everything; it is one and the same being reigning in the dark depths of nature and in eternal clarity, one and the same effecting the severity and isolation of things, and unity and kindness, the same thing that rules with the will of love in goodness and the will of anger in evil.[2]

We have given in some detail Schelling's argument in the *Of Human Freedom* because it expresses, in embryo, the major points of the philosophy of history which finally emerges from Schelling's metaphysical empiricism. *The Ages of the World*, to which we will now turn briefly, represents an extension of the analysis of process and its application to nature and history which was proposed in the *Of Human Freedom*. While *The Ages of the World* was begun in 1811, it was never completed, and the fragment which remains, which was intended to form the first book of a trilogy, was not published until after Schelling's death. Nevertheless, the work as it now stands gives the fundamental principles of Schelling's philosophy of history, as is evident by a comparison of what it contains with the content of the lectures which Schelling later delivered on this theme.[3] It therefore represents a synoptic guide to the philosophy of history which Schelling developed during the latter part of his career.

*The Ages of the World* is an extension of Schelling's earlier work on freedom in two major respects. It is, in the first place, a consideration of the relation of God and reality as a whole in a much more comprehensive metaphysical view than was furnished in *Of Human Freedom*. The latter work was concerned primarily with the problem of *human* freedom and only incidently with the problem of the free existence of being as such. To that extent, it would appear that Schelling had not worked out fully the question of the extra-logical character of reality until after 1809. For this reason, secondly, not

---

[1] *Ibid.*

[2] I, 7, 409. Gutmann, p. 90.

[3] F. De W. Bolman *op. cit.*, pp. 67–8. Bolman's Introduction to his translation of *The Ages of the World* is an indispensable contribution to the English reader's understanding both of this work and of its relation to Schelling's philosophy as a whole.

only do the chief actors in the drama of the development of reality appear specifically designated as "potencies"—as aspects of being as such—in *The Ages of the World*, but there is here presented a much more complicated schema of process than in *Of Human Freedom*. Whereas previously Schelling had presented the principles as completely activated, he now finds it necessary to distinguish a pre-cosmic, intra-divine process from the actual process of nature and history. In the latter, there will be reproduced the succession of the potencies which had been prefigured in the necessary dialectic of the "eternal nature" of God. Thus the distinction between what Schelling later called the negative and positive philosophies is now employed by him in the elucidation of the course of the development of reality.

Accordingly, Schelling's answer to the question, "Why is there anything? Why not nothing?"[1] in *The Ages of the World* is answered by an appeal to an ontology which is "recollected" as the pattern of being, as its logical structure, and which is confirmed by appeal to the facts of the historical process. The process which is discovered by an analysis of the nature (essential structure) of being represents the ideal aspect of reality. Reality itself, or the existing structure, confirms the philosopher's "recollection" through its furnishing to experience the events which the conceptual scheme demands. In other words, the philosopher finds, upon turning to history itself, the confirmation of his ontological hypothesis.

The hypothesis which Schelling erects to explain the nature of God and his relation to being follows closely his earlier construction in *Of Human Freedom*. To conceive of God adequately, Schelling argues, it is not sufficient to regard him as pure being, or undifferentiated essence. To the extent that he is conceived as personality, as living, an "eternal antithesis"[2] of positive and negative, of affirmation and denial, or expansion and contraction, corresponding to the light and the dark, must be posited as aspects of his one being.[3] For "as certainly as there is life, there is contradiction in primal nature."[4] The first potency, B, is the negating power which opposes itself to the affirming principle, A, just as that which presents a false life (B) opposes itself to the true life (A).[5] B is that which is not, the "privation" of Aristotle, which, to be sure, is not non-existent, but which

---

[1] II, 3, 7. Cf. *Supra*, p. 000ff.   [2] I, 8, 211. Bolman, p. 97.
[3] I, 8, 209–13. Bolman, pp. 95–99.   [4] I, 8, 219. Bolman, p. 105.
[5] I, 8, 220. Bolman, p. 107.

is not true being.[1] And like Aristotle's "privation" (στέρησις), B, the negating power, is "the necessary precedent (*prius*) of every movement."[2] Thus if God has a life, and if life implies process, B must be posited as the *prius* of God from which God's life takes its beginning. But even as A cannot be without B, and yet A stands as opposed to B, so the unity of God must be expressed in a third potency which is the unity of the two antitheses: A[3]. The dialectical relationship of these three potencies constitutes "a necessary concatenation"[3] of movements within the divine life.

Up to this point, the movement of the potencies in God is an eternal cycle in which each potency successively strives to be that which is. In order that this competitive struggle may cease, something higher must be presented to primal nature "before which it gladly and willingly recognizes itself as mere being, as what *is* not.'[4] This "something higher" is that which is "outside of and above God's necessity, which, in the three potencies, constitutes eternal nature." It is "eternal freedom, pure willing itself." Hence there must be assumed "a unity of necessity and freedom in the actual living God."[5] The result of this relation of the "nature" in God to his "pure Spirit", to "what is above being,"[6] is the re-alignment of the potencies so that each assumes its proper relation to each other and to the pure godhood. Thus A[3] of the divine nature, which is "that which in nature itself is free and spiritlike,"[7] becomes "subject" (in the sense of material) to the eternal freedom of God, while the other two potencies "sink," respectively, so that B is material for A[2] and A[2] is material for A[3].

Through this alignment, "life has thus voluntarily assumed organic constitution."[8] Further scrutiny of the characteristics of the potencies reveals that each plays a specific role in the expression of the divine life. A[3] is the "universal soul whereby the universe is animated..., the eternal bond between nature and the spirit world as well as between the world and God, the immediate instrument whereby alone God works in nature and the spirit world."[9] Hence the third potency, A[3], is a mediator between the godhood and the nature in God. B is the "potency of negation,"[10] or the potency of nature as

---

[1] I, 8, 221. Bolman, p. 108.　　[2] I, 8, 224. Bolman, p. 111.
[3] I, 8, 228. Bolman, p. 115.　　[4] I, 8, 233. Bolman, p. 120.
[5] I, 8, 239. Bolman, p. 127.　　[6] I, 8, 240. Bolman, p. 128.
[7] I, 8, 242. Bolman, p. 130.　　[8] I, 8, 253. Bolman, p. 142.
[9] I, 8, 252. Bolman, p. 141.　　[10] I, 8, 246. Bolman, p. 135.

such, while A², the second potency, is the potency of the "world of spirits." All three potencies, constituting God's nature, are united under that which is "nonpotent" [*Potenzlose*],[1] which is the principle of transcendence in God, God's freedom.

Such, in general, is Schelling's concept of God in *The Ages of the World*. Only when God is thus conceived, Schelling maintains, can "the story of that series of free acts whereby God resolved from eternity to reveal himself"[2] be understood. Still explaining hypothetically how God opposes a world to himself, Schelling describes how God as pure spirit, as "the still, essential primal cause"[3] through the very character he possesses as will, posits that "other" which eventually becomes the world. The separation which here occurs is not a division of God himself into two parts, but merely a setting-off of God's nature from his free will. In this way, God gives himself an "eternal past"; i.e. he is himself a succession of states which are posited as "past," "present" and "future" within the divine life. Thus God himself may be said to possess an "eternal time,"[4] as long as the succession of states in God is not conceived as temporal in the ordinary meaning of the word. In this way, Schelling maintains, God's "past" may be understood as that phase of his life which is represented by nature: for "in nature, the spirit of eternity discerns itself as he who *was*, because it posits nature as its *eternal* past."[5]

The transition to the actual existence of nature, however, cannot be merely hypothetically deduced. The freedom of the godhood cannot be subjected to any necessity. Hence, "if the godhead took the part of being, actually revealed itself through being (which we must recognize as really having happened), then the resolution for that could come only from the highest freedom."[6] Accordingly at this point Schelling makes a transition to what he later called his positive philosophy. The description of nature's powers, into which Schelling goes in great detail, is to be understood as the result of his deductions from the concept of God and the relation of God to nature. But up to the point where the facts of nature (and history) are appealed to, *The Ages of the World* concerns itself only with deducing the eternal structure which nature manifests. But nature, according to Schelling, has not only a structure but also a history. It is characterized

---

[1] I, 8, 234. Bolman, p. 121.    [2] I, 8, 269. Bolman, p. 157.
[3] I, 8, 258. Bolman, p. 146.    [4] I, 8, 260. Bolman, p. 148.
[5] I, 8. 264. Bolman, p. 152.    [6] I, 8, 300. Bolman, p. 189.

by epochs, by divisions, which mark off successive periods, each of which is characterized by the ascendancy of individual principles which, having appeared in the actual world, are the powers of being which were formerly potencies.

Historical existence in general, as this is now conceived by Schelling, is the result of a free decision by the godhead to reveal itself. That which is revealed of God, however, is not arbitrary, for it follows according to his nature. As Schelling points out, "Without a free beginning, there would be no real history of the world."[1] But once God decides to reveal himself, his revelation follows the deduced sequence of the potencies of his nature. Furthermore, with the decision to reveal himself, there is also given to God the necessity of successive revelations, according to the potencies of his nature. If God is No and Yes, as well as the unity of both, and is equally God in each of these three expressions of his nature, then "it follows that both [the Yes and the No] exclude each other with respect to time, or that God as Yes and God as No cannot be *in the same time*."[2] Hence the historical succession which follows from God's decision to reveal himself:

> breaks eternity ,and, instead of one eternity, posits a succession of eternities (aeons) or times. But just this succession of eternities is what we commonly call time. Therefore eternity opens out into time in this decision.[3]

The "past," which Schelling defines as the period of God's revelation in which God was revealed as No, as B, is the history of the world under the ascendance of nature. All of the various stages in the development of nature are set forth by Schelling in what he wrote of *The Ages of the World*. Unfortunately he never finished this work, and what he would have said about the "present" and the "future" can only be conjectured. Presumably, the two succeeding epochs would be described as the successive ascendancies of $A^2$ and $A^3$, and accordingly we would have been presented with the history of mankind, as well as with the "future history" of the world under the hegemony of spirit.

Enough of Schelling's philosophy of history is evident here, however, to display the direction in which his thought was tending

---

[1] I, 8, 305. Bolman, p. 194.     [2] I, 8, 302. Bolman, p. 190.
[3] I, 8, 302. Bolman, p. 191.

around 1811. From a concern with the problems of human freedom, out of which the question of the meaning of human history emerges, Schelling passed to a consideration of the meaning of being as such, and thus a completely new metaphysic emerges. While as yet he had not formulated all the critical questions and answers relating to the construction of a positive philosophy, the basic orientation for such a construction is already present. But what is most decisive, it would seem, in shaping the course of Schelling's thought from 1809 on, was his concern for a genuine understanding of human history. And whereas earlier he had been content to present history within the larger context of an essentially static metaphysics, he became more and more convinced that only a completely historical metaphysics could adequately account for the existence of the world in general and of man in particular. The philosophy which finally appears in Schelling's later lectures is one which is, by no means accidentally, completely "historical in spirit."[1]

---

[1] II, 3, 317.

# CHAPTER FIVE

# THE HISTORY OF MANKIND

## I. The Character of Human History

From the over-all philosophical standpoint arrived at by Schelling in the last period of his life, we are conducted to a view of human history in which it appears unmistakeably as a part of the larger whole of universal evolutionary process. Here at last the transformation is effected from a relatively static metaphysics which is a-historically oriented to a completely dynamic metaphysics which is itself historical in nature. Thus Schelling is able to bring to a culmination the drive which had motivated much of his thinking from the very beginning: to represent philosophically not merely the structure of the universe but also, and primarily, the process by which that structure is realized.

In order to understand adequately the significance of human history from the point of view of Schelling's later philosophy, we must therefore keep in mind the metaphysical context within which this history appears. The fact that human history represented the focus of Schelling's interest during this period is easily understood in view of his confession that it was just man who impelled him "to the final desperate question: Why is there anything at all? Why not nothing"?[1] But in formulating the metaphysical empiricism which would furnish him with an answer to this question, Schelling found that not only man, but nature and God, must also be explained metaphysically—not as separate data isolated from each other, but as organically related in terms of the whole. Thus Schelling's essentially monistic point of view is preserved throughout the various changes in his philosophical perspective.

If, then, according to the contention of Schelling during this period, not only man, but also nature and God, have a history, it will be necessary first of all to locate precisely the history of man within the larger context of historical process in general. As we noted from our survey of the *Of Human Freedom*, "the birth of spirit is the

---

[1] II, 3, 7.

realm of history".[1] And from the standpoint of that same work, history introduces the period of autonomy in opposition to God. But as we have also seen from *The Ages of the World*, there is a period "prior" to the creation of the world wherein "the progress of life is a necessary one".[2] This period, during which God's life achieves an equilibrium of potencies under the supremacy of the pure godhead, precedes the divine decision for creation and the inauguration of the temporal history of the world. It is in keeping with this distinction that Schelling later maintained that as surely as one can say there is "a time before creation, one can say that the world has arisen *in time*, namely, that the world is only the link of a time which transcends the world.

> In so far as this time before the world for itself is still non-time, one can also call it eternity. But not absolute eternity. It is eternity only because it is still non-time, not yet *actual* time, but yet *possible* time.[3]

Since, according to this conception, "the world is only a link of the true time, and in so far itself an epoch,"[4] one must distinguish three epochs of "true time": "...(1) pretemporal eternity, which is posited as past *by* the creation; (2) the age of creation itself, which is the *present*; (3) the age in which everything is attained by the creation and which stands as future eternity."[5] We may recall at this point that Schelling's project for *The Ages of the World* called for a division of that work into three parts, corresponding to these three epochs of "true time".

The distinction which Schelling made between his "negative" and "positive" philosophies is contained within this schema of epochs of "true time". Pretemporal eternity represents, from the point of view of the philosopher of history, the necessary course described by the moments of being, hypothetically deduced, or "recollected", by the philosopher. This, the "negative" philosophy, formulates the metaphysical structure of the universe according to the "potencies" which relate themselves dialectically to each other and which combine to form the pattern of the whole. The empirical history of the world,

---

[1] I, 7, 377.
[2] I, 8, 300. Bolman, F. DeW., *Schelling: The Ages of the World*, p. 189.
[3] II, 3, 307. Quoted by Bolman, p. 196, n. 44.
[4] II, 3, 308. Quoted by Bolman, p. 58.
[5] II, 4, 109. Quoted by Bolman, p. 58.

however, cannot be deduced in the same way, and hence the positive philosophy must turn to the facts of creation, the second epoch, which posits the pretemporal eternity as past, and find therein the confirmation of the deductions of the negative philosophy. From the point of view of the philosopher, of course, the third epoch, "future eternity", is still future. Nevertheless, it serves as a guide for the philosopher's vision of the destiny of creation; the final reconciliation of creation with the Creator.

While thus creation itself, the present, is to be seen as the second epoch of true time, and itself as called into existence as the result of a free decision on the part of the Creator, it must also be seen as embracing within itself a plurality of phases. Prior to, and in one sense including, the history of mankind, there is also to be distinguished "the entire history of the world."[1] The history of the world is marked by epochs, corresponding to the principles (formerly potencies) which characterize the phases of being in general. For in that the *whole* history of the world, and not just part of it, is to be regarded as "a progressive revelation of God,"[2] this revelation, when it occurs, must occur according to the sequence of potencies. Hence, Schelling maintains, "the sequence of potencies... stands therefore also as a succession of epochs."[3] The epochs of world history, according to *The Ages of the World*, are characterized by successive ascendancies of the principles B, $A^2$, and $A^3$, or the successive revelations of God as No, Yes, and the unity of both. From a slightly different perspective, the revelations of God may be regarded as successive revelations of the principle of will:

> ...what first enters being (what assumes being) is a negating, strictly necessary will, which, however, makes itself the ground of a higher will. The latter, although not really free (being love's pure will), is nevertheless intelligent will. Finally, above both rises the conscious and free will which is spirit in the highest sense, as the third principle was soul in eternal nature.[4]

In the same way, nature passes from a stage of undifferentiated being to differentiation through the attractive power of $A^2$. The first period, during which takes place the creation of the stars, finally gives way to that of the production of plants and animals; and at last, after many vicissitudes, conscious being, the highest power of

---

[1] I, 8, 305.    [2] *Ibid.*    [3] I, 8, 310. Bolman, p. 199.
[4] I, 8, 309. Bolman, p. 197.

nature, is brought forth upon the earth. But it is only here, at the
last stage, that the history of mankind is ready to begin.

The general schema of *The Ages of the World* may be taken as repre-
sensative of the way in which Schelling orients human history in
respect to the history of the world and the still more inclusive history
of reality as a whole. But inasmuch as a precise characterization of
human history is not possible without a closer scrutiny of the potencies (or principles) which mark the movements and configurations of
process in general, a survey of these "moments" will help to reveal
more adequately the nature of historical becoming. First we shall
consider Schelling's description of the potencies as set forth in the
negative philosophy.

The concept of "potency" was employed by Schelling as early as
the *Philosophy of Nature* to indicate how the Absolute differentiates
itself in its manifestations as real and ideal unities respectively.[1]
Even as the one Absolute may express itself, or be seen from, a
variety of perspectives, so the potencies serve to indicate the
"power" under which the Absolute is to be seen. From the point of
view of the *Philosophy of Identity*, each potency indicates "a certain
quantitative difference of subjectivity and objectivity"[2] in respect to
the one Absolute, which itself is the "indifference" of all potencies.
The potencies are forms of the Absolute, but as such they are "absolutely simultaneous".[3] The Absolute itself is without potency.[4]

Schelling's later philosophy, to the extent that it is "negative",
retains the concept of potency substantially unchanged, although
the individual potencies as such are related to one another in a somewhat different fashion. In keeping with the method prescribed by his
metaphysical empiricism, Schelling saw his task as that of differ-
entiating between knowledge of the "what" and knowledge of the
"that".[5] To the former belongs the logical determination of being; to
the latter the empirical verification of that which being has been
conceived to be. The philosopher proceeds, therefore, to the construction of his hypothesis relating to "the possibility of things"[6] in
order, later, to subject his hypothesis to the verification of experience. If we translate this logical determination of the "what" into
cosmological (or theological) terms, we shall see that it represents

---

[1] I, 2, 66f.      [2] I, 4, 134.      [3] *Ibid.*, p. 135.      [4] I, 6, 212.
[5] II, 3, 57–8.      [6] II, 3, 75.

the epoch of pretemporal eternity, prior to the creation of the world.

The potencies of being are set forth by the philosopher in fulfillment of his task "...first to discover... what true being is."[1] Assuming, as Schelling does, that "the general world process is based upon a progressive... victory of the subjective over the objective,"[2] or the imposition of form upon a previously formless content, the philosopher asks himself, in effect, What must I assume as regards the nature of being in order that this process may be conceived as realizable? To think "being as such" is, as Schelling notes, to demand of human reason an extraordinary exertion, inasmuch as one is required "to think of the absolutely non-objective in this, its non-objectivity".[3] In other words, one is required to do what, as such, is impossible for thought: to make an object of that which is by nature pure subject. This pure subject of being, the *primum cogitabile*,[4] must be arrived at by a process similar to that practiced in certain forms of Indian religion where the thinker withdraws himself from all objectivity, becomes "inward," and prepares himself to arrive at rational identity with the pure subject.[5] The pure subject of being, the first thing conceivable, is, as such, however, the mere possibility of being. As the first potency,—A, it is that which lacks rational determination, hence also true being. It is merely that which is "the point of departure for development."[6]

But care must be taken not to overlook the significance of this first potency in Schelling's metaphysical hierarchy. For here Schelling has expressed himself unequivocally in favor of a dynamic conception of the universe; and this first potency has the role of inaugurating the process which reality as a whole displays. As that which *is* not, as non-being, it is nevertheless *not* the non-existent.[7] It is a deprivation, a lack of true being, to be sure; but it is such, Schelling maintains, in precisely the same way as is Aristotle's "privation" ($\sigma\tau\acute{\epsilon}\varrho\eta\sigma\iota\varsigma$).[8] It is "the primitive germ of visible nature, that from which nature is developed in the succession of ages."[9] Furthermore— and what is most important from the point of view of reality as a process—as potentiality it is that which "*when* it elevates itself into being... it is that which *should* not be...[10] "Unless there were something which should not be, something whose presence had to be

---

[1] II, 3, 76.    [2] I, 10, 231.    [3] II, 3, 251.    [4] II, 1, 302.
[5] II, 3, 251–2.    [6] II, 2, 141.    [7] I, 10, 235.
[8] I, 8, 221. Cf. II, 1, 302.    [9] I, 8, 243. Bolman, p. 132.
[10] II, 3, 224, cf. II, 3, 285.

eliminated or made innocuous, process would not get under way. There would be no reason for movement from one thing to another, and we would be left with mere static being in which everything was as it should be. For, Schelling argued,

> The beginning is only beginning inasmuch as it is not what really should be, not that which is veritably and unto itself. If there is a decision, then only that can be posited for a beginning which distinctively inclines most to the nature of what *is* not.[1]

Here, according to Schelling, is the major difference between his system and all the systems "which wish to explain the origin of things by descent from above"[2] and which hence are necessarily emanationist in character. Such systems

> almost necessarily come to the thought that the emanations of the highest primal power at some time or other attain a limit below which there is nothing, and which, itself only a shadow of reality, a minimal degree of reality, can only to a certain extent be said to be, but really is not. This is the meaning of non-being among the Neo-Platonists, who no longer understood the true meaning of Plato.[3]

In contrast, Schelling affirms a principle of non-being too, but it is a non-being which is not the mere final lack of being. It is, rather, the first principle of all becoming; "it is not merely a deficiency or lack of reality, but active negation."[4] As such, therefore, evil, for Schelling, is represented by the activation of this first principle. Like sickness, it has "a real, a truly vital life,"[5] Like error, it is a real knowledge rather than a lack of knowledge, although it is a false knowledge. And so, while evil "is inwardly a lie and devoid of all true being,"[6] it is a being which *should* not be. And because that which should not be is posited as that which is first, process moves to the overcoming of that false being in order that, finally, true being may be installed in its place.

The first potency is, hence, in many ways the key figure in the drama of universal history. It is that which is the basis of process, and thus is denoted as "the genuine *sub-jectum* ($\dot{v}\pi o\kappa\varepsilon i\mu\varepsilon v o\nu$)".[7] In this sense, it is that which contains within itself the material for the

---

[1] I, 8, 220–21. Bolman, p. 107.      [2] I, 8, 244. Bolman, p. 133.
[3] I, 8, 244–5. Bolman, p. 133.       [4] I, 8, 245. Bolman, p. 133.
[5] I, 8, 267. Bolman, p. 155.         [6] *Ibid.*
[7] II, 1, 319.

determinations which reason, the second potency, will elicit from it. Thus, rather poetically, it may be characterized as "the mother and vessel of all visible things."[1] And yet, in itself, it is "a will within which there is no understanding."[2] It is the "nature in God" described in *Of Human Freedom* and *The Ages of the World*. As that which is "blind, dark, and unutterable in God,"[3] which resists the light and seeks to withdraw into itself, it is that which must be liberated from contradiction, and changed from that which denies God into that which ultimately affirms him.

The second potency is the complement of the first. Its law is "to repress the negating original power."[4] If the first principle is designated as blind, chaotic will, the second is to be understood as that which is without will,[5] but which "orders, confines and gives measure to the infinite, boundless will."[6] In other words, the second potency A, is the "principle of understanding,"[7] the idea, which brings form and order into being, and which represents the fulfillment of the aim of creation of "the raising of the Yes over the No."[8] The second potency stands to the first as object to subject.[9] But its relation to the first potency determines only part of its character. To be sure, it serves as the instrument by which the will finds an object for itself.[10] But within the larger context of process, A serves as the means by which that which ought not to be, the first potency, is rendered ineffective and brought into a higher unity. As "that which liberates [the first potency] from contradiction,"[11] it is, from one point of view, the ideal image which God has of the manifold possibilities within that which can be brought into being. Through the second potency, form is impressed upon—or, more accurately, brought forth out of, chaos. Hence this principle, "the savior and liberator of nature, must in any case be outside and above this nature, and just for that reason stand to it as the spiritual to the corporeal."[12]

The third potency completes the necessary determinations of being. In fact, from Schelling's point of view, all three potencies are delivered, in the first instance, by the attempt to arrive at a complete

---

[1] I, 8, 244. Bolman, p. 133.
[2] I, 7, 359. Gutmann trans., *op. cit.*, p. 34.
[3] I, 8, 244. Bolman, p. 133.
[4] I, 8, 250. Bolman, p. 138.
[5] II, 2, 112.
[6] I, 10, 289.
[7] I, 7, 363. Gutmann, p. 38.
[8] I, 8, 287. Bolman, p. 175.
[9] II, 3, 227f.
[10] II, 3, 214–15.
[11] I, 8, 246. Bolman, p. 134.
[12] I, 8, 248. Bolman, p. 136.

concept of being as such. Hence, following Fichte,[1] he maintains that the *complete* concept of being involves the positing of being first as subject, next as object, and finally "as subject and object in one, inseparable subject-object."[2] Thus, when, to this merely formal determination of being as such, there is added the specific content which the three potencies of being reveal in the theogonic process, the result is the characterization of the potencies in the manner already indicated. The third potency $\pm A$, is the unity of the first two potencies. As such, it is not only the "eternal end" of the necessary movement of being,[3] but also the identity of the infinite ($-A$) and the finite ($+A$), the ἄπειρον and the πέρας, unbounded and bounded of Plato.[4] Thus also, if $-A$ is the potency of nature, and $+A$ is the potency of reason, $\pm A$ is the potency of Spirit. In contrast to $-A$, the potency which should not be, $\pm A$ is that which should be. Hence it is to be seen as the good in contrast to evil, as "that which can be posited as such."[5]

Such are the "moments" of being as they reveal themselves to the philosopher who would have the complete concept of being. But as yet there is no assurance that they are related concretely to anything actually existing—and as we have seen, Schelling conceived the task of the positive philosophy to be that of showing how the potencies may be understood as actually descriptive of historical process. Hence the potencies of being must now be placed within the larger context of universal development. On the assumption that reality is to be conceived as primarily a theogonic process, in keeping with the point of view of *The Philosophy of Mythology* and *The Philosophy of Revelation*, we must assure ourselves of the relation of the potencies to God. If God himself is to be distinguished from the potencies, and yet is accorded an intimate connection with them, what is the nature of that distinction and that connection?

Schelling is most emphatic in his insistence that the three potencies are "not three beings, but rather *one threefold* being which presents merely three aspects."[6] Accordingly, "the difference of subject, object and subject-object is not a substantial difference, but merely a difference of determination."[7] It is one and the same being which, when it posits itself, does so first as object, then as subject, and finally as subject-object. If then, when these potencies are so placed

---

[1] II, 3, 77.     [2] *Ibid.*     [3] I, 8, 228.     [4] I, 10, 256.
[5] II, 3, 236.     [6] *Ibid.*     [7] II, 3, 237.

as to be actually regarded as principles of process, that process can be seen to have a definite beginning, middle and end, according to the ascendancy of the potencies as they display themselves successively.[1] But inasmuch as it is the whole which is reproduced in its entirety in each of the succeeding potencies, and such wholeness (i.e. such that "the part... is itself not less than the whole, and likewise the whole not more than the part"[2]) is the character of spirit ("*Geist*"), in the *complete* being, embracing all the potencies, there is given the Absolute Spirit.[3]

This complete spirit—which, as such, is to be distinghished from the third potency, in that the latter is "not the complete, absolutely free spirit"[4]—is the "pure godhead" of *The Ages of the World*. It is only this absolutely free spirit, the complete concept of which involves the distinction within him of potencies, which can be called God. He embraces all reality within himself; "the potencies are in the Absolute Spirit not *as* potencies but as = He himself."[5] But such inclusiveness does not prevent the possibility of the Absolute Spirit, "by nature eternal,"[6] of positing a non-eternal being which is distinct from Himself. Since God himself is free from the necessity of his own being, he is able to will a world distinct from himself. When and if he wills such a world (the proposition is still hypothetical), the potencies which up to that point were "merely forms of the Absolute Spirit and = He himself"[7] would become determinants of another being, i.e. of a being different from God as his concept delineates him. Being would be posited as the first potency, and each of the succeeding potencies would follow in order. Thus "the *three* forms would be represented to him (to the Absolute Spirit) as so many potencies of a future being."[8] As "basic categories of being"[9] (i.e. of the being distinct from God himself), they would appear as $A^1$, $A^2$, and $A^3$, or, respectively, as "that which might be," as "that which must be," and as "that which should be," thus reproducing in a world distinct from God the determinations found within God himself.

The freedom of God is safeguarded by Schelling's insistence that God as the Absolute, as free spirit, is not to be identified with any or all of the potencies, nor with being as such. As *actus purissimus* God himself is to be understood as materially different from the being which he creates. Furthermore he is formally free to decide if and

---

[1] II, 3, 238.  [2] II, 3, 239.  [3] *Ibid.*  [4] II, 3, 260.
[5] II, 3, 263.  [6] *Ibid.*  [7] II, 3, 264–5.  [8] II, 3, 267.  [9] *Ibid.*

when a creation shall take place. It is possible for him, if he so wills, either "to remain in that original—tensionless—being, or to egress into that tensed and self-contrary being."[1] God is truly God in that his will is not bound to anything outside of himself. He can be or do anything he wills.

On the other hand, God is not to be regarded as surrendering his being by creating a world. While God himself is not involved in the movement of process, the world is not a world apart from God. The being which is separated from God as a consequence of his decision to create a world "is indeed no longer God himself, but neither is it absolutely not-God."[2] It is the one God which *is*, fully, in each of the forms which being, or existence, displays. When God posits himself as —A, it is not God as he *should* be, to be sure; and to the extent that —A represents a form of being which is opposed to the final form, it is not-God. But by the same token, it *is* God in this opposed form of being. That which is real in the potencies "is always only the godly"; while "that which is not godly in them, or that whereby they are (mere) potencies, is that which is merely accessory".[3] In order to create a world, "in order to emerge *actually* from that rotatory movement which was necessarily posited with his original being, and to pass over into that opposed, i.e. rectilinear, movement, the complete spirit had no other means than, as beginning, middle and end in himself, to make himself actually unlike himself."[4] Thus while "the godhood or the divine being of the potencies is indeed suspended [during creation], at the same time only the form or manner of the divine existence... is suspended, but not the existence of God himself."[5]

In this way, Schelling maintains, it is possible to achieve an understanding, not only of historical process in general, but of historical process conceived as intimately dependent upon the activity of God. Since God is "the indissoluble unity"[6] of the potencies, and hence the one God in all the expressions of divinity, we are led, according to Schelling, to the concept of monotheism. But at the same time, from the kind of monotheism here envisioned, it is possible also to arrive at a systematic understanding of polytheism. For if we regard the potencies not in their relation to God, but as they appear reciprocally excluding each other, "we must recognize

---

[1] II, 3, 269.    [2] II, 3, 272.    [3] II, 3, 280.    [4] II, 3, 274.
[5] II, 3, 281.    [6] *Ibid.*

that, as such, they are posited outside of their godhood... outside of that *actus purissimus*..., but at the same time, as something *outside* of God (*praeter Deum*), they cannot be non-godly."[8] The potencies conceived as individual divinities (which in reality are not other than manifestations of the one true God) represent the point of view of polytheism. In this way, as we shall see, Schelling is able to present a philosophy of mythology and a philosophy of revelation which are not two separate philosophies, but the one general philosophical schema with these two phases.

But the question still remains: how and why did God inaugurate a process outside himself? The "how" of this question has already been partly answered. There can be no ground outside of God to which appeal could be made in order to explain this event. This "being-beside-God" of a world which opposes him can be explained by appealing "to the will of God alone".[2] That which is truly existent, "that ἐξιστάμενον begins with that which is opposed to the true God, but within which God himself is, as it were, concealed."[3] If, then, we can appeal only to God's will to explain the "how" of this extra-position of the Absolute Spirit, then the "why" of it may shed some light on the process itself. As Schelling notes, it is an ancient teaching that "God executes his intentions by way of antithesis."[4] Hence, with reference to the immediate question, God posits himself as —A, as "that which might be", *not* in order that he may be this —A, but because he has another intention. For as the first potency is (or may be) posited, so the second *must* follow, and finally the third potency will also be realized, and with it the true end of the theogonic process will be achieved.

The reason for this succession of potencies in the theogonic process may be suggested in various ways. In the first place, as Schelling envisions it, the succession of potencies within the divine being, prior to any actualization of them, is a constantly repeated sequence without beginning and end. The result of such a ceaseless succession is a "rotatory movement" which, for God, is a condition of lack of bliss ("*Unseligkeit*").[5] Therefore he welcomes an actual succession in which an end is put to that rotary movement, and each potency is brought to separate expression. But in order to accomplish this, the Absolute Spirit must be posited as beginning, middle and end of a process which is successively differentiated in each of its phases.

---

[1] II, 3, 283.　　[2] II, 3, 271.　　[3] II, 3, 272.　　[4] *Ibid.*　　[5] II, 3, 273.

But a more exact accounting may be rendered for the movement of the theogonic process if attention is directed to its final end, the positing of the third potency. If there is a final cause for the process as a whole, it can be discerned only in the creature which is the last and highest expression of its movement. Here in man, or more precisely in human consciousness, which is the goal of the theogonic process, there can be "brought back in [man] that principle which is the initiatory cause of the process and which during the whole process is that which exists *outside* of itself."[1] That which thus exists outside of itself during the process is that which, as a result of the process, "comes to itself, becomes consicus of itself."[2] If, then, "the whole process is merely a *successive* coming-to-itself of that which in man (as the highest and final creature) is conscious of itself,"[3] in human consciousness there shall be realized the reconciliation, through true science, of the being which through the process has been sundered from itself. It is for this reason, according to Schelling, that Plato rightly regarded all true science as recollection; and it is also the reason why the moments of being can be "recalled" by the philosopher in his attempt to erect the negative philosophy. And even as "we strive in science for the place where we, (i.e. the man in us) once were, so that striving for a truly central knowledge which surveys everything from the mid-point... is itself the most incontrovertible proof that human consciousness was originally in possession of this knowledge, and should be in possession of it again."[4]

Thus God himself is to be realized in the process which opposes his Absolute Spirit. But at this point, the relation of man and of his history to the movement of process as a whole must be scrutinized with some care. For while it is true that all creation achieves its climax in man, the appearance of man himself introduces a point of difference, an alteration of the character of process as a whole. For up to this point, where the creation of man occurs, there is "no being outside of God (in the sense of *extra*); everything hitherto has been confined within God."[5] But with the creation of man, a new beginning of process is made. For man through his freedom—his complete autonomy and independence of God—posits a world "not merely *praeter*, but rather *extra Deum*."[6]

In order to understand how this is possible, it is necessary to see

---

[1] II, 3, 287.          [2] *Ibid.*          [3] *Ibid.*
[4] II, 3, 287–88.       [5] II, 3, 353.       [6] II, 3, 353.

clearly the nature of man and the role he plays in creation. And it is here that the decisive importance of man's autonomy, as this was delineated initially in the *Of Human Freedom*, becomes manifest. It will be recalled that in this earlier work Schelling sought to arrive at a conception of man which would render the assumption possible that man is that one creature which is endowed with genuine freedom—not merely phenomenal freedom, which consists in ignorance of one's complete dependence on the Absolute, but a genuine freedom to act independently of any other determinant. Basically the same conception of human freedom was employed by Schelling throughout his later work in order to explain the course of human history. The reason why man introduces a moment of difference into creation is that he, of all creatures, is endowed with genuine autonomy and thus is able to initiate an extra-divine process based upon the principle, —A, which is opposed to God.

All of the creations of God prior to the creation of man are the result of the production by means of the potencies of beings which are still dependent solely upon the creative activity of God. This first creation is "absolutely and exclusively one which is immanent within God."[1] But with the creation of man "the potencies appear no longer as such, but now *actually* as divine personages, which, previously, they were only in concept and for a higher perspective."[2] Man is thus installed in creation as that creature on which these divine personages have impressed their stamp, and man is released from the domination of the merely cosmic powers and elevated to freedom.[3]

The fact that man is free is a result of the manner in which he was created. Like all created beings, man's existence derives from the decision of the Absolute Spirit to emerge from his self-containment [*aus seinem An-Sich hervortreten*] and, as it were, extend his being in a being distinct from himself. The being which thus emerges as distinct from the Absolute Spirit is, however, not a being *materially* distinct from God. It is *formally* distinct, to be sure, but it retains "the attributes of a being which exists entirely as a result of the Divine Will."[4] Hence the existent being distinct from God, while no longer God himself, retains within himself, by virtue of the manner of his origin, "the possibility of being brought *back*" to God himself, and is thus "at least *potentia* God."[5]

The potentiality of this reconciliation to God of a creation outside

---

[1] II, 3, 353.  [2] II, 3, 344.  [3] II, 3, 345.  [4] II, 3, 271.  [5] II, 3, 272.

of God is a potentiality possessed by man. But this potentiality cannot be realized immediately. For in the creation of man himself there
is involved the possibility of a further severance from God—a possibility which is realized in human history. In God's positing a being
outside himself, he necessarily sets in operation a process which involves the activation of the potencies in sequence—the sole aim of
which, however, is "the overcoming of the [being] which is excluded
from [God's] pure being."[1] But in the act of creation itself, God has
imposed a limitation upon the mode by which his purpose can be
accomplished. In endowing his creation with the attribute of being
separate from his pure being, and thus directing its activity *away*
from its origin, God has also imposed upon himself the necessity of
giving to this separated being "a *potentiality* of turning back to
[God]."[2] Since God himself no longer possesses or controls this separated being, he must give it the means of freely, i.e. willingly, returning to its divine source. But with the possibility of its turning
back there is given at the same time the possibility of its turning itself *against* its origin. As a result of this necessity, therefore, there
emerges in creation a creature, man, which is endowed with the
ability of voluntarily directing creation back to its origin in the
Absolute Spirit, on the one hand; but on the other hand, this same
freedom permits it (or him) to oppose itself both to the Absolute
Spirit and to the rest of creation.

The creation of man is, accordingly, the creation of a completely
autonomous being. To be sure, man's autonomy is not that of a self-
created being; but he possesses nevertheless the ability to direct himself according to the laws of his own being. As we noted in *Of Human
Freedom*, this autonomy of man is the mark of a being which is endowed with true selfhood, or spirit; for, as Schelling notes elsewhere,
"spirit is that which is able to tear itself free from (material) being...
that which is free over against that which is."[3] Man is free from being
both theoretically and practically; i.e. he is able both to represent, or
make objective, that which is, *ideally* (whence man's ability to know,
or to possess science), and to make that which is (the world) an object
for his independent (moral) activity, or to make being *really* objective. It is this spiritual power of man to which human history is a
living witness.

When, now, we re-survey the course of the development of process,

---

[1] II, 3, 347.    [2] II, 3, 347.    [3] II, 1, 402.

we see that in the creation of man God has created a being which is both (potentially) independent of him as its origin, and at the same time materially identical with him. Not only is man, as an aspect of that which has developed *praeter Deum*, a mode of the existence of God himself; he is also in respect to his *freedom* the same as God.[1] As spirit, man is free (potentially) both from God as Absolute Spirit and God as that which has been created in the process distinct from God. Man as the final cause of creation is free from the three potencies of process—even as God as Spirit is free from the necessity of his own being. And

> just this highest creation is man—man in his original being, it is understood—as he emerges from his creation immediately; the primal man ["*Ur-Mensch*"] who, therefore, in the oldest account is placed in a divinely enclosed and protected space, in Paradise.[2]

Thus in *almost* all respects, man as he is created originally is the same as God. The single difference is that man is a being which has been created. But this difference is all-important. At first man does not see the difference between himself and God. In blissful ignorance of the fact that the potencies are presuppositions of his own being, he is not aware of the difference "that God by *nature* is the *prius* of the potencies, whereas man is lord of the three principles only insofar as he *preserves* and does *not* suspend the unity with which they are posited in him."[3] But in that he is free to turn himself either against the potencies or against the Creator, and believing himself to be lord of the potencies, even as God is, "it is natural that he should turn himself against the potencies in order to be himself *like* God."[4] And here man is the victim of a great, albeit unavoidable, delusion. In seeking to set the potencies in tension, so that they will operate in sequence, even as God the creator had done originally, man displays his craving after the majesty of God. But instead of achieving this majesty, he falls victim to the aroused powers which he had dared to displace from their equilibrium. For the first time he is enabled to distinguish between good and evil, through the displacement effected in his consciousness by the actualization of the potencies. But at the same time, instead of achieving the majesty of God, or even preserving the relative majesty he himself had, man by his grasping for power sets free the first potency (which now becomes an independent principle).

---

[1] II, 3, 347.    [2] II, 3, 348.    [3] II, 3, 349.    [4] *Ibid.*

Inasmuch as this principle is the "basis of human consciousness" only so long as it remains in its proper place in relation to the whole, its emergence from that unity turns it into "a power transcending and... destroying human consciousness."[1] Instead of remaining subordinate to the power of man, the first principle becomes a self-contained, absolute power, endowed with a life of its own. As the enemy of God and man alike, it takes man captive and delivers him unto death.

This catastrophe is the immediate cause of human history. A new world, the world of peculiarly *human* affairs, is posited by this deed of man. Whereas the operation of universal process had previously been confined to an extra-divine movement, man "in putting *himself* in God's place... set the world outside of God."[2] This, the "fallen world" of Christian theology, to the extent that its existence is still dependent upon the prior existence of God, is not wholly extra-divine. But as far as human *consciousness* is concerned, from which the knowledge of the true God has been eradicated by the Fall, this world is known only as one which is outside of God. The consciousness of man has been wounded, torn loose from its true center—wherefore "philosophy has as its highest goal the restoration of that disrupted consciousness."[3] Such restoration, which is the true task of philosophy, is, as Schelling complains, all the more difficult in that "most people do not *want* to be healed at all and, like unhappy patients, raise an unruly outcry if one even approaches their wounds..."[4]

In spite of such opposition, however, the philosopher who would truly explain human history must presuppose the events leading up to the Fall, as well as to those which immediately followed. Having assumed the Fall of man and the excitation of the first potency, the philosopher is provided with "the basic fact of history."[5] The first potency (which now as a principle of historical change is designated as "B") was previously posited, in respect to nature as a whole, as eccentric; "but in man it again became central."[6] By this act, therefore, a new movement is begun, between which and the previous process there is "the great difference: the latter was a divine tension, posited by the divine will; this is posited by the human will."[7] Having placed himself in the position of the Father, and thereby having ex-

---

[1] II, 3, 350–51.    [2] II, 3, 352.    [3] II, 3, 364.
[4] II, 3, 365. Translated by Bolman, *op. cit.*, pp. 61–2.
[5] II, 3, 360.    [6] II, 3, 365.    [7] II, 3, 366.

cluded the Father from the process, man has invoked to power the potency which will make manifest the Son ($A^2$), but thereby also man "has separated the Son from the Father... as well as from the Spirit" ($A^3$).[1]

The character of human history may now be seen in its definitive form. Most assuredly must the process of human history which has been set in operation by the Fall of man be seen as a *theogonic* process.[2] It is at the same time "a completely extra-godly,"[3] hence natural process, especially as it expresses itself in the mythological systems of mankind. The theogonic process as a whole has "no other function than that which it had in creation, namely the overcoming of the opposed principle... by means of a purely natural or necessary operation."[4] In this overcoming of the opposed principle (B), "the second potency, through which God created everything, is the mediator."[5] The mediating potency, the Son, plays the decisive role in human history, for it is the instrument by which the creation which has fallen away from God in the excitation of the first potency is overcome and delivered again to the lordship of the Father. In fact, it is only with the fore-knowledge that the rebellious creation will be pacified and reconciled by the Son that the Father has decided for creation. Wherefore Christ declared that everything had been given over to him by his Father.

Accordingly the periods of human history divide themselves into two major parts: 1) the time or aeon of the Father, during which the Son had not been posited as an independent personage, which was also the time prior to the actual creation of the world; and 2) the time, or age, of the Son, which is "the entire time of this world."[6] These two major periods correspond to the first two epochs of "true time" referred to above: the age of "pretemporal eternity" and the age of the "present" respectively.[7] The age of the Son, or creation, is itself subdivisible into two periods: a) the time of His suffering, "during the entire age of paganism," during which the whole creation is held in the power of the first potency; and b) the time of his triumph, during which, as the second potency, He has been elevated to Lord of being.[8] These last two subdivisions are the major periods of human history, during which, respectively, mythology and revelation are the main characteristics. It is to the exposition of the

---

[1] II, 3, 367.   [2] II, 3, 368.   [3] *Ibid.*   [4] II, 3, 370.   [5] *Ibid.*
[6] II, 3, 375.   [7] II, 4, 103.   [8] II, 3, 377.

content of these two periods of the history of man in creation that we shall now turn.

## II. THE CONTENT OF HUMAN HISTORY

The philosophy of history, in the narrower sense of the term as an explanation of *human* affairs, must be able to explain "history as a whole."[6] Having surveyed the context within which Schelling places human history, we must continually keep in mind his contention that history can be properly understood only as a part of the larger whole of universal process. For, in Schelling's view, unless the philosopher is able to discern the true beginning of human history as such, he is deprived of that which is most essential for a delineation of its true character. Mere formulae purporting to be descriptive of various historical periods are useless without a grasp of the "reason why" of history itself.[7] History must be accorded a true beginning and a true end; and "since it goes without saying that that which has not discovered its own origin can neither discover its own end,"[8] it behooves the philosopher of history to investigate carefully the origins of human events.

As we have previously noted, Schelling distinguished the "present age," or the age of creation, from its presupposition, the age of "pretemporal eternity." While the latter age is "past," from the point of view of the actualization of God's decision to create the world, it must nevertheless form an indispensable part of the philosopher's understanding of human history. For even when we confine our attention to the present age, we must distinguish, in the first place, "historical and pre-historical time."[9] The various periods or epochs of historical time are themselves a part of a sequence which includes pre-historical time. Thus when, in the second place, the subdivision of historical time into the age of paganism and the age of revelation is made, the philosopher of history is able to see that the subordinate dichotomy of historical process is only provisional; for history as a whole has as its goal the suspension of all historical difference and the positing of the one, true God both in human consciousness and in His lordship over all creation.

Accordingly, Schelling maintains, it is not "a wild, unorganic,

---

[1] II, 1, 230.    [2] II, 1, 232.    [3] II, 1, 230.    [4] *Ibid.*

boundless time into which history conducts us; it is an organism... *a system of times...*"[1] But before we consider the various ages, or times, of history itself, it will be well, for the sake of perspective, to glance briefly at the situation of man prior to the Fall. In contrast to the temporal state of man after the Fall, when the knowledge of the true God becomes an ideal rather than a reality, man before the Fall had "a purely substantial knowledge of God."[2] Strictly speaking, this state of human consciousness cannot be termed historical. For human history, in the sense of a true sequence of events whose immediate occasion is the autonomy of man, does not begin until after the Fall. Wherefore Schelling designates this as the "supra-historical" period of mankind.[3] It is "original Man,"[4] or essential man, which occupies this place in universal process. None of the historical distinctions, such as individual men, nations, nor even "mankind," have yet emerged. For at that point man does not have true consciousness. That which is *potentially* human consciousness is that which in the supra-historical state is undifferentiated from God. The original man "posits God" immediately as the essential state of his being.[5] One cannot even say that original man *has* consciousness of God; he *is* that consciousness.[6]

While such a delineation of the supra-historical period of man may seem irrelevant to an understanding of human history, Schelling insists that, rightly understood, it profoundly affects such understanding. For as soon as one inquires as to the origin of religious representations among mankind, he is forced to commit himself to an hypothesis as to the original relation of human consciousness to God. Failure to realize this has led to the false assumption that consciousness *comes to* God from an originally godless state. But "consciousness does not come *to* God; its first movement is ...away from the *true* God."[7] And even as the first self-conscious act of man brings about the excitation of the first potency, with the resultant loss of the true center of human consciousness, so the movement of human history itself is to be understood as a restoration to man of that which was originally his: an immediate relationship to the one true God.

Thus if the Fall of man results in the disruption of that immediate rapport with the true God, are we to assume that mankind is directly

---

[1] II, 1, 235.    [2] II, 1, 185.    [3] II, 1, 184.    [4] *Ibid.*    [5] II, 1, 185.
[6] II, 1, 187.    [7] II, 1, 186.

conducted to the known sequences of recorded history? On the contrary, Schelling carefully distinguishes two periods which, although a part of the general scene of the historical, are yet anterior to historical time in the restricted sense of recorded history. These two periods are designated by Schelling as the "absolute prehistorical" and the "relative prehistorical."[1] If we distinguish the various ages of history in respect to the purely formal criterion of our possessing recorded information about them, and, accordingly, employ the term "historical" only in reference to those for which records survive, we must designate *both* the "absolute prehistorical" and the "relative prehistorical" as prehistorical in this sense. But if one distinguishes *"Geschichte"* and *"Historie"*—"the former is the series of occurences and events, the latter the information about them"[2]— then the "absolute prehistorical" is to be denoted as the *"vorgeschichtliche"* time and the "relative prehistorical" as *"vorhistorische"* time.[3] Both of these ages antedate *"historische"* time; but the "absolute prehistorical" age is innocent of distinguishable events and is the time of *"complete historical immobility"*,[4] whereas the "relative prehistorical" age is full of events, although its events have not been recorded. As we shall see, these three divisions represent for Schelling the major periods of the age of human history.

In our (necessarily) sketchy survey of these periods of human history, we shall consider first the "absolute prehistorical" age. While it is true that this age contains no true succession of events, "by this it is not meant that nothing at all happens therein."[5] On the contrary, Schelling avers, the sun rose and set, men lay down to sleep and rose again, were born and died. But since the same events repeated themselves ceaselessly, "there is no progress, and hence no history"[6] to be discerned in this era. It is basically a "timeless time," in which there is "no true before and after since it is a kind of eternity, as the Hebraic expression (*olam*) which is used for it in Genesis signifies."[7] Prior to this age there is only the supra-historical.

But this was the precious Golden Age of the World, the time when "the human race was as yet one and unseparated."[8] Neither cities nor nations had arisen: and this alone of all the situations of the human race might "rightly be named the *state of nature*".[9] Here the

---

[1] II, 1, 235.    [2] *Ibid.*    [3] II, 1, 236.    [4] II, 1, 234.    [5] *Ibid.*
[6] *Ibid.*    [7] II, 1, 235.    [8] II, 1, 175.    [9] *Ibid.*

human race dwellt together in "peaceful unity."[1] As yet there were no fixed boundaries, no settled habitations. Men lived as nomads, wandering at will over the face of the earth, untroubled by enclosures or private property. And later on, when this way of life was abandoned by the rest of mankind, certain groups, such as the Rechabites among the Hebrews, persisted as "the last survivors of this oldest race" by whom settled dwellings, the planting of vines and the sowing of seeds were regarded as religiously tabu.[2]

The explanation for this "absolute prehistorical" age is not to be found, however, in any factors relating to the socio-economic circumstances of the people who lived at this time. On the contrary, these circumstances are rather an effect of the universal process which works itself out in human consciousness and expresses itself in the *religious* situation of mankind. If, therefore, we survey this age from the point of view of the theogonic process which now has installed itself in human consciousness, we shall recognize it as the result of the excitation of the first potency, "that principle of the beginning,"[3] by the freely-willed act of man. As a result of this act, pictured in Genesis as the eating of the forbidden fruit, man is cast forth from Paradise and human history begins. Indeed, as Schelling remarks, "history, as a new world of movement, could not have been posited at all if man had not once again moved and shaken that foundation of creation by which everything should attain to peace and to an eternal stability."[4] But the "eternal stability" of creation lies in the far distant future; and as a result of man's initial act, that potency which "should not be" is immediately installed as the dominant principle, "B," of historical process. Thus human consciousness "finds itself in the power of... B," at the same time that it is led out of its original situation of immediate rapport with the true God. At the beginning of human history, in the "absolute prehistorical" age, the consciousness of man is dominated by the anti-godly principle, B, which has usurped the place of the true God through man's own decision.

Here, for the first time, mankind acquires a religion. The principle, B, which now "has made itself the master of consciousness,"[5] has through its revolt displaced the proper order of the potencies. Whereas originally it was the basis, or substratum, in respect to the higher potencies, through man's act it excludes the higher potencies and

---

[1] II, 1, 181.    [2] II, 1, 154.    [3] II, 3, 382.    [4] II, 3, 385.    [5] II, 3, 386.

manifests itself as blind will which puts itself in the place of the true God. The unity of mankind which is characteristic of this first age is thus affected by "a blind power, independent of human will and thought."[1] But while the religion of this age can be called a mono- theism, it can be so called only relatively, viz. "in contrast to the later *poly*theism which was produced out of its disintegration."[2] For "at the beginning of history, which Kant rightly designated as the Fall, into the consciousness of man, in place of the absolute-One there entered the relative-One... the relation to [which] was not the true religion."[3]

That the One which was the first object of mankind's worship was not the true God could be known only later when "the relative ceased to be absolute and was declared to be relative."[4] As we shall see, it was only after many vicissitudes extending over a long period of time that that part of mankind which was subject to "paganism" was released from this error. But an interesting sidelight on this distinction is thrown by Schelling in his discussion of the concept of God in the Biblical book, Genesis. Here, Schelling thought, it is possible to discover the traces of belief in the "relative-One" as it existed in the first age of mankind, as well as to show how the Hebrews alone had revealed to them the true God, while, with the separation of the nations, the rest of the human race instead turned into the tortuous paths of polytheism.

The distinction between the "relative-One" and the "absolute- One" is to be discerned, Schelling maintained, in the two names for God, "Elohim" and "Jehovah," which were used by the author(s) of Genesis and the other "Mosaic" books of the Old Testament. In the beginning of history, the Hebrews—as yet unseparated from the rest of humanity—designated God by the term "Elohim," a "general denotation," which refers to the God who is "the *immediate* content of consciousness."[5] It was only later that the term "Jehovah" was used to refer to the God "who is *distinguished* as the true [God."][6] It is Schelling's thesis, accordingly, that, if "Elohim is the God who is yet *indistincte*, whereas Jehovah is the God distinguished as such,"[7] then it was only at a later date that the true God was distinguished by the Hebrews and prior to that time *true* monotheism (which is equivalent to knowledge of the true God) did not exist.

The evidence for this contention may be discovered, according to

---

[1] II, 1, 137.   [2] II, 3, 389.   [3] II, 1, 144.   [4] II, 1, 145.
[5] *Ibid.*   [6] *Ibid.*   [7] II, 1, 146.

Schelling, by an examination of the genealogy found in the fifth chapter of Genesis where the account not only omits the names of Cain and Abel, but traces the descent from Adam through Seth and Enos. It is only from Enos on that men began to call upon Jehovah, thereby distinguishing him as the true God from the relative-One, Elohim. For "with Enos a *second* race of mankind actually begins—a second race... because it is no longer the same as the first race stemming immediately from Adam."[1] It is this second race, the descendants of Enos, which, through revelation,[2] comes to a knowledge of the true God, and thenceforth call him "Jehovah."

The later distinction between the Hebrews and the nations of mankind is based upon the adherence of the Hebrews to faith in the true God, while the nations of the world became polytheists. At first, however, there is no distinction between the Hebrews and the "nations," since the latter do not appear until the mythology of the second age makes its appearance. Prior to Noah, however, the solicitations of the second God, the God of the age to come, provokes marriages between "the sons of God" and "the daughters of man," whence are born a race of giants. The wrath of Jehovah because of such unfaithfulness is vented upon mankind in the form of the universal Flood, from which Noah and his family alone are spared because he did not forsake Jehovah and yield to the solicitations of the pagan god.[3] It is after the Flood that Jehovah sees "that the human race cannot be kept back from the transition to polytheism."[4] With polytheism, "mankind" as such disappears from the earth. Henceforth one must distinguish the Hebrews as a race ["*Geschlecht*"] from the rest of humanity which is now divided into peoples, or nations ["*Völker*"]. In an obvious reference to Lessing's theory in his *Education of the Human Race*, Schelling maintains that the Hebrews alone preserved and extended the knowledge of the true God; for from the time of the Flood not only is there found among them alone the distinction and worship of the true God which began with Enos, but also

> there exists revelation—which indeed can only be revelation of the true God—no longer among mankind in general, for this as such has disappeared... and just as little does it exist among a people—for everything which is called a people ["*Volk*"] has already lapsed into polytheism—the knowledge of the true God

---

[1] II, 1, 148.    [2] II, 1, 155.
[3] II, 1, 150–52.    [4] II, 1, 152.

exists among a single race which has remained outside of the nations.[1]

Thus it is the Elohim which the Hebrews honored originally with the rest of mankind. It is the Elohim "whom the nations and the heathen fear,"[2] as well as "the universal God by whom Abraham is tried, after the manner of the heathen, to slaughter his son for a burning sacrifice"[3] although "it was the Jehovah who appears [to Abraham] to restrain him from the consummation"[4] of this act. In fact it was Abraham to whom Jehovah first revealed himself; but since "the immediate content of Abraham's consciousness remained the primal God, the Elohim,—when the true God appeared to him, the first God necessarily remained "the ground of the appearance of the second." Wherefore the true God, for Abraham, "is never the *existing*, but invariably the *becoming* ["werdende"]."[5] Hence "Jehovah is to Abraham merely the primal God in his true, persistent essence."[6] But what is most important, from the point of view of our discussion, is that the monotheism of Abraham "had for its presupposition the same God which is the presupposition of polytheism."[7]

The "absolute prehistorical" age as it was experienced elsewhere than among the Hebrews presents some rather interesting features in addition to those already noted. The Elohim of the Hebrews is the first principle, B, which by its revolt has subjugated human consciousness and installed itself as the one false God in place of the true God. By this act, however, B has torn itself loose from the unity in which it should find its proper place by "subordinating itself to the higher potency"[8] next above it. But since in its blindness it opposes itself to the higher potency and its proper place in the hierarchy, there "arises a struggle in which the principle which has exalted itself to a false life no longer suffers the still power of that divine necessity... as center, as spirit, but wills, rather, to present *itself* as spirit."[9] As a consequence of this struggle, the principle, B, which seeks to be the One, is "unavoidably torn into multiple parts,"[10] and

---

[1] II, 1, 155.    [2] II, 1, 163.    [3] II, 1, 164.    [4] *Ibid.*    [5] II, 1, 165.
[6] II, 1, 168.

[7] II, 1, 170. It may be of interest to note that Schelling rejects the hypothesis that the presence in Genesis of the two names for God is an indication that they are derived from two independent sources. For, he argues, the names of God "do not change arbitrarily," but are used with intentional discrimination "according to the matter under discussion." II, 1, 163.

[8] II, 2, 171.    [9] *Ibid.*    [10] II, 2, 172.

consciousness is presented with a One which is a manifold. The One does not will this fragmentation and hence seeks continually to posit itself as nothing but unity. But it cannot entirely escape the attractive power of the second potency; and as a result consciousness is confronted with a plurality which is "*actually* only the *One posited as* plurality... a *unum versum.*"[1]

It is this situation of human consciousness which produces that ancient astral religion which "did not so much regard the stars as gods as, on the contrary, the gods as stars."[2] At first glance, this appears to have been a system of polytheism; and, in fact, Schelling refers to it, at least once, as "the first simultaneous polytheism."[3] But the fact that it is a simultaneous polytheism distinguishes it from the later successive—genuine—polytheism. For the religion of this age does not consist in a worship of several distinct deities, but rather of the One deity which is seen in the several stars. What these people worshiped in the stars was rather "the principle which was the inner, concealed *ground* of all heavenly or sidereal movement."[4] The stars, in other words, were not regarded as gods so much as manifestations of the one God in multiple.

This astral religion is called "Zabism" by Schelling—a term by which he sought to distinguish it from the so-called "Sabeism" which was the religion of a particular group of Arabians.[5] The name "Zabism" is derived, according to Schelling, "from the Hebraic and Arabian Zaba, the host (*exercitus*), and then in particular the heavenly host, whence comes also the Old Testament name Jehovah Zebaoth, Lord of Hosts."[6] In that Mohammed was called a "zabi," Schelling believes, he was so called, probably, by the idolatrous Arabians who saw in his doctrine of the one God a reversion to Zabism.

But whatever the religion be called, its distinctive features are unmistakeable, in Schelling's view. It is the religion of that part of mankind which has not yet achieved an historical life, has not yet, that is, been separated into peoples or nations. It is the religion of nomads who, ruled by that One principle, find their natural abode in the wilderness. Man has not yet achieved a concrete life, settled dwellings and circumscribed locations. He is "a stranger on the earth, as bereft of a homeland as a wandering star."[7] Only the dead have a place to rest; the living must wander ceaselessly. Urban society

---

[1] *Ibid.*        [2] II, 2, 174.        [3] II, 2, 172.
[4] II, 2, 177.    [5] II, 2, 179–80.     [6] II, 2, 180.      [7] II, 2, 182.

arises only after man has acquired stationary possessions. But since "only that can possess something which possesses itself,"[1] and since man is, at this point, "estranged from himself, put beside himself,"[2] ruled by a blind power and hence possessing no power over himself, he has no possessions—("To possess something means to have something in one's power"[3])—but is ruled by the same power which holds the stars in their courses.

The main reason why this was regarded by later ages as the Golden Age is that the man of the "absolute prehistorical" age was completely determined in his consciousness by the One god, "that King of the Heavens,"[4] who had completely ousted the true God and who, at first, is entirely successful in repelling the advances of any god which might challenge his supremacy. Man did not feel himself *unfree* in this age, for "only he feels himself unfree who is ruled by two principles and is irresolute betwixt both."[5] Hence the man of this age felt himself perfectly free, even though his actual state was that of perfect determination. From the point of view of a later age, therefore, whose consciousness is torn between competing principles, the state of prehistorical man appears as perfect bliss. That it was *not perfect* bliss, but a false bliss, could be known only by an age or a people to whom the perfect bliss of the *supra-historical* age, the age of man in Paradise prior to the Fall, was glimpsed and striven for. Hence only the Jews and Christians, to whom the true God is *revealed*, can have a true idea of human felicity, which is "not of this world." Paganism knows only the Golden Age of an historical existence. But, as Schelling notes,

> at both termini of the moral life, freedom and necessity appear as one; the *pure* necessity. by which the man of the present moment is governed, is experienced as freedom, just as at the opposite terminus freedom in its highest self-consciousness again appears as operative with necessity.[6]

In this way alone, Schelling maintains, can one explain "the *peace* and *stillness* of the prehistorical age, which is comparable only to the deep, solemn stillness of the heavens."[7]

Specific instances of this religious situation are to be discovered, according to Schelling, in the traditions of many widely separated peoples. Among the Greeks, for instances, it was Ouranos who was "the absolutely universal God,"[8] and whose hegemony antedates

---

[1] *Ibid.*     [2] II, 2, 183.     [3] II, 2, 182.
[4] II, 3, 388.     [5] II, 2, 183.     [6] *Ibid.*     [7] II, 2, 185.     [8] II, 2, 287.

Kronos and Zeus. But it is the Chinese empire of Schelling's day which, of all modern nations, preserved most nearly the character of this prehistorical time. In fact, in Schelling's view, it is incorrect to designate the Chinese as a nation; "they are, rather, a pure humanity... an arrested portion of the *Absolute* prehistoric humanity."[1] Whereas other people were formed by the divisive effect of the mythological process, China "remained completely outside the mythological movement."[2] China proceeded only to the point where the Heavenly One, which China with the rest of mankind once revered, was displaced from its heavenly position and became worldly; i.e. the principle of heaven [became] the all-powerful ruling principle of all of Chinese life and of the State."[3] Thus, for the Chinese, the ruling principle of that astral religion of prehistoric humanity became embodied in the State, and particularly in the Emperor, with the result that the same *form* of religious life (although not the same content) was preserved in China after the rest of humanity had been swept along in the mythological process. In China itself, which is nothing less than the earthly form of the Heavenly Empire, there is to be found "the mid-point, the center, the entire power of Heaven."[4] Moreover, the monosyllabic language of the Chinese is itself a remnant of the primal languages of the human race before the confusion of tongues produced a multitude of polysyllabic languages.[5] In this as in other noteworthy respects, the Chinese indicate their close association with the characteristics of the "absolute prehistorical" age.

Up to this point, we have not encountered a genuine historical process. During the entire "absolute historical" age, human consciousness is confined within a circle of "necessary and involuntary representations."[6] The sideral principle, B, appears to consciousness "as masculine, as Ouranos, as Lord of the heavens."[7] It is not until the next principle, $A^2$, approaches that a true succession of qualitatively different historical ages is inaugurated. For Schelling maintains, "in an exact sense historical time begins with the completed separation of peoples."[8] But inasmuch as this separation of peoples takes place as a result of a crisis in human consciousness, induced by the approach of $A^2$, which approach is hence the occasion for the separation, the transition to historical time is actually prehistorical.

---

[1] II, 2, 522.    [2] II, 2, 527.    [3] II, 2, 529.    [4] II, 2, 533.
[5] II, 2, 541ff.    [6] II, 3, 389.    [7] *Ibid.*    [8] II, 1, 181.

Historical time, properly so-called, is characterized by a theogonic process. To the extent that the Ouranic god imposes immobility upon the age in which he rules, there can be no true succession, and hence no theogonic process. *Successive* polytheism (as distinguished from the "simultaneous" polytheism of Zabism) is what Schelling regards as mythology in the genuine sense of that term; and "mythology is above all a *historical* phenomenon."[1] But what is most important from our point of view is that Schelling regards the appearance of mythology as itself indicative of a "necessary process"[2] by which mankind is led out of that state of undifferentiated unity in which the revolt of B places him, and conducts him through a series of moments of historical time toward the rehabilitation of his consciousness in the knowledge of the true God. And since "objectively regarded, mythology is... *actual theogony*, history of the gods,"[3] the meaning of which can be delivered only by an understanding of the process as a whole, its true significance will be grasped only when mankind has finally been led to the point where mythology itself has come to an end and revelation of the true God has taken its place.

The "relative prehistorical" age which succeeds the age of Ouranos marks the (eventual) establishment of polytheism and with this the separation of mankind into peoples and nations. This, the age of paganism, has a long and involved history, only the outline of which we can indicate here. The next higher potency to B, $A^2$, never wholly ineffective even during the age of the complete ascendancy of B, finally forces the illegitimate principle to concede some of its power. As a result, B is transformed into a feminine principle, and Ouranos becomes Ourania, the Queen of the heavens. Here, Schelling maintains, in the idea of Ourania, "is the transition, the first foundation, of mythology."[4] Zabism is, as such, unmythological; and to the extent that mythology arises only as a result of successive polytheism, Ouranos himself, through his exclusiveness, cannot be rightly designated as a mythological figure. Zabism as such can be regarded "only as a yet unhistorical religion, and therefore also it is the religion of as yet unhistorical (prehistorical) mankind."[5]

But with the appearance of Ourania, Ouranos himself is provided with the means to becoming the first member of a (necessary) mythological process. This transition has already been effected by the time the first principle, B, having "materialized itself,"[6] or become

---

[1] II, 1, 55.    [2] II, 1, 193.    [3] II, 1, 195.
[4] II, 3, 389.    [5] II, 3, 390.    [6] II, 2, 193.

maternal, is worshipped, according to Herodotus, as Mylitta among the Assyrians, as Astarte among the Arabians, and as Mitra among the Persians.[1] Among the latter, the old astral religion was still followed, but in a corrupted form, in that not only the stars but also the sun, moon and the elements were also included in their devotions. But the significant fact for the mythological process as a whole is that "with this first feminine deity the second potency has achieved a place... in consciousness."[2]

This principle, $A^2$, is not at this point in complete possession of the human consciousness. In fact, several actions and reactions in the theogonic process must take place before complete victory is won by this liberating power. The god which corresponds to the principle $A^2$ will later, in Greek mythology, make his full appearance as Dionysos. But before he does so, he must prepare human consciousness for final liberation through successive attacks upon the power of B. Thus, rather than overwhelming his opponent with one mighty blow, as it were, he woos mankind by a gradual subjugation of the principle of evil. In this way, Schelling believes, it is possible to account for the "so-called contradictions of mythology,"[3] by which is meant the numerous appearances of the same god in entirely different guises. Dionysos is the one principle, $A^2$, running throughout the extent of mythology, who in various ways works for the liberation of consciousness from the power of B. But by the same token, Dionysos is "another god in that moment when he is only first born into reality, without yet operating,... another in the following moment when for the first time he *begins* to operate, and still another god in a yet later moment when his work is done and he has completely vanquished the opposition."[4] As we shall see, $A^2$ achieves its full dominion over the fallen creation only in Christ. The age of polytheism is the age of paganism in which the liberating potency "must work not according to its will but only according to its nature."[5]

With the appearance of Ourania, "*actual* polytheism is posited for the first time."[6] But as yet the two gods, Ouranos and Dionysos, do not directly influence one another. It is merely the approach of the strange god which has transformed Ouranos into Ourania and provoked, at the same time, an adulterous relationship to him on the part of his devotees—as witness the practice of sacred prostitution among the devotees to the Babylonian Mylitta, as reported by

---

[1] II, 2, 199–200.   [2] II, 3, 390.   [3] II, 3, 392.
[4] *Ibid.*   [5] II, 3, 376.   [6] II, 2, 237.

Herodotus.[1] Such a practice is to be explained, according to Schelling, by the approach of the strange god, Dionysos, whose name is not yet known, but who yet is powerful enough to effect what are felt as illicit relations between himself and the devotees of the feminized Ouranos.

The moment of actual struggle between B and A[2] is introduced with the arrival of the God known in Greek mythology as Kronos. This is the point at which Dionysus is not merely latent, but actually begins to operate upon human consciousness. Whereas formerly Ouranos had been merely feminine and yielding, now, under the pressure of the effective activity of Dionysos, he again becomes masculine and unbending. He resists with all his power the approach of the principle which seeks to deprive him of his sovereignty. This stern, intolerant God "is the god of the nations which next appear in history and in the mythological process, the Phoenicians, the Tyrians and the Carthaginians, as well as of the Canaanite peoples."[2] He is known as Baal among the Phoenicians and as Moloch among various other peoples, but the Greeks know him as Kronos, the god of an earlier age.

Dionysos now makes his appearance in human consciousness, but not as yet in the form of complete divinity. To the extent that Kronos opposes him and seeks to bar him from actuality, Dionysos "cannot appear *as* God, but only as an inconceivable demi-being between God and man,"[3] Thus in his first appearance, Dionysus is God "in concealment, in negation, abasement."[4] He must first acquire divinity. Hence Dionysos is discovered initially in this form, according to Schelling, in the mythology of the Phoenicians as Melkart, but frequently referred to as the Phoenician Herakles. As Herakles in Greek mythology, he embodies the same idea which is found in a variety of mythological systems: "Herakles is, so to speak, a precursor... an earlier appearance of Dionysos."[5] Kronos is the false god who has usurped the place of the true Father. He is the intolerant principle, brought into actuality by man; and jealous of his falsely acquired sovereignty, he seeks with all his might to keep the true Son (Herakles) from assuming his rightful place in reality. Hence the Son must suffer. Instead of enjoying the status of a Son, he is reduced to the level of a servant, "just as the Messiah of the Old Testament appears not as the Son but rather only as the sorrowing

---

[1] II, 2, 238ff. cf. II, 3, 391.
[2] II, 3, 393.          [3] II, 3, 394.     [4] *Ibid.*     [5] *Ibid.*

and suffering *Servant* of God."[1] Thus Herakles in pagan mythology is laden with labors and suffering, although he is otherwise regarded as in all respects the friend and helper of man. In Phoenician mythology, Herakles does not achieve a higher status. But the idea is carried farther by the Greeks, among whom, eventually, Herakles becomes a god after he has overcome the curse of mortality.

At this point, according to Schelling, a new moment is introduced into the mythological process. Just as, earlier, Ouranos was transformed into a feminine divinity, Ourania, so now also Kronos becomes feminine upon the occasion of the approach of a new principle, $A^3$. The new divinity which appears as a result of the transformation of Kronos into a feminine deity is Cybele "who first appeared among the Phrygian or Phrygo-Thracian racial stock."[2] Here, where the actual overcoming of the first principle, B, begins, Cybele appears as "the Great Mother of the gods, *magna deum mater*, viz. of the future material gods."[3] But here we must pause briefly to explain the significance of this appearance of a new principle in the mythological process.

It is only with the appearance of Cybele, according to Schelling, that mythology achieves fullness of expression, for it is only at this point that the third potency becomes effective. At the beginning of history, only the first potency, B, in the form of Ouranos, ruled man's consciousness. Gradually and reluctantly, room was made for the second potency, $A^2$, first by the transformation of B into a feminine deity, Ourania, and then by the installation of the demi-god, Herakles, who as one form of $A^2$, was subjugated by the reaction of B in the form of Kronos. But even here, the foundation was laid for the eventual overthrow of the principle which "should not be." His exclusive lordship over human consciousness was broken, and the first stages of his subordination and return to his rightful position of "ground," or basis, of reality were accomplished. But so far only two principles had entered into the movement of process. It is with the appearance of Cybele, whose presence is evoked by the approach of the third principle, that the totality of potencies is achieved. Inasmuch as these three potencies "are the real, basic principles... of process, and to the extent that they appear to consciousness as gods, they are the *essential* gods, entering successively into consciousness and... mythology is nothing but the successive coming of these gods."[4]

[1] *Ibid.*    [2] II, 3, 395.    [3] II, 3, 399.    [4] II, 3, 396.

Accordingly, Schelling suggests, the mythological process may be divided into four parts. The first part represents the epoch in which Ouranos rules alone. But the next three parts represent the era during which Dionysos gradually achieves ascendancy. The second period is the epoch of Ourania, but it is also that of the *birth* of Dionysos. The third period is the epoch of the actual *operation* of Dionysos (the age of Kronos), but also the age of transition to the coming of the third potency. The third potency, the Spirit, can be fully realized only after the first potency has been fully subjugated. But since Kronos is still in command of this age, the Spirit's coming must be deferred while the second principle reduces Kronos to impotence. It is at the end of this third period that Cybele appears, as a token of the age to come. It is in the fourth period that the final overthrow of the first principle is accomplished and the actual coming of the Spirit takes place. At this point mythology comes to an end.[1]

Here, in the last epoch of the mythological process, when all three potencies have been brought into operation, three complete and independent mythologies make their appearance: the Egyptian, the Indian and the Greek. Each represents, in its entirety, the operation of the three potencies. But only in the Greek does a consummation of the mythological process as a whole come to expression. Egyptian mythology is that in which "the bitter struggle against the blind principle still continues, in which, therefore, this principle itself, although besieged, for the last time... extends the fullness of its power."[2] Typhon is the god in Egyptian mythology around whom everything revolves, and who, in his death struggle... which is indeed the death struggle of the real principle, B, as such—fights against the Dionysiac god, Osiris. But so uncertain is the outcome that the Egyptian consciousness "feels this struggle, at one time, as a dismemberment of Typhon, at another as a dismemberment of Osiris."[3] It is only with the birth of Horus, the third principle, that the victory over Typhon is assured. Thereupon Typhon is assimilated with Osiris and becomes the ruler of the underworld. Thus his independent power is brought to an end and he is returned to his proper place of subordination. Isis, the mother of Horus, and wife of Osiris, is (presumably) the feminine form of Typhon whose main function in the process is to bring the spiritual principle, Horus, to birth. But Egyptian mythology as a whole is dominated by the first principle.

---

[1] II, 3, 396–97.      [2] II, 3, 401.      [3] *Ibid.*

The Indian mythology "appears to be the complete opposite of the Egyptian."[1] For while the Egyptian mythology finds its center of gravity, so to speak, in the real principle, the Indian, on the contrary, is organized around the ideal principle. In fact, for the Indian consciousness, that principle of the beginning, B, "is completely overpowered by the higher potency and reduced to impotence."[2] Brama, the first principle, is wholly without worshipers, and appears only as a god of the distant past. In his place rules Siva, not in deference to Brama, but in complete independence of his predecessor. The third principle, Vishnu, is likewise detached from his predecessor, Siva. As a result, Schelling contends, the Indian consciousness is split into multiple parts. Lacking a genuine principle of unity, its unhappiness is only increased by the competing systems of Buddhism and mysticism.

It is only in Greek mythology, Schelling contends, that the mythological process as a whole achieves its consummation. Here "consciousness is brought back to its true center... the declining god not forsaken but preserved as a spiritual god."[3] This is the consummation of the mythological process because it represents the subjugation of the first potency by the second in such a way that it (B) again becomes the basis for that organic wholeness of reality under the lordship of $A^3$ which was destroyed by the Fall. Hence Greek mythology "is the quiet death, the true euthanasia of the real principle."[4] Herein that primal god who, as Ouranos, had subjugated human consciousness to the blind power of B, is finally vanquished, but not so as to destroy his effectiveness so much as to redirect it. As Hades, he is made the true *subjectum*, and "presents himself to human consciousness as the god who exists in *all* the gods—the essence of all—who existed in Ouranos, in Kronos, and who now exists in Zeus, the head of the manifold of gods which has now emerged."[5] Once more the real principle has become a mere *potency*; and since, as potency, he no longer excludes the other potencies, but forms the true basis for all, the mythological process comes at last to its true end. Even as at the time of the immobility of the Ouranic age, during which a simultaneous polytheism was posited, so now, also, in this latter age, "that simultaneous polytheism, whose summit is the Greek Zeus, can emerge again."[6]

The establishment of this mythological system among the Greeks

---

[1] II, 3, 403.    [2] *Ibid.*    [3] II, 3, 405.
[4] II, 3, 406.    [5] II, 3, 408.    [6] II, 3, 407.

was, of course, not accomplished immediately. In fact, pacification of the real principle and the final enthronement of Dionysos is not effected until Greek thought has run the course of its development through the mysteries of the Hellenistic age. At the end of the third epoch into which Schelling divides the mythological process, as we noted previously, Cybele appears in response to the actual operation of the Dionysian principle as a result of the "materialization" of Kronos. The stage is now set, as it were, for the final overthrow of B under the lordship of the third principle, $A^3$. As yet, with the appearance of Cybele, only the birth of Dionysos is accomplished. Before the coming of the Spirit can take place, the Dionysian principle must achieve complete control over the Ouranian.

Accordingly, in the fourth period of the mythological process, at the point where Dionysos is not only able to effect the feminization of Kronos but also to achieve a relationship to consciousness as such and in his own right, another feminine divinity appears. This goddess is Demeter, by whom the actual overthrow of the real principle is made concivable.[1] But, it must be stressed in respect to this overthrow, Demeter "is at first merely the *conception* thereof, insofar as consciousness still clings to and depends upon the real god."[2] Demeter first appears among the gods of the age of Kronos as the wife of Poseidon. As such, she is the wife of "the still entirely material representation of the god which in the future will become spiritual.[3] But at this time she gives herself immediately to the influence of Dionysus and thus prepares the final overthrow of the real principle.

At this point human consciousness is enabled to represent objectively the distinction between the real and the Dionysian principle, which it does by "positing the real god as a particular person."[4] That which in Demeter was bound to the real god is separated from him by a kind of birth, as Persephone. Thus Persephone represents that part of human consciousness which was still inextricably associated with the real principle of the past. The celebrated "rape of Persephone" thus is to be understood as the act whereby the god of the past (now become Hades) takes with him into the underworld, the realm of the past, that part of human consciousness with which it had formerly been associated. Nevertheless human consciousness feels this act as a plunder of something which is precious to it— wherefore Demeter is the sorrowing mother.

---

[1] II, 3, 412.     [2] *Ibid.*     [3] II, 3, 413.     [4] *Ibid.*

So far the theogonic process has been represented in the "purely exoteric mythology."[1] But now, with the reconciliation and appeasement of the sorrowing and angry human consciousness, resort must be had to the mysteries where the highest god will be proferred as a substitute for the god which has been displaced. Here especially in the mysteries of Demeter celebrated in Eleusis, the substitute god, Dionysos, the embodiment of the second principle, will come forward, placate Demeter, and the mythological process will be brought to a close. Dionysus, a relative late-comer to Greece, finds his full expression in the mysteries.

Because of the importance of the mysteries, in Schelling's view, as a culmination of the mythological process, a word of explanation concerning them must here be inserted.

> The mysteries are to us a natural and necessary product of the *mythological process* itself; they result from it and could not have preceded it. They do not negate the plurality of divinities, but rather contain the reason, so to speak, the actual secret thereof— not a secret which stands in contradiction to it and is *outside* of it, but rather the secret which this plurality conceals within itself.[2]

In other words, the Greek mysteries contained the key to the mythological process. In this respect, therefore, they stood not only as an explanation of all that had previously transpired therein, but themselves were "the final crisis... of the mythological consciousness itself."[3] In that they "contained the same esoteric history of mythology"[4] which is reproduced in the philosophy of mythology, they introduced the celebrants both to the death struggle of consciousness with the real principle and its release from that power by the Dionysian principle itself.

Here, at last, Dionysos appears in three-fold form. The old Ouranic god is overcome by the second potency, Dionysus, who by this act becomes Dionysos Zagreus, the chthonic Dionysus. Bacchus, the Dionysus form of the present age, who accomplishes this task of reducing the real principle to his proper subordination to the higher potencies, in accomplishing his task, is raised to a higher form "as existing, enduring spirit, exalted above manifoldness, as well as above the change of the world of sense."[5] Here at last the completion of the mythological process is effected as Iacchus, the third form of Dionysos, appears in his final form. At the same time, Demeter,

---

[1] II, 3, 414.      [2] II, 3, 442.
[3] II, 3, 443.      [4] II, 3, 444.      [5] II, 3, 474–75.

sorrowing for her daughter, is also appeased. Although she cannot return to the underworld, the abode of the ancient god, and yet must find satisfaction for the loss of her daughter, she can be reconciled only by a relation to the potency which has been the cause of her loss. In becoming the mother of Iacchus and Kore, Demeter is finally appeased, and the mysteries close with the sacred marriage of Iacchus and Kore. Thus "consciousness is completely released from the necessity of the mythological process, and a new world, although represented only in the deepest secret of the mysteries as purely future, begins for consciousness."[1]

We have now reached the point in Schelling's exposition of the content of history where we can better appreciate the perspective from which that which has gone before was delivered. Implicit in all of Schelling's discussion of the history of mankind, and of the nations into which it was divided, is the assumption that only a "higher" point of view can discover the true meaning, the actual connections, of historical events. This higher point of view is that which finally achieves full expression in the *Philosophy of Revelation*. As Schelling remarks, in his discussion of the Resurrection of Christ, such events are "like flashes of lightning in which the higher, i.e. that true, internal history breaks through into the merely external history."[2] Merely "external" history, the bare facts of human events, is empty and dead "when it is robbed of its connection with that inner, divine, transcendent history, which is above all actually the *true* history, the history κατ' ἐξοχήν!"[3] Outside of such a connection with this divine history of the universe, the true understanding of history is quite impossible. It is therefore the task of the philosophy of revelation to provide the requisite insight into history.

From this point of view, the operation of the mythological process as it reaches its culmination in the mysteries of the Greeks may now find its fullest explanation. In paganism merely the external unity of the potencies was represented. Their relation to the Spiritual unity which is exalted above the potencies, i.e. to the *true* God, was not achieved: "everything which paganism achieves is only a *simulacrum* of the Unity."[4] The tension in which the potencies were originally placed by the Fall of man was not entirely transcended. If it had been, the rapport with the true God would have been achieved in

---

[1] II, 3, 488.   [2] II, 4, 219.   [3] II, 4, 220.   [4] II, 4, 86.

paganism itself. Hence, since in paganism "the tension is only exter-nally (*actu*), not internally, transcended, the third potency does not become present."[1] The third potency is *known* to paganism, but its actuality still remains future. This is the limit within which the mythological process is necessarily confined. Thus, in the mysteries, paganism ends on a prophetic note—a prophecy, in fact, of the coming of Christ by whom the third potency will be made a present reality.

Thus Christ is to be understood as "the eternal Reconciler."[2] When his work is seen against the background of the whole of human history, it is obvious that in Christ the world which fell from God is restored to the true Father. Even as history itself began with the installation of the first principle—which should not be—in human consciousness, so Christ, as the full embodiment of $A^2$, mediates the recall of consciousness to its true center, in God. The Holy Spirit, $A^3$ is the true goal of human history. As such, he is "the *third* Lord of the human consciousness, even as we found him in mythology."[3] In him the striving of all paganism is fulfilled.

When Christ is understood in his true character as $A^2$ of the theogonic process, it is realized that "from the beginning, i.e. from the Fall, the Son of Man took upon Himself the divine wrath and placed Himself between this wrath and the being which was apostate from God..."[4] Even in paganism Christ (although not recognized as such) was the true mediator and savior of human nature. Since this was his eternal vocation, he could not do otherwise than identify himself with the being which had become an enemy of God. And al-though he does not give himself to this being outside of God, he nevertheless willingly takes upon himself the guilt which mankind bears. Hence "he who knew no guilt has through his love made him-self guilty."[5] Thus Christ has truly borne the sufferings and the sor-rows by mankind. He is the true Messiah.

But Christ is not an end in himself. His function is that of medi-ator. Thus, as long as he lives in particularity, in a life apart from the Spirit, he is himself involved in the tension of the potencies. Thus, according to the New Testament, as Christ begins his work, the Holy Spirit draws near as a token of the completion of the work which he is to undertake. Hence "this approach of the Spirit is a new proof of the tension within which Christ was placed and which is

---

[1] *Ibid.*      [2] II, 4, 81.
[3] II, 4, 83.    [4] II, 4, 196.    [5] *Ibid.*

released for the first time when he appears *as* Christ."[1] But the Spirit can come only after the Father is fully reconciled. The death of Christ is the event by which Christ overcomes the last enemy, death. By his death Christ sacrifices his selfhood completely, and his spirit becomes identified with the Holy Spirit itself. After the Resurrection, "the man Christ is, *by himself alone*, one with the *entire* Godhood; in it there is the original Man... restored." [2]So the Christian, who in baptism, enters into the fellowship of his death, also enters into his life which is eternal. Thus when Christ is finally glorified, and has reconciled all creation, the Holy Spirit (A[3]) comes; and that which for paganism was purely future is made a present actuality.

As yet we have not made sufficient note of the part which Judaism plays in this drama of redemption. At the beginning of our discussion of the mythological process, we did call attention to the fact that Schelling regards the Hebrews as a race apart, and thus as not having entered into the historical process in the way in which the nations (which are distinct from the Hebrews) did. It is precisely this exclusiveness of the Hebrews which, in Schelling's view, permits one to distinguish between a "sacred" and a "profane" history. If one assumes, as Schelling does, that the mediating potency, A[2], is, in a sense, the prime mover of human history, and that outside of its operation no history takes place, one is obliged to ask for the role of this potency in respect to the history of the Hebrews. "Profane" history is the history of paganism, within which the mythological process runs its course. In this history, the mediating potency is not known as Christ, but as Dionysos or one of his counterparts. But in the history of the Hebrews the true God *is* known by revelation. Thus we must assume that, if the Hebrews, along with the rest of mankind, were deprived of the knowledge of the true God by the Fall, then that knowledge must have been restored to them in a way which is not found among the nations of the world. In brief, it is Schelling's contention that knowledge of the true God was revealed to the Hebrews—at first to Abraham—and that therefore the history of the Hebrews is a "sacred" history and quite different from that of other nations.[3]

Here we will do little more than summarize what we observed earlier in respect to the Hebrews. For them, the first (historical)

---

[1] II, 4, 84.     [2] II, 4, 219.     [3] *Philosophy of Revelation.* II, 4, 119ff.

knowledge of God was of the Elohim. But this God is the false god, corresponding to Ouranos among the pagans. It was this god who commanded Abraham to take his son, Isaac, and offer him as a burnt sacrifice.[1] This god was the same god who ruled the consciousness of the nations of mankind. Jehovah, the *true* God, however, reveals himself to Abraham as he is about to perform the deed commanded by Elohim. It is this god, accordingly, who is revealed to the Hebrews—not directly, to be sure, but by his *angel* which, therefore, may be regarded as the manifestation of the second potency.[2] The mediating potency, the angel of Jehovah, is the instrument by which the Hebrews, through Moses, the Law, and the prophets, are ever afterward led. To the Hebrews alone, of all the people of the world, revelations—not one, but several—are the means by which they are gradually conducted to knowledge of the true God. But throughout the history of the Hebrews, the "dark principle", the Elohim, forms the substance of their consciousness. This "Kronic" principle is conceived as "the Lord of heaven and earth."[3] And to the extent that its reality remains effective, the Hebrews are continually tempted to succumb to the attractions of the pagan gods. The "dark principle" in Hebrew consciousness is itself the reason for the necessity of revelation; and thus "Christ is the *end* of revelation, just as He is the end of paganism."[4]

Christianity, as it appears in history, is incorporated in the Church. As soon as Christianity entered the world, "it had to submit itself to the general conditions and laws to which all development in the world is subject."[5] Hence, as is indicated in the Parable of the Tares, the Kingdom of God is that to which Satan has access, and its development must be subjected to the same strains and stresses to which any natural, historical phenomenon is heir. By the Kingdom of God, Schelling means the visible Church within which the Christian "idea" is contained and transmitted.

For the destiny of Christianity is that it be extended to all the peoples of the world, and this can be effected only through the medium of an historical institution, the Church. This institution begins at the moment when Christianity becomes a world religion, and acquires an existence in the world.[6] But historical Christianity is not all of a piece. It divides itself into three parts, corresponding to the three potencies, each part to be identified, according to Schelling, by

---

[1] II, 4, 121–22.   [2] II, 4, 123.   [3] II, 4, 125.
[4] II, 4, 124.   [5] II, 4, 294.   [6] II, 4, 298.

its participation in the character of three major figures of the New Testament: Peter, Paul and John. We shall consider each of these, briefly, in turn, for "these three names may be taken as representing three ages of the Christian Church."[1]

The Church of Peter is most closely identified with the figure of Moses in the Old Testament. Even as Moses stands for that which is stable, real and substantial in the Old Testament, so the Church of Peter, the law-giver, is that part of the Christian Church which is the basis of all the rest. Without the church of Peter, the rest could not be; "if the Church was to have... historical ground and make progress, Peter had to rule first."[2] It was Peter who was selected by Christ to be the head of His Church, to establish it upon the earth, and to give it corporeal existence. But by the came token, the church of Peter inherited all of his weaknesses. Its striving for political power, upon which it came to depend, was the chief cause of its overthrow at the time of the Reformation. Its conservative nature prevented it from looking beyond itself, and it sought, therefore, to make itself the *exclusive* basis of Christianity—as the dark principle, B, sought to make itself the true God. But, Schelling maintains, "the concept of the ground is so little exclusive that, much rather, it has significance only insofar as it *requires* another succeeding it and outside itself."[3]

The Pauline church acquires its character from the figure of Elijah, the founder of prophecy and the opponent of legalism. Elijah is "the fiery spirit who... moves toward a yet unknown future."[4] Paul, the Elijah of the New Testament, established the principle of freedom within the Church. In contrast to Peter, Paul is the active, forward-looking figure. In the Epistle to the Galatians, Paul proclaims his independence of any human source for the Gospel which he preaches. And in his personal activities within the early Church, he opposed the legalism, the authoritarianism and the conservatism of Peter. In Paul moves "the ideal, eccentric... principle."[5] But, in the course of the history of the Christian Church, it is the spirit of Paul which finally comes to full expression in the Reformation. Hence "the Apostle Paul is the first Protestant."[6] It has been his spirit more than any other which has guided the destiny of Christianity in relatively modern times.

But "the true Church exists in neither of these forms alone."[7] The church of John, whose character is shaped by the last of the prophets,

---

[1] II, 4, 309.    [2] *Ibid.*
[3] II, 4, 301.    [4] II, 4, 303.    [5] II, 4, 309.    [6] II, 4, 310.    [7] *Ibid.*

John the Baptist, is "the church of the future."[1] According to Schelling, the church of John is the true end of the movement of the whole history of the Church. The church of Peter was the foundation, the church of Paul the means, by which the illegitimate authority of the earlier church was broken, and the church of John is the church wherein the Holy Spirit shall dwell in all its fullness. Protestantism "should recognize that it is merely a transition, a mediation, that it is something only *in relation to* something which is yet higher..."[2] So, Schelling concludes,

> As in God himself there are three distinctions, so three chief apostles appear within Christianity. Just as little as God is in One Person, just as little is the Church in one of the apostles alone. Peter is the Apostle of the Father. He looks most deeply into the past. Paul is the Apostle of the Son, John the Apostle of the Spirit —he (John) alone in his Gospel has... the glorious Word from the Spirit, which the Son will send from the Father—and which... will conduct to all truth.[3]

In the church of John, no nation, no state, no particular group will be dominant. The church of John will be the Church of all mankind.

---

[1] II, 4, 303.     [2] II, 4, 321.     [3] II, 4, 327.

# CHAPTER SIX

# CONCLUSIONS

Now that an opportunity has been presented to survey the full extent of Schelling's reflections on the nature of human history, the reader may be in a better position to estimate the claims which were put forth at the outset in their behalf. It would seem that, on the whole, and aside from the defects which are evident in various aspects of his philosophy, Schelling did advance the cause of an evolutionary metaphysics beyond the point reached by any of his contemporaries, and that by so doing he provided a more adequate ontology for the understanding of human history than had been furnished up to this time. In general, Schelling's evolutionary ontology—or theology—as this receives expression in his "positive philosophy", would appear to be a laudable attempt to overcome the defects of a static metaphysics, of the type embraced by the Enlightenment, in an appreciation of the complexity and uniqueness of human history in general and of religious history in particular. On the other hand, Schelling's grasp of many of the problems raised by the attempt to understand history philosophically may be questioned as to its adequacy, as well as its originality. We should, therefore, attempt a brief critical appraisal of Schelling's labors in this field.

When seen against the background of the Enlightenment conception of history, and the criticism of that conception by European thinkers from 1750 on, Schelling's earlier attempts to furnish a philosophical scheme for its interpretation do not appear to have been very significant. It is true, of course, that from the outset Schelling proposed a dynamic metaphysics. Whether the dynamism which is basic to his early philosophy derives from the pure activity of Ego, from the nature of the Absolute, or from God—however the ultimate principle be defined—Schelling insisted that reality must be understood as possessing movement or change as an essential characteristic. But this dynamism was obviously derived from Fichte; and at first Schelling's interests lay mainly in the direction of offering a philosophy of nature which would fill a gap left by the Fichtean philosophy. Schelling's interest in history was not developed until considerably after the beginning of his career.

It was not until 1800, with the appearance of the *System des transcendentalen Idealismus*, that Schelling had moved to a point, philosophically, where he was ready to treat history as a field requiring special consideration. A deciding factor in his conception of history in this work may well be the fact that he approached it from the point of view of his earlier philosophy of nature. For in seeking to define the significance of human history, he felt called upon, apparently, to designate its characteristics so as to explicitly differentiate it from subhuman nature. From a "transcendental" point of view, Schelling regards nature and history respectively as real and ideal sides of the one Absolute Ego; and thus, while preserving the connection between nature and history, he yet distinguishes them sharply from one another. The significance of this treatment of history by Schelling would appear to consist in the circumstance that it was certainly among the first of the attempts of the German idealists at a metaphysics of history. And while, in this respect, Schelling's ideas were faithful to the suggestions proposed by Kant, and were in some respects anticipated by Schiller and Friedrich Schlegel, no one in Germany, it seems, had previously attempted a philosophical system which was sufficiently comprehensive to embrace both nature and history.

But while it is true that Schelling's metaphysics during his first period is dynamic in character, its dynamism is incomplete. In this respect, indeed, Fichte and Hegel, among the German idealists, may be said to have been more dynamically minded than was Schelling. We had occasion to note earlier that, on the whole, Schelling's first period is a-historically oriented. For even when he had achieved the standpoint of objective (as contrasted to Fichte's subjective) idealism in the system of identity, he still maintained that both nature and history, as real and ideal respectively, have as their goal the transcending of this dualism in an absolute identity. Whether the final synthesis be achieved in the intellectual intuition or in art, the result is the same. Mysticism eventually makes the insights of both natural science and the philosophy of history irrelevant. All knowledge outside the Absolute is partial and, to that extent, false.

It is only in Schelling's second period, from the appearance of his treatise on human freedom in 1809, that he achieves a metaphysics which is not only thoroughly dynamic but evolutionary as well. To be exact, the evolutionary theology does not achieve its complete expression until three or four years later. But Schelling's later philosophy is largely an amplification of the position taken in *Of Human Freedom*. From this time on, Schelling not only repudiated the idealism of his earlier period, but he launched also a vehement attack against all forms of rationalism, particularly Hegel's, and sought to conceive of reality primarily as a gradually evolving process.

While there is no way of proving conclusively that it was any one factor which motivated this shift in Schelling's philosophical perspective, it does not seem absurd to suggest that at least part of the answer lies in Schelling's desire to provide more adequately for a historical treatment of reality. As we noted earlier, beginning with the *Of Human Freedom*, Schelling's investigations were strongly influenced by the writings of the theosophist, Jacob Böhme. Particularly, it seems, it was Böhme's conception of the theogonic process which captured Schelling's imagination. The mystic's analysis of this process into a three-fold pattern of creativity, in which God is to be viewed as the primal ground or ungrounded which achieves expression through the "nature in God," the will, provided Schelling, no doubt, with the fundamentals of the metaphysical scheme which he embraced in his positive philosophy.[1] Thus, with Böhme's emphasis upon the processing character of the life of God, and Schelling's own earlier interest in the religious construction of human history, as evidenced in *Die Methode des akademischen Studiums*, it was an easy transition to the point of view of his later philosophy in which he sees the whole of reality as essentially an evolving theogonic process.

Schelling approaches an historical ontology, thus, somewhat obliquely. Yet it would also appear to be true that his preference for this conception of the nature of things was in keeping with the general trend of the Romantic movement itself, as this was delineated in our opening chapter. And if, in addition, we attend to Schelling's own confession in his *Introduction to the Philosophy of Revelation* that it was "just he, man, who impelled me to the final imponderable question: Why is there anything? Why not nothing?"[2] it would seem that Schelling's concern to set forth reality's history (and not merely its structure) is accounted for. For in Schelling's view, and in the view of most of his contemporaries, human nature is most adequately displayed in human history. And since human history does not re-

---

[1] Cf. F. DeW. Bolman, *op. cit.*, p. 19ʏ.     [2] S. W. II, 3, 7.

peat itself, but develops and progresses, its movement must be conceived teleologically. An historical ontology receives justification,
therefore, in Schelling's view, as a means to an adequate philosophical understanding of man. If one is to supply an ultimate context for
man and his activities, he is obliged, Schelling contends, to formulate
a universal history within which the history of man would find a
place. Whence did man originate? Where is he tending? Such
questions can be answered, according to Schelling, only by a philosophy which is through and through historical.

This is the point also, it would seem, of Schelling's strictures
against the ontological argument, both in its ancient form and in its
most recent Hegelian expression. Following the Kantian criticism,
not only Fichte, but also the early Schelling and Hegel, embarked
upon metaphysics with the assumption that Reason is ultimate
reality and that, accordingly, first philosophy achieves expression
through Reason's making itself its own object. Schelling does not
dispute the legitimacy of the *purpose* which had prompted such an
assumption and consequent procedure. But now—in his second
period—he denies that the metaphysics of Fichte and Hegel has
adequately discharged its task. If metaphysics' task is the determination of an ultimate context for human experience and human
activity and thus the stipulation of the "whence" and the "whither"
of process—assuming, as these philosophers do, that reality is
basically an activity or process rather than a static structure—then,
Schelling declares, idealism has not achieved its goal. For while
everything else may be accounted for by idealism, it cannot account
for the existence of reason itself. The question still remain: Why
reason? Why not unreason? Reality must be more than rational if
reason itself is to be explained metaphysically. If reason, then, is not
original, but itself something which has evolved, then traditional
idealism is helpless in trying to account for it.

It is, accordingly, the evolutionary ontology which is expressed in
Schelling's later philosophy which gives his thought a genuinely
historical orientation. It is primarily because he now maintains that
"God himself... is not a system but a life"[1] that he denies the ability
of rationalism to plot the necessary determinations of being a priori.
Since life is characterized by growth, by development, by a process
of unfolding from what is implicit to what is explicit, from lower to

_____

[1] S. W. I, 7, 399. Gutmann trans., *op. cit.*, p. 78.

higher or more complex, philosophy must proceed by way of description rather than deduction. One cannot assume a Most Perfect
Cause at the beginning whose nature it is to exist, and by appeal to
which all the difficulties of accounting for a world of imperfection
and evil are "explained" away. Rather one must undertake a patient
investigation of how the world may be *supposed* to have evolved. Only after one's hypothesis has been verified *a posteriori* does one have
the right to say that he has "explained" the world as it actually
exists. In the conviction that the universe has come to be what it
now is as the result of an evolving process wherein something which
"ought not to be" is gradually overcome, Schelling turns his back
with finality upon traditional, static metaphysics.

In spite of Schelling's positive contributions, however—and it
would seem that his contributions to the criticism of Hegelian
idealism are of permanent value—there are several defects discover-
able in his philosophy when it is examined from the point of view of
his attempt to construct a genuinely "historical" ontology for the
interpretation of human history. In the first place, many will
question his appropriation of the theosophy of Böhme as an instrument for the elucidation of the course of human history. If, as Schelling himself declared, "the uterances of theoretic mystics are indeed
to a great extent incomprehensible,"[1] and "mysticism expresses the
contrast with formal, scientific knowledge,"[2] the question might well
be asked whether the employment of notions taken from such sources
are really adequate to furnish us with a knowledge of history—even
if we assume, as Schelling does, that human history is to be understood as a part of the life of God. To propose that a theogonic process
is, as such, verifiable in the events of history seems to bespeak an
audacity which few, if any, reliable commentators on history would
sanction at the present time. The point is, however, that while to the
mystic or theosophist history may be a theogonic process, the
question still remains whether such a judgment about history as a
whole is verifiable, and whether our knowledge of history is increased
by making such an assumption as to its contents.

But a somwhat graver defect seems to lie in the determinism which,
in spite of himself, Schelling assigns to the course of history. It is
obvious, of course, that Schelling makes a valiant effort to escape the
determinism which traditional rationalism has assumed in its ability

---

[1] S. W. I, 10, 185. Gutmann, *op. cit.*, p. xlix.
[2] S. W. I, 10, 191. Gutmann, p. li.

to deduce the pattern of historical events. While he was not too successful in this respect in his *System of Transcendental Idealism*, inasmuch as in this work he still sees the "spontaneity" attributed to human actions as taking place within a determined framework, he nevertheless does, to some extent, remedy this defect in his *Of Human Freedom* wherein he endows the human will with unconditioned autonomy. From this time on, Schelling conceives of man's life as a part of the life of God; and since God himself lives in the autonomous life of man, there is nothing outside of man's will—or so it would seem—which can limit its freedom of expression. But still the outcome of history is never in doubt. The principles of the theogonic process describe a determined course in the actions and reactions of historical movement. Hence the philosopher *can* deduce in advance the pattern which history will follow. He may have to appeal to the facts of the religious consciousness to verify his speculations, but the possibility of calculating history, according to a determinate scheme, is implicit in the nature of the investigation which Schelling undertakes, as well as explicit in many of his utterances. Schelling, thus, certainly exaggerates the contrast which he sees between his own philosophy and Hegel's. It remained for later philosophers, such as Bergson and others who took up the cause of an evolutionary metaphysics, to banish this remnant of rationalism.

Indeed, as we pointed out in Chapter IV, Schelling seems not to have been aware of the fact that his "metaphysical empiricism" involved the fallacy of affirming the consequent. Certainly many will also point out that some established scientific procedure of today involves, formally, the same fallacy. But Schelling's whole position would have been inestimably improved had he recognized the nature of the investigation which he undertook in his Philosophy of Mythology and Philosophy of Revelation. Had he suggested that his philosophy was more in the nature of a hypothesis of dubious verifiability when applied to the religious history of mankind, he would no doubt have attracted a much more sympathetic audience.

It is, of course, notoriously easy to pick flaws in the work of a thinker, especially when he launches such an ambitious project as did Schelling, and when his defects have become more evident in the light of later philosophic developments. His metaphysical scheme, for example, hardly gives an adequate account, even on its own terms, of how the second potency renders ineffective the first potency and thus provides the impulsion by which historical process is directed toward the final redemption of human consciousness from the power of "that which ought not to be."[1] Schelling suggests that the disequilibrium caused by the introduction of the first potency to a position of dominance is that circumstance within being as a whole which causes the (inevitable) reaction of the remaining potencies so as to produce that movement by which the offending member, the first potency, is put back into its rightful position. To the question, how does the second potency influence the first? Schelling *might* have answered that the second potency is the instrument by which being as a whole nullifies the influence of "that which ought not to be," just as a living organism musters an antibody to counteract a poison. But Schelling does not dwell upon this rather important aspect of his metaphysical scheme, and leaves unanswered, accordingly, a key question relating to the "reason why" of process as such.

Similarly, but for somewhat different reasons, many Christians have been offended by Schelling's use—or misuse—of Christian theology in his attempts to render an interpretation of the general course of human history. He has—perhaps rightly—been called a Gnostic; and in this respect, at least, he belongs more in the tradition of Eastern Christianity than in that of the Western Church. But such a judgment depends, at least in part, upon one's estimate of mysticism, or theosophy, as such. Certainly it cannot be disputed that many others in the Christian tradition have set a precedent for Schelling in this endeavor.

A final estimate of Schelling's efforts to provide an ontology for a better understanding of human history can be made only in the light of the more general philosophic context in which he wrote and lectured. To the extent that he did at last arrive at an evolutionary metaphysics, he must be credited with bringing to a culmination, in some respects, a trend which had been developing since European criticism of the Enlightenment set in. As a Romantic, he obviously shared many of the ideas of his contemporaries—to most of whom he did not acknowledge his indebtedness—but from whom he derived the major portion of his thought, especially in the earlier portion of his career. As an admirer of Böhme, he made a somewhat dubious attempt to construct a theogony of human history. And as an idealist in the German tradition, he was one of the first to see the defects in that school and seek to remedy some of its weaknesses, especially in

---

[1] *Supra*, p. 134.

its method of interpreting human history. Later philosophers, while discarding Schelling's speculative apparatus, have nevertheless benefited considerably by his attempts to express more truly and cogently the meaning of human history.

# BIBLIOGRAPHY

## A. SOURCES PERTINENT TO THE PRESENT STUDY

Bolman, F. deW., *Schelling: The Ages of the World*. New York, Columbia University Press, 1942.

Brown, Andrew, "John Locke and the Religious 'Aufklaerung'", *The Review of Religion*, XIII, 2 (January, 1949).

Brunschwig, Henri, *La crise de l'état prussien a la fin du XVIIIe siècle et la genèse de la mentalité romantique*. Paris, 1947.

Cassirer, Ernst, *Rousseau, Kant, Goethe : Two Essays*, translated by James Gutmann, Paul Oskar Kristeller, and John Herman Randall, Jr. Princeton, 1945.

—, The Myth of the State. New Haven, Yale University Press, 1946.

Creed and Boys Smith, *Religious Thought in the Eighteenth Century*. Cambridge, Harvard University Press, 1934.

Croce, Benedetto, *The Philosophy of Giambattista Vico*, translated by R. C. Collingwood. New York, 1913.

Dilthey, Wilhelm., "Fortentwicklung von der absoluten Vernunft zur Gottpersönlichkeit, dem Willen als Grund der Welt und der Annerkennung des Irrationalen und Geschichtlichen," *Gesammelte Schriften*, Vol. IV. Leipzig, 1921.

Erdmann, J. E., *A History of Philosophy*, translated by W. S. Hough, New York, The Macmillan Co., 1909.

Fischer, Kuno, *Schellings Leben, Schriften und Lehre*. Heidelberg and München, 1872–77.

Flöter, Hans, H. F., *Die Begründung der Geschichtlichkeit in der Philosophie des deutschen Idealismus*. Halle, 1936.

Furhmans, Horst, *Schellings letzte Philosophie : Die Negative und positive Philosophie in Einsatz des Spatidealismus*. Berlin, 1940.

Gutmann, James, *Schelling: Of Human Freedom*. Chicago: The Open Court Publishing Company, 1936.

Hegel, G. W. F., "The Phenomenology of Mind", Introduction, *Hegel Selections*, J. Loewenberg, ed. New York, 1929.

—, *Lectures on the Philosophy of History*, J. Sibree, ed. London, 1894.

Herder, J. G., "Auch eine Philosophie der Geschichte zur Bildung der Menschheit, 1774. *Werke*, ed. Suphan, Vol. V.

—, "Ideen zur Philosophie der Geschichte der Menschheit," 1784–91. *Werke*, vol. XIII.

Heussler, H., "Schellings Entwicklungslehre," *Rheinische Blätter für Erziehung und Unterricht, 1882*.

Hobbes, Thomas, "Philosophical Rudiments Concerning Government." *The Philosophy of Thomas Hobbes*. F. J. E. Woodbridge, ed. Minneapolis, 1903.

Hume, David, "The Natural History of Religion," *Essays and Treatises...* London, 1768.

Jankélévitch, Vladimir, *Le Odysseé de la Conscience dans la dernière philosophie de Schelling*. Paris. 1933.

Kant, I., "Recensionen von J. G. Herders Ideen zur Philosophie der Geschichte," 1785. *Werke*, Vol. VIII. ed. Königlich Preussischen Akademie der Wissenschaften. Berlin, 1912.

—, "Idee zu einer allgemeinen Geschichte in weltbürgerlichen Absicht," 1784. *Werke*, Vol. VIII.

—, "Muthmasslicher Anfang der Menschengeschichte," *Werke*, Vol. VIII.

—, "Kritik der reinen Vernunft," *Kant's Gesammelte Schriten*. Vol. III. Berlin, 1911.

—, *Prolegomena to any Future Metaphysics*. Translated by Paul Carus. Chicago, 1933.

Kroner, Richard, *Von Kant bis Hegel*. Tübingen, 1921–4.

Lessing, G. E., "Die Erziehung des Menschengeschlechts," 1780. *Werke*. Berlin, n.d.

Lisco, Heinrich, *Die Geschichtsphilosophie Schellings, 1792–1809.*

Locke, John, *An Essay Concerning Human Understanding*. London, 1690.

—, *Second Treatise on Government*. London, 1690.

Lovejoy, A. O., *The Great Chain of Being*. Cambridge: The Harvard University Press, 1936.

—, *Essays in the History of Ideas*. Baltimore, 1948.

Mehlis, Georg, *Schellings Geschichtsphilosophie in den Jahren 1799–1804*. Heidelberg, 1907.

Randall, J. H., Jr., *The Making of the Modern Mind*. Boston, New York: The Houghton-Mifflin Co., 1940.

Rousseau, J. J., "Discours sur l'origine et les fondements de l'inégalité parmi les hommes." *Oeuvres Completes de J. J. Rousseau*. V. D. Musset-Pathay, ed. Paris, 1823.

Royce, Josiah, *The Spirit of Modern Philosophy*. New York, 1892.

Russell, Bertrand, *Introduction to Mathematical Philosophy*. New York and London, 1919.

Schelling, F. W. J., *Sämmtliche Werke*, edited by K. F. A. Schelling. Stuttgart and Augsburg: J. G. Cotta, 1856–61. Division I, Vol. 1–10; Division II, Vol. 1–4.

Schiller, Friedrich, "Simple and Sentimental Poetry," *Essays Aesthetical and Philosophical*. London: Bohn Library, 1875.

Schleiermacher, Fr., *Reden über die Religion*. 1799.

Schreitmüller, Heinrich, *Das Leben Gottes in Schellings Philosophie der Offenbarung*. Landshut, 1936.

Schröder, Christel M., *Das Verhältnis von Heidentum und Christentum in Schellings Philosophie der Offenbarung*. Munich, 1936.

Tillich, Paul, *Mystik und Schuldbewusststein in Schellings Philosophischer Entwickelung*. Gütersloh, 1912.

—, *Die religionsgeschichtliche Konstruktion in Schellings positiver Philosophie, ihre Voraussetzungen und Principien*. Breslau, 1910.

—, *The Interpretation of History*. New York, 1936.

Vico, G. B., *La Scienza Nuova*; translated as *Principes de la philosophie de l'histoire* by Jules Michelet. Brussels, 1835.

Voltaire, *Essays and Criticisms*. New York, 1915.

Wiener, Max, *Fichtes Lehre vom Wesen und Inhalt der Geschichte*. Kirchhain, N. L., 1906.

Windelband, W., *A History of Philosophy*, translated by J. H. Tufts. New York: The Macmillan Co., 1910.

## B. SCHELLING BIBLIOGRAPHIES

1927   Jost, Joh. F. W. J. Schelling: Bibliographie der Schriften von ihm und über ihn. Bonn.

1933  Gray-Smith, Rowland. Bibliography, supplementary to Jost's in *God in the Philosophy of Schelling*. (Philadelphia), pp. 17–20.
1936  Gutmann, James. Bibliography, supplementary to Jost's and Gray-Smith's, in *Schelling : Of Human Freedom* (Chicago), pp. 119–23.
1942  Bolman, Fredrick deWolfe, Jr. Bibliography supplementary to Jost's Gray-Smith's and Gutmann's, in *Schelling : The Ages of The World* (New York), pp. 241–243.


## C. ADDENDA TO JOST'S, GRAY-SMITH'S, GUTMANN'S AND BOLMAN'S BIBLIOGRAPHIES

1939  Rotenstreich, Nathan: Bayath Haetzem Baphilosophia meKant ad Hegel. (The Proplem of Substance in Philosophy from Kant to Hegel.) Jerusalem.
1942  Schelling, F. W. J. von. Vom deutschen Genius. Dokuments der deutschen Bewegung. Leipzig.
      Gedanken von Schelling. Berlin-Zürich.
      Tsanoff, R. A. "The Idealistic Quest of Spiritual Unity," *The Moral Ideals of our Civilization*, p. 359–72.
1946  Essais. Trad. de S. Jankélèvitch. Paris.
      Introduction à la philosophie de la mythology. Trad. de S. Jankélèvitch. 2 vols. Paris.
      Die Weltalter. Fragments. In den Urfassungen von 1811 und 1813. hgg. V. Manfred Schröter. Munich.
      Copleston, F. C. "Pantheism in Spinoza and the German Idealists." Philosophy, XXI: 78.
      Fuhrmans, Horst. "Zu Schellings Spätphilosophie." Blätter für deutsche Philosophie. XIV: 3.
1946  Nobile, E. Panteismo e dualisme nel pensiero di Schelling. Naples.
1948  Schelling: Clara. hgg. von Manfred Schröter. Munich.
      Dempf, A., "Philosophie der Romantik in München." Geistige Welt. Munich.
      Meyer-Abich, A., Naturphilosophie auf neuen Wegen. Stuttgart.